C0-ATI-817

SHOESTRING INVESTING MADE E-Z

John Santosuosso, Ph.D.

MADE E-Z PRODUCTS, Inc.
Deerfield Beach, Florida / www.MadeE-Z.com

WARNER MEMORIAL LIBRARY
EASTERN COLLEGE
ST. DAVIDS, PA. 19087

5-17-2000

HG 4527 .S267 2000
Santosuosso, John.
Shoestring investing made
E-Z

Shoestring Investing Made E-Z™

© 2000 Made E-Z Products, Inc.

Printed in the United States of America

MADE E-Z
PRODUCTS

384 South Military Trail

Deerfield Beach, FL 33442

Tel. 954-480-8933

1 2 3 4 5 6 7 8 9 10   CPC   R   10 9 8 7 6 5 4 3 2

This publication is designed to provide accurate and authoritative information in regard to subject matter covered. It is sold with the understanding that neither the publisher nor author is engaged in rendering legal, accounting, or other professional services. If legal advice or other expert assistance is required, the services of a competent professional should be sought. From: *A Declaration of Principles jointly adopted by a Committee of the American Bar Association and a Committee of Publishers.*

Shoestring Investing Made E-Z™

John Santosuosso, Ph.D.

Limited warranty and disclaimer

This self-help product is intended to be used by the consumer for his/her own benefit. It may not be reproduced in whole or in part, resold or used for commercial purposes without written permission from the publisher. In addition to copyright violations, the unauthorized reproduction and use of this product to benefit a second party may be considered the unauthorized practice of law.

This product is designed to provide authoritative and accurate information in regard to the subject matter covered. However, the accuracy of the information is not guaranteed, as laws and regulations may change or be subject to differing interpretations. Consequently, you may be responsible for following alternative procedures, or using material or forms different from those supplied with this product. It is strongly advised that you examine the laws of your state before acting upon any of the material contained in this product.

As with any matter, common sense should determine whether you need the assistance of an attorney. We urge you to consult with an attorney, qualified estate planner, or tax professional, or to seek any other relevant expert advice whenever substantial sums of money are involved, you doubt the suitability of the product you have purchased, or if there is anything about the product that you do not understand including its adequacy to protect you. Even if you are completely satisfied with this product, we encourage you to have your attorney review it.

Neither the author, publisher, distributor nor retailer are engaged in rendering legal, accounting or other professional services. Accordingly, the publisher, author, distributor and retailer shall have neither liability nor responsibility to any party for any loss or damage caused or alleged to be caused by the use of this product.

Copyright Notice

The purchaser of this guide is hereby authorized to reproduce in any form or by any means, electronic or mechanical, including photocopying, all forms and documents contained in this guide, provided it is for non-profit, educational or private use. Such reproduction requires no further permission from the publisher and/or payment of any permission fee.

The reproduction of any form or document in any other publication intended for sale is prohibited without the written permission of the publisher. Publication for nonprofit use should provide proper attribution to Made E-Z Products.

Table of contents

Introduction to Shoestring Investing Made E-Z™

Shoestring Investing Made E-Z understands the world where many folks live. Daily they face the financial challenges and problems of life, and they have limited financial resources to confront them with. They make ends meet but may see few prospects for a brighter future. Some are young, with minimal incomes and growing family responsibilities. Others are in occupations and professions where salaries tend to be modest. Still others may have had past possibilities destroyed or severely damaged by periods of illness, unemployment, or some personal crisis.

Shoestring Investing Made E-Z's goal is to convince its readers that even with very modest monetary assets, they can make solid, realistic progress. It also furnishes help on how to avoid the mistakes and traps that look so enticing but do not work or can even be harmful. For numerous people, it will open up roads that are safe to travel but which they never knew existed or were largely unexplored territory. This guide is not a route to great wealth quickly, or even slowly. What it does promise is a realistic opportunity to improve your financial situation. The approach is one for all seasons, good economic times and not-so-good ones, bull markets and bear markets. Obviously, there are benefits to starting young, but those of any age can adopt these techniques.

Shoestring Investing Made E-Z stresses the opportunities and safety provided by diversification, and gives practical suggestions on how the small investor can participate sensibly in a variety of financial situations. Cash investments, stocks, bonds, mutual funds, real estate, and international markets are among the areas included. Appropriate strategies such as dollar averaging, closed-end funds, and methods for doing your own financial research are explored. Those that small investors should not attempt, including options and futures, are carefully discussed and their pitfalls explained. *Shoestring Investing Made E-Z* also shows how to benefit others with your investments while at the same time you benefit yourself. In addition, an extensive annotated bibliography of financial books is included.

For those seeking guidance in financial areas outside of investing, *Shoestring Investing Made E-Z* can point the way to sound decisions. Help is offered on insurance, wills, living wills, and those times when borrowing is absolutely unavoidable.

Shoestring Investing Made E-Z is for people who want to make tomorrow better. They wish to take charge of their financial future and are seeking the tools that will enable them to successfully reach their goals. Here is where they can find them.

Chapter 1

Toward a brighter tomorrow

What you'll find in this chapter:

➠ On living paycheck to paycheck

➠ It's never too late to begin to save

➠ Fear and time—the two major negatives

➠ The miracle of compound interest

➠ Watch for stumbling blocks and get going

It can be good to dream, if the dreams are worthwhile, realistic ones. There is so much we would like to do if only we knew the way. Improving our financial situation would help in many cases. But is it possible?

This guide shows the way. It is for those meeting life's typical daily financial challenges. Plenty of excellent works are already available. Some of these are listed in the back of this volume. They are worth reading, but no source, no matter how good, can meet everyone's needs. Numerous ones are extremely valuable for experienced investors and for those who have considerable assets to put to work. Others may need different strategies.

> **HOT spot** Many people hope tomorrow will be brighter and more prosperous than today.

Various books provide proven insights, but may also present approaches and methods that might be uncomfortable for some people, especially the inexperienced investor. Then there are also those which decline to discuss such matters as dividend reinvestment plans, because they see these as too slow or too conservative; but these concepts are ideal for certain folks.

Living paycheck to paycheck

There is a seemingly countless number of people who live from paycheck to paycheck. Often they tried to make financial headway and feel they have failed. Some have not tried because they believe the effort would be futile. Many others may give up because they become thoroughly confused by investment styles and products they never used or understood. On occasion that fear may be healthy. It can keep us out of trouble. In other instances it is not. Most of us, the first time we encountered a bicycle or a computer, probably looked upon these contraptions with a certain degree of suspicion. Eventually, maybe with the shedding of a few tears, we learned how to master them and discovered they could even be fun.

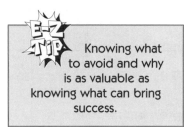

Knowing what to avoid and why is as valuable as knowing what can bring success.

This book is designed primarily for those who have been living paycheck to paycheck. It intends to encourage them to meet the task of riding the bicycle, and to accomplish that with as few bumps and bruises as possible. It also takes a look at things that do not work. Understanding why past efforts fell short of the mark can spare us from going down the wrong road once again. It is also helpful to know what paths might be worth exploring for some people, but not for others. Persons who live paycheck to paycheck, or nearly so, cannot always copy the investment style of someone who is already reasonably financially secure. In fact, to do so may well prevent them from achieving their own financial security.

What we discuss is definitely not intended to be some sort of miracle cure. It is not a plan designed for someone about to face, or in the midst of, a serious financial crisis, such as bankruptcy or unusually large medical expenditures. Such people are urged to seek professional counsel so they can deal with these challenges as effectively as possible. However, debt in itself is no reason to give up in despair. The methods examined should work for many people who are at least able to meet the payments on the debt they may have incurred. In fact, they may well strengthen the resolve to get out of debt permanently and to use credit in a more constructive manner.

It's never too late to start

The person who begins at fifty or even later has a better chance of living more comfortably, both physically and psychologically, than the person who never begins at all. No matter when you begin, there is still time to achieve a sense of financial accomplishment and of being in command of your financial life. Reaching such a point is really to obtain a genuine source of wealth.

HINT One is never too young or too old to try some of what is presented here. Obviously, it is better to begin earlier rather than later. Anyone who has ever taken even a brief look at the workings of compound interest will understand that.

Those looking here for rapid solutions to all their financial problems and worries will most definitely be disappointed. If you are not wealthy now, do not expect to be wealthy by the time you finish reading this book. In all probability, you will not be wealthy ten years from now. Most people never will be. However, if what you are seeking is a map which is understandable by nearly everyone seeking command of their financial life and a tomorrow which is more economically secure, then proceed with all due deliberation. Remember you are not alone. Others made this trip before you. They know that discouragement can seem to be lurking behind every bush and tree. So there is no need to go wandering off the path into the shrubbery. Stay on the road, and you will arrive at your chosen destination. Along the way you may, perhaps to your surprise, discover that the trip can be exciting, even exhilarating.

note The longer your money has to work for you the better job it can do.

We are about to embark on a journey, an exploration of potential financial opportunities. Along the way you will be invited to consider a variety of possibilities. Not surprisingly, few, if any, will need or want all of them. Each individual's situation is unique. It is much like going into a good restaurant. Take a close look at all the entrees on the menu. Then carefully select what appeals to you.

The longest journey

Far too many high school graduation speeches have said something to the effect that, "the longest journey begins with a single step." As simple and overworked as that statement may be, there is some valuable and overlooked truth to it. It does take but a single step to get started. That is obvious. It is also difficult to do, and that is not so obvious. Far too often procrastination is the order of the day.

 Even though rationally we may comprehend action is needed, and needed now, nothing happens. We need to learn to walk first. Running is possible, but only after that is accomplished.

Each one of us could make our own list of reasons why beginning a regular investment program is so difficult. Near the top may be the *fear* that we are not bright enough, clever

 enough, or quick enough to do such a thing. That mystique which often seems to hang over the stock market may encourage such negative thinking. Of course, the only way to prove that our fears have no factual basis, that no special or secret skills are needed, is to begin.

Time is another factor that subtly destroys plans to get started. On the one hand we may believe we are now too old to bother. There is not enough time to accomplish anything significant. The sooner one gets started the better, However, we often have far more time than we realize, and need to do

note Money needs time to earn money. The more time we give it, the easier it is to get the job done.

financial planning for an extensive period of years. Today, many of us can count on a fairly lengthy retirement. In many instances there will also be the need to provide for a spouse who might outlive us, particularly if he or she is several years younger than we are. The point is to start now. If we

think we are too old to bother, it certainly will not help to wait until we are older.

 On the other hand, we can also be convinced that there is plenty of time to begin later. Starting later is better than not starting at all. However, the longer we wait the harder we have to work to have the same success we could have had if not for procrastination. The money we earned as interest or capital gains will have time to earn still more. The so-called "miracle of compound interest" is correctly named. Interest allowed to compound over a lengthy period of time begins to do amazing things, even if in the early years it appears to be growing at a snail's pace. It is never too early to start.

Possibly the strongest stumbling block of all is the feeling that present financial circumstances will keep us from ever devoting enough money to develop a meaningful investment program. Earlier, this book admitted it would not make you rich. That admission will be made again. However, it does not take the investment of impossibly large sums of money to significantly improve an individual or family financial situation. About the only way to prove this to one's personal satisfaction is to actually begin. Once the change begins to be noticeable, and that is usually much

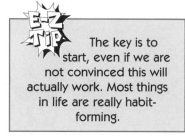

The key is to start, even if we are not convinced this will actually work. Most things in life are really habit-forming.

sooner than we might think, the determination to continue and to even accelerate an investment program can become quite strong. The key is to get started. Stop and reflect on the things you do without thinking but do nearly every day. They are part of your everyday routine. In reality they are habits. Once investing is another habit, it becomes almost automatic. It is hard to think of not doing it.

It is almost time to get started. Before we do, it will be worthwhile to look at some things not to do. Avoiding mistakes saves time and money, sometimes a lot of each.

Chapter 2

Swinging for the fences and other disasters

What you'll find in this chapter:

➠ What smart investors can learn from baseball

➠ About fraud and opportunities that aren't

➠ How to spot the legitimate companies

➠ About infomercials, MLM and Ponzi schemes

➠ The right questions to ask of anyone

A baseball story

Around Philadelphia, folks will long remember Richie Ashburn. Ashburn was for many years a radio and television broadcaster for the Phillies, until his untimely death during the 1997 season. However, the old timers will tell you that they were fans of Ashburn's well before he got into broadcasting. They recall the Whiz Kids, and Richie most definitely was one of the Whiz Kids. Who were the Whiz Kids? Why, none other than the 1950 Philadelphia Phillies, a bunch of baseball players who brought that team their first National League Championship since 1915 and, at that time, only the second in the franchise's entire history. Ashburn played center field and played it well. He was one of the most popular of all the Whiz Kids. Without him there would have been no championship.

On the last day of the regular season Richie, who was never known for having a great arm, threw a tremendous strike from center field to throw a Brooklyn Dodger base runner out at home plate, and the Phillies went on to win the pennant with a tenth inning victory. Had the runner scored, the

Phillies would have been forced into a playoff game to decide who would be league champion and earn the right to go on to the World Series. They might have won that game, but chances were just as good they might have lost. The modest Ashburn later remarked, "I only ever made one throw, but I made it when it counted."

Richie Ashburn did know how to get the job done when it counted. However, it was usually not with his arm—but with his bat—that he was victorious. Ashburn did have some things going for him. He was fast, he was smart, and he was not embarrassed to bunt his way onto first base. The end of a typical season would usually find him the owner of a better than .300 batting average with more than his share of stolen bases.

There was only one thing Ashburn did not do very well, and that was hit home runs. On average he got about one per season, and sometimes that was of the inside-the-park variety made possible by the determined use of his speed. One year the St. Louis Cardinals decided to take down a right field screen in the city's old Sportsman's Park. Ashburn responded by hitting two shots in one game for home runs into the bleachers that stood behind where the screen used to be. The Cardinals went into a near state of shock. Back up went the screen the following year.

No matter how hard he might have tried, Richie Ashburn would never have been a power hitter. Fortunately, he had the wisdom to know it. Richie simply found other ways to beat you—the stolen base, the single that his speed turned into a double, and the infield grounder that became a legged-out single rather than just another out. One amazed sportswriter called Ashburn "the .100 hitter with the .300 average." There was at least some truth to that. Ashburn knew the things he could do. He knew the things he could not, and he possessed the wisdom to know the difference. He worked hard at the things he could do. That made him and his team champions. It may not hurt to also add that in a day when baseball salaries had not shot past the rings of Saturn, the "Nebraska Cornhusker," as he was sometimes called, was known as a smart ball player for another reason. He invested his money wisely.

The "moral" of the story

What does all this baseball talk have to do with "real life?" It is simply this. Most of us are not "long ball" hitters. If we insist on swinging for the fences, in all probability what we will accomplish is another strikeout.

Refusing to face this can hurt in another way. It can blind us to seeing the constructive things we can do, things that we can make work. We can do the financial equivalent of bunting, stealing a base, getting a walk, and wind up winning some exciting one-run ball games.

That may sound logical and even easy, but the temptation to try something a bit more spectacular can be overwhelming if we are not alert to it. We look around us and see others enjoying "the good life." They drive nicer cars, take better vacations, and can afford at least a modest pool for their house. Meanwhile we seem to "enjoy" higher credit card debt, dental bills and, literally, a leaking roof. It is the old story of not being able to keep up with the Joneses. It can feel even worse if the Joneses are the same people with whom we went to school or whom we know have less education or work experience than we do.

> **The key is to become a smarter batter. Yes, we may on occasion be rewarded with a "round tripper," but of greater importance is getting on base more often and scoring more runs.**

Maybe life for the Joneses is not quite as sunny as it appears to be. Maybe ours is not as grim as it may seem at times. That may make little difference. We react to the world we perceive, not the one that is actually there.

> **Definition:** If all those around us appear better off than we are, we are apt to feel poor even though in actual terms we may not be. Sociologists call that *relative deprivation.*

Sudden and unexpected expenses, the desire to finance a college education for a son or daughter and, even in particular cases, a reduction in salary or benefits can all add to the burden. Perhaps we desperately wish to please family members and provide them with the things they want and which we feel they should have. As we grow older we may begin to be haunted by the fear that we will not have financial security in our retirement years. That fear may be real rather than a mere spectre. Many Americans are faced with rising medical expenses at the time in their lives when they are forced to survive on Social Security and perhaps an all too inadequate pension. We may also wonder what the financial health of Medicare will be at the time we need it.

Faced with these kinds of circumstances, the temptation to step up to the plate, look for a nice fastball, and try to drive it over the fence for a grand slam home run can be all too tempting. We want to win the game so badly, and it feels as if we must be in the bottom of the ninth inning. Time seems to be running out. We need to win quickly.

Scams, plans, and false opportunities

It is an understandable feeling. It is also one that may lead to financial destruction leaving us worse off than before. We are all too likely to swing wildly, swing at almost anything, and be fooled over and over again. One report indicated that confidence men selling "investments" which ranged from highly suspicious to just plain fraudulent knew that a person who fell for their sales pitch once would probably be an even easier mark a second time. In fact, numerous people desperate to recoup earlier losses would hand over additional hard-earned money and retirement savings as many as six times!

Of course, not all the seeming "opportunities" we encounter are fraudulent. A good number just do not work for most folks. Unfortunately, on very rare occasions, they do. Yes, somebody will win the lottery. However, we actually have a better chance of being struck by lightning, unless the lottery of course happens to be jury duty! Evidence of that rare winner can lure us right into the trap.

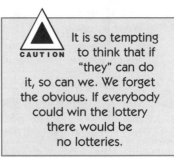
It is so tempting to think that if "they" can do it, so can we. We forget the obvious. If everybody could win the lottery there would be no lotteries.

Chains and pyramid scams

Modern versions of the old chain letter scam are another potential total disaster. "Investors" put up a certain required amount of funds, get to add their name to a list and recruit others to join them. The name at the top of the list receives money from the new members and is removed. Supposedly, when your name rises to the top, you receive back your original contribution plus a handsome profit. This does not work, and it is also illegal. Not only do desperate people lose money, they also sometimes find themselves involved in criminal investigations, although they may have gotten involved with no

HOT spot Tragically, even the Internet is now being used to "market" investment clubs and plans to the unsuspecting. One company in Italy used cyberspace to lure in participants from literally around the world.

intentions of any wrong doing. To make matters even worse, some of these so-called plans and clubs give their victims absolutely no chance of winning. Names on the list may be those of nonexistent persons or members of the family of the con-artist who put the fraud together in the first place. The only people whoever "invested" any money in the entire operation are his marks.

Work-at-home schemes

Ironically, even a sincere effort to work hard or be creative can lead to financial pain. While there are occasional legitimate offers, the majority of work-at-home schemes are just that. One popular version of this calls for persons to buy supplies to make craft items which can then be sold back to the supplier. When the finished items are offered, the home worker discovers they do not come up to the supplier's "standards." Other variations are more outrageous. The information, provided for a fee, informs the homeworker to place advertisements in magazines offering opportunities to work at home. The victim is encouraged to become the victimizer.

CAUTION Work-at-home schemes may extract relatively small sums of money from their targets, but they can be particularly cruel since they tend to take it from those who can least afford to lose it.

Marketing your own idea

Much larger sums are involved with certain traps aimed at those who may believe they really have something marketable to offer. For example, how much do you really know about that company that offers to represent you and present your invention to potential manufacturers? Is it willing to furnish you with references and the names of inventors who have successfully used its services? More than one inventor has paid thousands of dollars and received nothing of value in return.

Multi-level marketing plans

In a different category from the things we have been discussing are multilevel marketing plans. There are several companies with high-quality products and services that distribute in this manner. Some of their distributors have done well. If you think you have the personality and drive for this kind of work, there is probably little harm in giving it a try for a limited period of time. However, if you find your efforts produce less than success, do not let this discourage you from investment strategies that might work for you.

The big problem for many people who try multilevel marketing is that, in these plans, there is normally no such thing as a protected sales territory. Those who can sign up others as sales persons receive credit for a percentage of the new recruits'

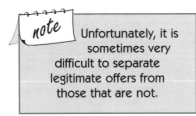

Legitimate companies will not object to you checking on them and will probably help you do so.

sales. These persons are then encouraged to go out and do the same thing. Thus, if you have several levels of sales people working under you, you increase dramatically your profit potential. Unfortunately, before very long, the market is saturated with too many people trying to sell the same thing to too few customers while still seeking to sign up yet more sellers. Many will get frustrated and quit. Expenses could also be incurred as a result of buying products to meet sales quotas but for which there is no resale market, and for traveling to meetings where your attendance may not exactly be required but will be strongly encouraged.

note Unfortunately, it is sometimes very difficult to separate legitimate offers from those that are not.

What kind of results has multilevel marketing produced in the past? A 1987 study of 1,002 participants by the Quebec Consumer Protection Office indicated the average income earned was $2.50 per hour. A 1997 study by the same office found that 48.8 percent who tried it lost money, 27.5 percent made none, and only 3.1 percent reported making a "moderate" amount. There is little reason to believe the situation is much different in the United States than in Canada. As noted, you may want to try one of these plans, but if it does not work for you rather promptly have the wisdom to see that, and go on to something that does.

Too-good-to-be-true opportunities

There are companies that do market genuine prepackaged business opportunities which enable buyers to go into business for themselves, although these often require a substantial investment. However, a 1995 *Wall Street Journal* article reported on steps by both the federal and state governments to stop a large number of business-opportunity scams, involving approximately 100 companies. They promised to establish people in a variety of businesses including vending machines, amusement games, telephones, display racks for cards and computer software, and auto parts. The prospects of the people running these firms were those who had no jobs or were in need of additional income. Those feeling a sense of desperation often will not take the time or effort to do the research, and the fraudulent operations know it. They will make wild profit potential claims and offer poor-quality merchandise. Some have even used shills to pose as highly satisfied participants. Starting your own business may be both satisfying and profitable, but it may take more time, money, and work than it appears. Even then, there is no guarantee of success.

note One marketer even admitted that 80 percent of the people who bought his plan never acted on it at all.

Infomercials

Perhaps closely related to this problem are television infomercials. They can pop up at anytime, but seem to be most prevalent late at night. Many involve real estate. Many of the others, although it may not be apparent at first, are based on mail order or something similar. Again, it is a problem that these things do work for a few people, but for most they do not. Sometimes, within a few days or weeks after viewers bought a course, they have been contacted by high-pressure sales persons trying to sell them expensive goods or services which are

HINT If it were as easy to make money as the infomercials claim, why would they bother to sell you the system? The marketers could simply use it themselves and make all the money they wanted.

"needed" to make the proposed business venture successful. On those rare occasions when you might actually find an operational vehicle rather than something now reduced to little more than scrap metal at a government auction, expect to compete with experienced professionals if you are serious about bidding on it. True real estate bargains are likely to draw the same kind of competition.

Ponzi schemes

From time to time, local scams seem to crop up which can separate those seeking a better financial life from what financial resources they may already have. These come in almost endless varieties. They may involve some alleged fantastic new product or process, real estate, or other business ventures. The unsuspecting are often introduced to the "opportunity" by friends, business acquaintances, or even fellow church members. If they are fortunate, all they will lose is their "investment," which in some cases has been their life savings.

DEFINITION

Many of these are completely illegal, nothing more than *Ponzi schemes*, where the early investors receive some of the money invested by later ones. Tragically, some of the schemes have destroyed families and old friendships, and created embarrassment and legal problems. Even the opportunities which may be legal usually are little more than a concept or an elusive dream.

Look before you leap

No matter how well you may think you know someone, never invest in anything until you have thoroughly checked it out. Do the people in charge of the project have experience in the field? How liquid is the investment; can you sell at anytime you want out? Can the company furnish bank references? Are its financial records regularly audited? Are the promises of profits just too good to be true? Even if you get satisfactory answers to all these questions it may be best to look elsewhere for financial opportunity.

We could continue looking at it indefinitely. By now, some common strains are probably obvious. Nearly all of these approaches make outlandish claims of profit for relatively little effort. They are designed to appeal mostly to those who are feeling financial stress and strain, who are ready to grasp at almost anything that seems to offer a bit of security and the hope of a better life. Some extract rather small sums of money, while with others it may be extensive. All get people blindly swinging for the fences and striking out.

Are there better ways? Yes, but they require time and work. They probably will not make you a millionaire either. But they can bring you a solid degree of financial success and security plus the personal satisfaction that comes with that. They are intended to have you not just working for money, but to have your money working for you. They are all based on the well-established, well-tested concept of investing. You can start with the basics, and with minimum risk or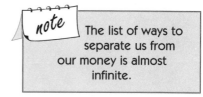

The list of ways to separate us from our money is almost infinite.

money. In time, if you desire, your approach can become considerably more sophisticated, and most likely more rewarding. There is no guarantee of success, nor can there be. But, there is nothing mysterious or magic about it either. You may already be doing some of this, but like Richie Ashburn, our goal is to play smarter. If you are curious, then read on to discover some ways to find your first investment dollars.

Chapter 3

Finding those first dollars

The small investor

Some excellent publications claim to be written with the small investor in mind. Unfortunately, their idea of the small investor often seems to be anything less than a major financial institution. Of course, there are others that are sensitive to the needs of those of us who do not quite command the assets of the interior of Fort Knox (the government gold depository). But even these may frequently appear to be writing for persons who are relatively financially comfortable and are looking for something constructive to do with cash that is not needed to meet basic monthly expenses.

The May 1995 issue of *Better Investing*, a monthly magazine, gives us a more accurate view of the genuine small investor. An editorial entitled "I Want to Invest, but I Don't Have Much Money," indicates that the publication daily receives letters from people with this problem. For example some might feel they could spare $300 or $500 dollars a year for stock purchases, but brokers tell them to come back when they have $5,000. *Better Investing* offers two very constructive suggestions for those in this situation. Dividend reinvestment plans and investment clubs provide ways to invest small amounts of money regularly and constructively. You will find both discussed elsewhere in this book, and both are highly recommended.

Certainly, if you are investing $500 or less a year in stocks or mutual funds you are a small investor. Even if you could invest several thousand a year, you would still be in that category. However, if you have been living essentially paycheck to paycheck, even finding $500 a year may seem like an impossible task. In fact, you may be questioning whether you can prevent yourself from sinking deeper into debt. You are being called upon to do something different, where there may be no experience on which to draw. That can not only make it difficult, but a little frightening as well. At the very least, you may wonder if you can really do it. If this is the case, then it is just as important to know what it is necessary to avoid as well as what to do. Even if you believe you can come up with a few hundred dollars a year to start, it may help to discover some ways to possibly increase that and to be aware of a critical pitfall which can be a dangerous trap.

> **note** We said that the longest journey begins with that single step. We should also note that this first single step may be the most difficult you will have to take.

Borrowing to invest

It is important to know what not to do as well as what you can do. Perhaps every rule may have an occasional exception, but for the small investor this one probably has none: *Never,* under any circumstances, borrow money for investment purposes. The reason for this is quite simple: If your proposed investment is a sound one, with no more than prudent risk, then it is almost impossible for it to earn you more money in a year than you will have to pay in interest for the money you borrowed. If it does have the potential to earn more than the interest you will owe, most likely it is not an investment but a *speculation.* It is questionable that large investors should speculate. Small investors most definitely should not. They simply cannot afford to lose frequently (occasional modest losses will not be fatal and can be considered tuition you pay to learn).

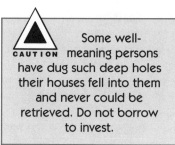

Some well-meaning persons have dug such deep holes their houses fell into them and never could be retrieved. Do not borrow to invest.

If you borrow for a profitable investment, it is unlikely it will earn as much as your borrowing will cost, and you will also be under the additional financial pressure to make the monthly payments on your loan. Despite some of the phenomenal annual returns of the stock market in the 1990s, it would be dangerous to expect your return would be greater than the cost of the loan every year, or even most years. If you borrow for what was indeed a prudent investment, but still turned out to be a losing one, then you have the extra burden of having to make up the losses plus still pay off the loan. You are now in a deeper hole than when you started.

Investing while in debt

While some may, on good grounds, disagree, I do not believe it is absolutely necessary to be completely debt free before starting an investment program. As noted elsewhere, certainly it will be beneficial to work on reducing your outstanding debts as you invest, but investing regularly can help inspire some people to work harder at getting their entire financial house in order. Too many people might never begin to invest if they first waited until they were completely debt free, or had only an outstanding mortgage.

If your current debt obligations can be met each month without unreasonable financial strain, then, quite possibly, you are financially strong enough to begin an investment program. If later on your situation should deteriorate, despite your best efforts to prevent this, then temporarily there is nothing wrong in reducing or even totally suspending your investment program until you can safely resume it.

If you speculate you may win once in awhile, but you will lose most of the time, and in the end you will lose the money you borrowed plus probably more.

Getting your family's support

The kind of investment approach advocated here is one that will benefit from family support. Share your investment goals with your spouse, and if you feel they are mature enough to respect the confidentiality of all of this, perhaps even your children might learn from knowing some of what you are striving to accomplish. If you have the family's understanding and cooperation, then your task will be much easier. In their own way, each family member might even be enthusiastic enough to help by being a little more frugal and cutting back on unnecessary expenses, such as running the air conditioner at a lower temperature than necessary or using the clothes dryer to dry a single item or two.

> *note* If you are trying to pull back the throttle while the family is crying, "full speed ahead," your job may not be impossible, but it certainly will be more difficult and, in the beginning at least, it already seems quite challenging enough.

However, confidentiality is absolutely essential so, if necessary, wait to bring children into all of this until they are mature enough to understand. Nothing can be more discouraging for new investors than to have others, whether intentionally or unintentionally, ridicule their efforts. Some well-meaning friends and associates may not discourage you but will offer all kinds of tips and suggestions. You do not need that kind of advice. Some of it may actually be sound, but it is usually close to impossible for the beginner (sometimes even the experienced) to tell which is and which is not. Some offered "help" may actually be more detrimental than the ridicule. Once you have had a degree of experience and are a bit more seasoned at all of this, you can use your judgment as with whom and to what extent you discuss investment and other financial matters.

Establishing a cash reserve

Although they may somewhat differ on the amount you need, a number of financial experts would probably say wait to invest in stocks, mutual funds, and other kinds of investments until you have an emergency cash reserve. Probably three months take-home pay would be the minimum, while others might advocate at least six months. Actually, there is much to be said for this position. Access to liquid resources for those unexpected needs and emergencies can be critical. If you have already been saving something with this kind of purpose in mind, it would be wise to continue. However, if you have been living paycheck to paycheck, it may be that the sum total of your liquid savings is a figure between zero and a few hundred dollars. While it would be ideal for you to build up your savings first, it may seem like such an obstacle that the job will not get done and you will never get around to other kinds of investment approaches discussed in these pages. It is these investment strategies that ultimately offer the best opportunity to achieve a level of financial security that offers something beyond paycheck to paycheck existence. It is essential to have cash reserves and other liquid assets. That is stated numerous times in the pages ahead, but you will need more than that to get where you will want to journey.

If you are starting with either no or very minimal savings, and you do not feel up to the challenge of first building a cash reserve, you might try a *compromise strategy.* If your starting goal is to find $50 a month to invest, than put $25 into a bank or credit-union savings account, or some other place where it will be reasonably safe, draw a little interest, and not be so readily available that you will be unduly tempted to spend it. Series EE United States Savings Bonds, which can be purchased for as little as $25 and redeemed any time after being held for six months, are also all right. You can order these through your local

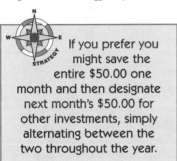

If you prefer you might save the entire $50.00 one month and then designate next month's $50.00 for other investments, simply alternating between the two throughout the year.

bank. The remaining $25 will be available for the kinds of investments we review in the chapters ahead.

By dividing the money between the two categories, you may make it easier to maintain and even increase your enthusiasm to contribute to both. If you cannot possibly find $50, then pick a lesser amount with which to start. If you can set aside $100 or more, then by all means do so. At the very beginning of this trip, the fact that you are investing something is far more important than the actual dollar amount.

As noted, the first step is the important one, and often the most difficult. It cannot be demonstrated scientifically, but it seems that once we start investing we develop the ability over time to find just a few more dollars to put into our efforts, and then later we find still a few more beyond that. Eventually, you may be investing a monthly amount you would have originally never thought possible. You will also discover that you are no longer just working for money. The money you have invested is now working for you. Interest, dividends, and capital gains will begin to accumulate, and your earnings on your investments will start to have earnings of their own. The magic of compounding will start to take place. Probably, you will also get the incentive to get your entire financial house in order, and you will simultaneously start to see your debts decline. But, none of this will ever happen if that first step is not taken. Take it, no matter how small it may have to be.

> Are you in the habit of eating out for lunch? Brown bag it, and invest the savings. Save $1 per working-day this way, and in a typical month you have over $20 for investing.

Once you decide on a monthly target, the next task is to find the money. Do not get discouraged if, at first, you do not have complete success. Take what you did find, and start putting it to work. Revise your target downward if you must, upward if you can. Stay flexible.

Finding hidden money

Now, you can start devising ways to make your "grub stake" appear. Try some of the following:

- If your job provides any overtime, you might consider setting aside some of your overtime money for your investment objectives.

- Should you receive an increase in wages, leave present spending where it is (yes, that is difficult) and put the additional funds into your investments.

- If you are in the habit of making long-distance calls that last more than a minute or two, cut that phone bill by writing letters (or use e-mail if you have a computer) at least some of the time.

- If you pay somebody to wash your car or mow your lawn, give thought to doing these chores yourself and banking those savings.

- Dine out less, and choose modest places when you do.

- Watch all utility usage for waste that can be eliminated.

> **HOT spot** Remember, if you start, chances are excellent that, in time, more funds will become available. It is those first dollars that are the most elusive. Do not give up until you find them. Once you do, keep searching for more.

- Cut back on hobby-related and recreational expenditures.

- If nothing else will work, and it will not jeopardize your health, family, or present job, look for a second part-time job, even if for minimum wage.

This is not a complete list of strategies or even the best list. Hopefully it will give you some ideas, and you can come up with additional ones, ones that will be best for you. With practice, like most things, it gets easier. If the family assists and it becomes a team effort, it is easier still. If one month you do not make your goal, or things even go into reverse, forget it, and put it behind you. Go on to the next month. In time you will get there.

Your monthly budget

While you are meeting this challenge, you may want to draw up a monthly family budget. If you know where your money is going, then it becomes much easier to control it. Make your estimated expenditures realistic. Do not play tricks on yourself. If your estimates are reasonable (try to include a contingency category for the unexpected expenses), and you stick to them, you may be able to find those first dollars for investing. Then each month pay yourself first, not last as we are often likely to do. Give your investments top priority, and before long it may be difficult to imagine not making them.

Now, it is time for us to look at what can be done with those elusive dollars once they are firmly in your grasp. They can develop into good workers.

Chapter 4

The security of cash investments

What you'll find in this chapter:

⮕ Why hold an emergency fund?

⮕ How much to hold in reserve

⮕ The best ways to hold on to reserve funds

⮕ Factors to consider for a financial institution

⮕ A close look at different banking accounts

A major theme throughout this book is that small investors are different. They cannot afford to bear as much risk as those whose financial situation is more secure. For this reason alone, some of their resources should always be held in the form of cash or cash equivalents. There are other reasons as well. Money that you know you are going to need in the near future should not be exposed to market risk. Among other things, this might include funds that will be required within approximately the next three to five years for a college education, down payment on a house, or some other important major expenditure. Should financial markets decline there would not be enough time to rebuild the nest egg. If you are particularly risk adverse you might even be more comfortable with a greater time horizon.

A commendable habit would be to establish, over time, some sort of emergency fund which is the equivalent of possibly three to six months take-home pay. Withdrawals can be made from it to cover unexpected home or car repairs, temporary layoffs, or other unpleasantries. Again, since such needs can come with little or no warning, the money set aside to handle them should be very secure. Emergency cash needs to be fairly liquid cash.

Still another factor is that holding some cash tends to reduce our anxiety levels and makes it psychologically easier for us to take more, but prudent, risks with the remainder of our assets. We know we are not betting the "family farm" and, as a result, our investing decisions are likely to be more rational and profitable.

How much cash to hold

What percentage of our resources needs to be held in cash? There is no precise answer for that question. Every family's situation differs. The chapter on asset allocation should provide some insights into what might be a suitable amount. Cash investments can also be supplemented with other kinds, such as bonds, which are less conservative but also less volatile than stocks and much more liquid than real estate. Newer investors may be more comfortable holding a greater percentage of cash while they are learning about potentially more rewarding investment opportunities. Market

note Knowing you have assets that are safe helps prevent you from doing the wrong thing at the worst possible time.

conditions can be still another factor. When everybody in the world is screaming they want to buy stocks, it may be a good time to sell them some of yours and bank the cash until sanity returns to the financial markets.

Which ways to hold cash

There are various ways to hold the necessary cash reserves. As with other kinds of investments, each has its own advantages and disadvantages. Generally, there are probably only three reasons why you want to keep money in a bank. However, all three are good ones. Possibly the most important is that all of your accounts in a bank are insured up to a combined total of $100,000 by the federal government if the bank participates in the Federal Deposit Insurance Corporation's program. Credit unions are eligible for a similar government program administered by the National Credit Union Administration. It does not get much safer than this! A rule with absolutely no exceptions whatsoever is that, in the highly unlikely event you encounter a bank, credit union, or some other bank-like type of financial institution that does not participate in one of these programs, do not deposit or maintain any money with that organization. If you have doubts about its membership, do not hesitate to ask. Members will be happy to tell you. You are not interested in the nonmembers. Never settle for some sort of state or private insurance plan as a substitute for federal protection.

note Everyone needs some assets in the form of cash. On the other hand, because of the ravages of inflation and the danger of lost opportunities, the veteran investor normally will not find it prudent to be entirely in cash.

Most small investors will not have to worry about such matters, but it does not hurt to remember that insurance coverage is limited to a total of $100,000 for all accounts, not each account. There is nothing to stop you from opening another account with a different bank or credit union (not just another branch) and obtaining additional coverage this way. Of course, having to collect on this kind of insurance is inconvenient, may take considerable time, and is especially alarming if you have a critical need for your funds just at the moment the institution fails. You may feel it is worth the modest sum to get a report on your prospective bank's financial stability from *Weiss Research, Inc.,* or some other reputable rating agency. Weiss can be reached at 800-289-9222. Another established rating company is *Veribanc* of Wakefield, Massachusetts. The telephone number is 800-442-2657.

A second factor to consider when selecting a financial institution is convenience. Does the bank have branch offices you might wish to use? An increasing number of us like to use automatic teller machines (ATMs)

note

CAUTION An increasing number of banks provide various brokerage services. While there is nothing wrong in using these, remember there is no federal insurance on any of the financial products a bank may sell in this manner.

or bank by telephone or the Internet. To what extent does the institution provide these services, and what are the fees? Are there Saturday hours? Are safe-deposit boxes available for rental? Perhaps you might want to bank by mail. All of these are factors to consider.

Closely related to the convenience factor is the matter of fees. What does the institution charge you for the various services it provides? Unfortunately, in recent years there has been a tendency for banks to raise fees substantially and invent new ones. Some even charge for transactions with a teller. Minimum amounts which must be kept on deposit to avoid fees have also been raised.

It pays to shop and compare, and the matter of fees is one place where a credit union might possibly save you money.

Finally, while it is certainly not mandatory, in the event you need a loan a bank might smile more favorably and promptly on your application if you have been doing

HINT

other business with it. Of course, you want the best interest rates possible on money that you deposit with a bank or credit union, but in all honestly you can usually do better elsewhere. What you really want from a bank is the security of insurance, convenience, and possibly a loan. Many financial matters can be handled more profitably with other institutions such as mutual funds or brokerage houses.

The basic services that you may want are available from both banks and credit unions. Depending on the institution, they will come with a variety of packages and the fees to accompany them. Do some comparison shopping, and do not pay for bells and whistles you neither want nor need.

Types of bank accounts

Checking accounts are probably the most basic bank accounts you can have. They enable you to pay bills more easily and safely. Since most do not pay interest, keep only sufficient funds in the account to cover your monthly expenses or to prevent a service charge. The remainder should be put to work and earn at least a little interest.

Some checking accounts do pay interest. It does not hurt to look at what is offered by your financial institution, but in most cases interest-paying accounts require you to maintain a rather high balance. Usually, you will do better by taking a regular account and putting the money you would have kept on deposit to earn interest in some sort of savings or money-market account, where the interest rate is normally higher.

Regular savings accounts can usually be opened with a rather minimal deposit, and additional amounts of any size can normally be added at any time. There may be a limit on the number of withdrawals you can make over a particular period, although you could always close out the account and receive the entire balance if necessary. Such accounts offer liquidity and safety. They are a good place for your unexpected emergency funds. They are also an excellent way to start if you have never saved any money or if you want to gradually put money aside for a special purchase. Like a checking account, virtually every family needs at least one savings account. Their interest rates are rather low, but will be as good or better than on checking. Some banks have savings accounts less attractive than they used to be with more restrictions, fees for inactivity, and other inconveniences. Credit unions may permit you to open one with as little as $5. As usual, do some comparative shopping.

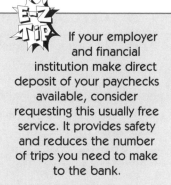 If your employer and financial institution make direct deposit of your paychecks available, consider requesting this usually free service. It provides safety and reduces the number of trips you need to make to the bank.

Some families may also want to maintain a **money-market account**. These pay higher rates of interest, but come with certain limitations. There will be a higher initial deposit required to open and maintain the account, perhaps $2,500 or more. While checks can often be written on these accounts, they may have to be for a specified minimum amount such as $100 or $250. The number of withdrawals per month either by cash or check may be limited. The inconvenience is not all bad. A money-market account makes it easy to get your funds, but not quite as easy as a checking or savings account. The temptation to use the money is somewhat lessened as a result. As you get into serious saving, a money-market account is worth considering. It may be an excellent place for your emergency fund.

Finally, banks and credit unions offer **certificates of deposit**, or **CDs**, as they are commonly called. *Certificates of deposit* obligate you to leave your money with the institution for a stated period of time. Normally, this will be from six months up to as much as five years, although sometimes a CD can be obtained for a period as short as one month. Interest rates are higher than you will receive on savings or money-market accounts. Typically, the longer you agree to let the bank or credit union use your money the higher the rate of

DEFINITION

interest. However, due to the peculiarity of financial markets, occasionally the rate may be slightly higher for a shorter time period. Even within a city rates are usually competitive, so check with several institutions.

Certificates of deposit

CDs issued by banks, but offered by some brokerage houses without sales charges, can provide attractive returns. The minimum investment will be at least $1,000. Broker CDs normally pay interest twice a year and, unlike CDs sold by banks, it may be possible to withdraw your money early without paying interest penalty. However, you will get the price available in the secondary market some brokers make for these. If you are seriously considering broker CDs, make sure you understand all the details before you make your purchase.

> **HINT** Although less convenient, banking by mail or the Internet may make it practical to consider out-of-town institutions in some instances.

There are a number of factors the bank or credit-union CD shopper needs to consider before committing to the final purchase:

- CD money should be money you are reasonably certain you will not need until the certificate matures. Yes, if necessary you can redeem the certificate early, but there will be an interest penalty for doing so (should you absolutely have to do this, make sure you deduct the penalty on page 1 of Form 1040 of your federal income tax return). If the redeemed certificate is a relatively new one, you could walk out of the bank with less than your initial deposit.

- Another basic question is how much can you invest in the CD? Different institutions will have varying minimums for the certificates they offer. Often it may be $1,000 or more, but sometimes as little as a couple of hundred dollars may qualify.

- Once you have decided on the amount and length of time of the investment, what to do with the interest becomes an important decision. While you may not touch the CD principle without penalty, you may have the interest it earns. It can be deposited into a checking or savings account if you wish, or it can be rolled back into the certificate to compound and earn additional interest. This raises still another question.

• How often is the interest compounded and paid? The ideal situation is daily compounding, because this means your interest immediately begins to earn additional interest. The frequency of compounding does not determine the schedule for payment. Some CDs pay monthly. Others may do so only once a year. Obviously you do not have access to the money until it is paid into the account. Also remember, once the interest is paid into a checking or other account rather than rolled back into the CD, it is no longer compounding, and the annual yield will be reduced accordingly.

• Finally, although for small investors it will not make a great difference in the total results, it is good to know if the interest rate is based on what in banking terms is known as a *CD basis,* or whether it is a *bond equivalent basis.* The "year" for "CD basis" is 360 days rather than the 365 days for "bond equivalent basis." This means that certificates with a "CD basis" will give you five days more additional interest over the course of a calendar year.

DEFINITION

When checking CD rates always get both the basic rate and the annual yield, which reveals what your money will earn with the assistance of compounding.

Some CDs do come with various bells and whistles. These may allow for upward adjustments in the interest rate or permit additional deposits before the maturity date. Such things are nice to have, but probably are not worth accepting less initial interest and yield in order to obtain them.

Certificates of deposit can be a useful part of your savings and investment program. Like checking, savings, and money-market accounts, they are eligible for federal deposit insurance. They are thus safe, and they are not subject to market risk. Because of their interest penalties, they lack just enough liquidity to make it easy to cash them in and spend the money. Some people may find short-term Treasury securities can do as good a job for them (see the chapter on bonds), but for many of us, CDs are an excellent choice.

Money-market accounts

A little less convenient, and with no federal insurance, are the money-market accounts sponsored by various mutual funds. In almost all instances, money-market accounts reward you for the slight additional risk and inconvenience you accept with a higher interest rate than banks or credit unions pay. These funds normally make checking available as well, but if you accept that option, make very sparing use of it, as it can make for rather complex record keeping. Checks may also have to be

> *note* The shorter the time to maturity, the safer and more conservative is the fund.

written for a certain minimum amount in order to be accepted. You can have money wired from your fund to your bank or credit-union account, or have the fund mail a check to you.

These kinds of money-market funds in many ways resemble a typical mutual fund. You buy shares in them, but the funds maintain the price at an even $1.00 per share. They do this by investing in various government and private financial instruments which on average will mature in no more than 120 days. Many average a period of forty days or less. Money-market funds invest in such things as Treasury bills, commercial paper, certificates of deposit, and bankers' acceptances. It is not necessary to know precisely what all these things are. Just remember the

> HINT Generally, the larger the money-market fund, the more likely its expenses will be lower, since there are more people to share the burden.

funds that invest exclusively in Treasury instruments are considered safer and also may pay somewhat less interest than those who also purchase nongovernment items. They may also have some tax advantages. Some funds are designed to be exempt from both federal and state income taxes. They invest strictly in certain short-term municipal securities and will usually provide a lower interest payout than their taxable counterparts.

While money-market mutual funds are not insured, very few have ever had any financial difficulties. They can be a good place to store money which needs to be relatively risk free. Look for a fund from a reputable company with adequate financial resources. Be sure to compare management and other fees, as these play a major role in determining how well the fund will reward its shareholders.

Also available are United States Government Series EE, HH, and I bonds, whose principal value does not fluctuate, and thus are as good as cash and almost as liquid. In addition, they provide tax benefits. See the entire separate chapter devoted to these.

Loan-participation funds

We conclude by taking a brief look at loan-participation funds. In the strict sense of the word, these are not cash or cash equivalents, since their net-asset value can fluctuate. However, the fluctuations in net-asset value and market price are less than in nearly every other noncash investment, so these can be considered rather safe. The funds are exactly what the name implies,

DEFINITION

pools of loans. They trade as closed-end funds in the over-the-counter market, but a few do trade on the New York Stock Exchange. Interest-rate yields can be quite good. For those looking for a little more income, but with only slightly less safety, they may be a good idea. *Barron's* includes a list of them in its closed-end fund section.

>))) It probably would
> HINT   be helpful to
> consult with a broker if
> you are interested in loan-
> participation funds.

Careful management of your cash investments is just as vital as that of more advanced investments. For those just getting started at some kind of savings and investment program, they may comprise all or the greatest part of their assets. Handled wisely, cash investments can serve you well and help lay a solid foundation for a more financially secure future. However, because they provide limited returns, and inflation and taxes can eat heavily into these, once the foundation is in place it is time to explore other possibilities. Cash is never trash. However, stuffing your mattress full of it is not the final solution either. Plain vanilla ice cream is good, but ultimately you will want to sample some of the more exotic flavors as well.

Chapter 5

United States Savings Bonds

Perhaps as a child you remember a favorite relative or someone else presenting you with a United States Savings Bond as a gift for a special occasion. If you still have that bond, take a good look at it. Chances are it will pleasantly surprise you when you redeem it. Older bonds, those issued before December 1965, can quietly earn interest for up to forty years. All other E and EE bonds have a maturity of thirty years, while H and HH bonds will be hard at work for twenty. There are a number of other reasons why these bonds are worth the consideration of investors of virtually any age.

E and EE bonds

Before November 1982, the United States Government issued E and H bonds. We'll look at H and HH bonds a little later. However, E bonds were attractive gifts for children. They could be purchased at relatively low prices and were about as safe an investment as one could find, since they were guaranteed by the United States government and, after an initial holding period, could always be redeemed for their original cost plus the accumulated interest. The one thing that made such bonds unattractive to serious investors was that the interest rate was so low that, after inflation and taxes, the rate of return could be somewhere between negligible and negative. EE bonds were introduced in 1982, and the new bonds had all the good qualities of their old E counterparts without their drawbacks.

> *note*
> EE bonds still are one of the few attractive investments for the investor who is highly risk adverse.

EE bonds can be an alternative to a bank federally insured certificate of deposit. The United States government guarantees payment of both principle and interest, and unlike other kinds of government bonds EE (and HH) bonds are never subject to market price fluctuations.

Very few investments can offer protection against both inflation and deflation, but until a few years ago EE bonds did. On the deflationary side, the bonds were guaranteed if held five years or longer to pay at least the minimum rate of return in effect when the bond was originally purchased. This was compounded semiannually and ranged from a high of 7.5 percent to a low of 4 percent. In 1995, the guaranteed interest rate was abolished for new bonds, but remains in effect for those already owned, with certain limitations. The inflationary protection is still in place for all bonds. Bonds purchased since May 1, 1997, earn a market-based interest rate which is 90 percent of the average yield, during the time the bonds are held, of marketable Treasury securities with five years remaining to maturity. Those held less than five years are subject to three months interest penalty. The rate of payment is adjusted every May and November. Interest rates can fluctuate, but your principal is always intact. EE bonds can be redeemed at any time after an initial holding period of six months.

> HINT
> EE bonds are one of those few investments where you do not have to worry about the value of your holdings fluctuating with the whims of the market. In addition, this is a very liquid investment.

For bonds purchased before May 1997, it would be best to check with a bank which accepts orders for EE bonds as to what their current value and rate of return may be. From time to time, the Treasury Department changed the guidelines, and the situation can be very confusing. Probably, you should inquire about any possible recent changes before making new purchases. Those with Internet access may also obtain information at the Treasury Department's Bureau of the Public Debt web site (http://www.savingsbonds.gov).

Advantages of EE bonds

There are considerable tax advantages to EE bonds as well. They are never subject to state and local income taxes, a factor which makes them particularly inviting in states where such rates are high. Federal income tax must be paid, but it can be deferred for literally decades until the bonds reach final redemption. On the other hand, you have the option, if you prefer, to pay the federal tax annually. Bonds registered in the names of children, if treated in this manner, usually will be subject to no taxes at all. Once a method has been selected for handling applicable federal taxes, it cannot be changed. Subject to certain age, registration, and income limitations, EE bonds purchased in 1990 and later, if used to provide a college or university education for the buyer, spouse, or dependent, are also exempt from federal income taxes.

Check with the Internal Revenue Service or your bank for the current income and registration restrictions on EE bonds.

Still another advantage for the small investor is that EE bonds can be conveniently purchased with relatively small sums that may be available for investing. New bonds sell for 50 percent of their face value (the redemption value may be more than the face value). Denominations currently available are $50, $75, $100, $200, $500, $1,000, $5,000, and $10,000. This means one can be obtained for as little as $25. Buyers are limited in a single calendar year to bonds with a total issue price of

Some thoughtful companies make a payroll savings plan available to their employees. Bonds in denominations between $100 and $1,000 can be obtained through this Bond-A-Month plan, which encourages regular saving in a relatively painless manner.

$15,000 if registered individually or $30,000 if registered with a co-owner. Small investors, except in most unusual circumstances, will hardly need to concern themselves with such limitations.

Obtaining bonds

The bonds are easy to obtain. Many banks will take orders for them, with the bond then being mailed several weeks later from a Federal Reserve Bank. They may also be able to provide you with information and an order form for placing your orders directly with the Federal Reserve Bank, if you plan to order bonds in denominations of $100 or higher. Bonds may also be purchased on a regular basis by direct withdrawal from your bank account.

note The easiest way to redeem your bonds is to take them to a bank which accepts orders for purchase. It need not be the bank where the bond was originally obtained.

Bonds can be registered in the name of one individual with or without a designated beneficiary. They can also be registered by two persons, either one of which has full redemption rights. Upon the death of the first, the other becomes full owner. Purchasers of bonds which qualify for the educational exemption should be at least 24 years old. And, these bonds should never be registered individually or jointly in the name of a dependent child whose education they are expected to help finance.

Bonds earn interest from the first day of the month in which an order for them is received, so those purchased late in the month, in effect, earn a free month's interest. If you have bonds purchased earlier than March 1993 or after April 1995, check carefully with your bank before asking it to redeem them. If not timed properly, you could lose from one up to six months interest, as interest accrues to the bonds only semiannually. For bonds bought since March 1993 through April 1995, this problem was eliminated, but cash those bonds

CAUTION All EE bonds older than thirty years or HH bonds more than twenty years old no longer earn interest and should be redeemed as soon as possible.

(and any others) as close to the first of the month as possible, as they will not earn interest for any final partial month in which you hold them.

HH bonds

At the same time that the Treasury Department introduced EE bonds to replace the old E bonds, HH bonds took over from the earlier H bonds. There are some similarities between the two. HH bonds are not directly purchased, but can be obtained in exchange for E or EE bonds which are no less than six months old and have a minimum total redemption value of at least $500. HH bonds are currently available in denominations of $500, $1,000, $5,000, and $10,000. Unlike holders of EE bonds, owners of HH bonds are paid the interest owed them twice a year. Check with your bank for the current rate before making an exchange. The interest rate is set for a ten year period, but may be changed at the end of this time.

> **HINT**
> Financial institutions which take orders for EE bonds can also assist in obtaining and disposing of HH bonds at virtually any time.

HH bonds do have certain advantages. As in the case of EE bonds, the interest they earn is never subject to state and local income taxes. They also permit the further deferral of payment of federal taxes on interest from EE bonds which are exchanged. Since all EE bonds have a final maturity after thirty years, and HH bonds after twenty, this means the taxes due on EE bond interest, but not that from HH bonds, could be deferred up to a total of fifty years!

> **HOT spot**
> HH bonds also are attractive to people who want a safe, steady source of income without market price fluctuations, and they are nearly as liquid as EE bonds.

There is one drawback to HH bonds, and there are times it can be serious enough to make them unattractive. Unlike EE bonds, their interest rate is not adjusted every six months, but can only change after a lengthy ten-year interval. In periods of rising inflation this means the HH bonds could actually produce a negative return. This is especially true when federal taxes are taken into consideration. Unlike EE bond interest, that received from HH bonds must be included in your taxable income for the year in which it is received. When the HH bonds are redeemed, the tax bill also comes due on all deferred EE bond interest used to help purchase them. HH bonds normally should be obtained and held only when inflation is low, and the HH bond interest rate is reasonably competitive with what could at least be obtained on a certificate of deposit. When these conditions do not exist, redemption of the bonds should be seriously considered.

I bonds

In 1998, the Treasury Department began to also issue I bonds. These in many ways are similar to EE bonds, but there are several important differences. Although issued in the same denominations as EE bonds, the I variety sells at its face value rather than 50 percent of it. Interest remains tax-deferred, but the rate is determined in a different manner. Part of it is based on the rate of five-year, inflation-adjusted Treasury notes. The second part will be adjusted every six months. It is based on the Department of Labor's *Consumer Price Index* (the CPI) for urban residents. Issue I bonds are designed to provide some basic protection against the ravages of inflation, something that has at times devastated the returns of bond holders. They are also protected from deflation in the event the CPI were to drop so that the decline is greater than the fixed rate portion of the earnings.

Probably most small investors need to examine the possibilities of EE and I bonds. They can be an attractive addition to a nicely diversified portfolio. They cannot tantalize you with the potential of some more exotic investments, but they are a lot safer. Most likely, only a complete collapse of the federal government could bring about their default, and that is highly improbable. EE and I bonds also have tax and other advantages which small investors will not easily obtain elsewhere. For some, HH bonds may also fill a need. Most banks can furnish additional information, or you can write to the Public Affairs Office, U. S. Savings Bonds Division, Department of the Treasury, Washington, DC 20226. The Treasury Department web site given above can also be helpful. Unlike other federal debt instruments, only American citizens and certain aliens either resident or working in or for the United States may own EE, I, and HH bonds.

Chapter 6

Stocks or mutual funds?

What you'll find in this chapter:

- ▸ Why diversification is so important
- ▸ The power of dollar averaging
- ▸ The option of mutual funds families
- ▸ Differences between load and no-load funds
- ▸ How to avoid the expense in buying stock

The beginning investor rather quickly encounters the question—which should I buy, stocks of individual companies or mutual funds? As with so many other investment questions, there is really no single, simple answer. Let us take a look at several factors and possibilities.

Mutual funds

Some financial advisors, especially those with a long-term view, feel that mutual funds are the best investment vehicle for most people. Several of the reasons for this are obvious. Stock mutual funds, because they purchase shares in a variety of companies, offer diversification. Diversification in turn offers safety. If several stocks in the portfolio turn out to be disappointing, others most likely will yield better than expected results.

For a small fee, mutual funds provide the investor with professional management. Such managers have access to information and help the individual investor could not hope to possess. At least in some cases, professional managers are probably far better able to handle the psychological aspects of handling money.

Many mutual funds allow the investor to get in with a moderate amount of money. Account minimums are on the rise these days, but a number of funds still permit entry for $1,000, or even a substantially smaller sum for an IRA account. Additional money can then be invested at any time. Most funds have a minimum of $100 for additional investments, but for some it is less. Mutual funds will also assist you in instructing your bank or credit union to automatically transmit a monthly payment from your checking account to your mutual-fund account. This can be extremely helpful if you want to dollar average, a powerful tool for the small investor and one we will look at more closely later.

> HINT   Really good managers may be less likely to get caught up in the "herd mentality" that often drives financial markets and causes people to buy and sell at precisely the least advantageous times.

DEFINITION

Companies that offer a variety of mutual funds, *mutual fund families*, provide still another sometimes useful service. Either for a very nominal charge or for free, mutual fund families, will permit you to transfer all or part of the balance in one of the company's funds to another. Small investors should avoid market timing and jumping in and out of investments, but there are instances when a switch from one fund to another makes sense. It is comforting to know that if such an occasion arises, it takes nothing more than a phone call to accomplish it.

For investors large or small, who have little time or inclination to do their own research, mutual funds make a great deal of sense. Mutual funds provide a convenient, relatively safe way to participate in the financial fortunes of a variety of companies, both domestic and foreign. For the small investor, mutual funds are usually—and sometimes—the only practical way to buy into foreign markets. Invest in quality mutual funds, add to your holdings regularly, become a long-term investor with a time horizon of five years or longer, and it is difficult to imagine that you will not make money. Mutual funds deserve some place in the plans of most small investors.

Load and no-load funds

DEFINITION

Of course, nothing in this life is perfect. Mutual funds are no exception. Some funds, known as *load funds,* levy a sales charge. That means a percentage of your money will not be invested at all. It goes to pay commissions. You can also buy *no-load funds* that have no such charges, but you will then have to do your own research to decide what funds are best for you, or pay someone else to do this for you.

All mutual funds, whether load or no-load, will assess to the fund holders a management fee for handling the fund's investments, and the fund will be responsible for other expenses as well. Well-managed funds can usually keep these expenses down to 1 percent or less. Expect to pay more if the fund invests primarily in foreign stocks or other more specialized or exotic investments. Smaller funds also tend to have higher expense ratios, since there are fewer investors to share the costs. While 1 or 2 percent may seem to be very little, over a period of years it will significantly lower what your money would have earned if you had not been required to pay it.

> **note** Although fund expense charges and fees are an unpleasant reality, if you are in a well-managed fund they will be worth the pain.

It is not always true, but often in life you do get what you pay for. Pay nothing, and that may be exactly what you will receive.

Disadvantages to mutual funds

Another more subtle problem is that when investors buy a mutual fund, they do surrender a lot of control over their investment. Of course, if they are unhappy they can always liquidate their holdings or switch into another fund, but short of that there is little they can do. The fund's portfolio managers determine what stocks are purchased and at what price. They also determine when they are sold. If they are short-term traders and, unfortunately, many often are, again you must either endure this approach or take your money elsewhere.

DEFINITION

In severe stock market declines (*bear markets*), mutual funds can suffer from yet another serious problem. It is the financial equivalent of a melt-down. By law, mutual funds have to allow investors to redeem their shares at *net-asset value* (the price which an individual share is worth) at anytime. If a financial panic sets in, fund holders may rush to redeem before they feel their holdings will decline in value. Even though fund managers may believe that the drop in stock prices is temporary, they may be forced to sell stock they want to keep in order to raise cash to meet demands for redemption. As more and more funds find it necessary to do this, it puts further downward pressure on prices, which in turn causes more people to panic and rush to liquidate their holdings. Eventually, rationality does return to the markets and, in time (on rare occasions it could be a long time!), prices recover, but an investor who experiences such a course of events is not likely to soon forget it. It is very painful to say the least, and one could get caught up in the panic selling almost without realizing it. Still those who have a clear idea of where they want to go and how to get there should not be mauled too badly by the bear. They understand nothing goes up forever, or down either.

In investing, knowledge is often power. If you know what mutual funds can do both for and to you, you will be in a better position to weigh how heavily they should fit into your investment strategy. A careful, objective evaluation will probably encourage you to commit a good deal of your investment money in their direction, despite their several drawbacks.

Stocks

Stocks of individual companies are also worthy of the small investor's consideration. Perhaps the major advantage of owning shares directly

HOT spot Every small investor should be aware of both the advantages and risks of mutual funds.

rather than through a mutual fund is that the investor now has complete control over decisions to buy and sell and at what price these transactions take place. This may be more beneficial in bear markets than in bull markets. Owning the shares directly, and assuming they have not been bought on margin, protects you from being forced to liquidate against your will. Small investors who know the difficulties of market timing can choose to ride out the bear if they own their own shares and have the wisdom and courage to avoid panic. For the reasons we have already seen, mutual fund managers do not always have this option.

There is another advantage to direct ownership, one that is largely overlooked: Owning shares in a mutual fund often does very little to encourage investors to become familiar with the industries and companies in which the fund invests. There are exceptions, of course, but it is too easy to leave that kind of research to the managers. After all, it is what they get paid to do. If you are going to make intelligent purchases of specific companies, doing some basic research on your prospective investments becomes almost inevitable. Such knowledge will not only help in making the initial investment, it will also assist in confirming whether the initial decision was correct or not. No one is perfect. Sooner or later every investor will make an investment that turns out to be a mistake. However, if you do your homework the mistakes will tend to be realized earlier and be less costly.

It is also probably easier to develop a long-term investment horizon if you invest in individual stocks. You are more likely to become a true investor rather than a trader, and this is particularly helpful for the small investor who will find frequent trading can often lead to losses or at best marginal gains. Come to know a company well enough to buy into it in the first place and you will probably be encouraged to stick around. Further, if something does begin to go wrong, the information you acquired will help you determine if the situation is serious enough that you should sell and begin to look elsewhere.

note Although in the midst of one it may seem that a bear market will never end, it eventually does, and stocks usually go on to new highs.

Still another benefit is that, as you research companies and industries, you will discover (almost without realizing it) that you are obtaining an education in economics and business. Not only is this helpful in making investment decisions, it can also be an immense source of personal enjoyment and pleasure.

Disadvantages to stock investing

Certainly, there are disadvantages to owning individual stocks. Diversity is more difficult to achieve, but in time you can buy shares in additional companies and more or less create your own "mutual fund." This will not be achieved overnight, but it can be done, and it can again help encourage a long-term horizon for holding shares.

HINT One need not be confined solely to American companies, unless you prefer to restrict yourself completely to the domestic market.

If you wish to go international for some of your investment budget, small investors may well find that sometimes mutual funds will provide greater opportunity. They will usually find it impractical to purchase shares traded only on foreign exchanges. However, a rapidly increasing number of foreign firms do list on both the New York and American exchanges and the NASDAQ.

Probably the biggest drawback for the small investor is the expense involved in buying stock in a particular company. One helpful way to overcome this is to use **dividend reinvestment** and **cash purchase plans** where these are available. Such plans are so useful for small investors that you will find an entire chapter devoted to them. For the moment, however, we note that while many companies have one of these plans in place and they can make it possible to purchase small amounts of stock economically, others do not. Commissions, even from a discount broker, make it uneconomical to purchase a small number of shares in most instances. Unless you place your order before the stockmarket opens in the morning, you will also be assessed an additional

> Many good companies just are not suitable choices for the small investor to own directly. If you want to own these, it would be best to seek out mutual funds.

charge of twelve and a half cents a share (one-eighth of a point), known as the *odd-lot differential* if you buy less than a round lot, or 100 shares on the New York or American Stock Exchange. If a stock sells for $10 or $15 a share, you may be able to avoid the odd-lot differential and also feel the brokerage fee for a round lot is reasonable. However, if the shares trade at much over $30 or $35, you may not feel you could afford to accumulate many in a reasonable period of time even through a company-sponsored cash purchase plan. Certainly, those over $100 are not very good candidates for the typical small investor.

DEFINITION

Investor temperament should play a role in determining whether mutual funds or individual stocks are best for you. If you want diversity quickly, or you find financial research painful and boring, then mutual funds are the way to go. If you want the maximum control over your investments, give careful consideration to individual stocks. However, it does not have to be an either/or situation. Many small investors would do well to add some additional diversity by investing in both mutual funds and individual stocks. Surprisingly, this rather basic and logical approach often is not suggested. If you give it a try, you may discover you are quite comfortable with it and that you appreciate the distinctive benefits that both of these kinds of investments have to offer. After you experimented with this awhile, you may find yourself leaning more to one type of investment than the other. That is fine. You can adjust your holdings as you see fit, but you may still feel there are strong advantages to owning both mutual funds and individual stocks. The perfect investment has never been created. Selecting several different kinds can make your investing safer and more rewarding.

Chapter 7

About brokers and the stock exchange

Even the thought of dealing with a stock broker may be intimidating to the potential small investor who never needed one before. In reality, it is much like shopping for a car or a major appliance. If you know what you need and what you are looking for, the whole experience can be a reasonably comfortable one. If you have no idea, then there could be problems.

To broker or not to broker

Investors who buy only no-load mutual funds directly from the companies who market them can get by without a broker at all. If you buy certificates of deposit or money market funds from a bank you do not need them either, and safe, conservative investments such as these should be included in most small investors' portfolios.

HINT

However, sooner or later, you may find a broker helpful or indispensable. Some mutual funds are sold only through brokers. Investors who do not feel comfortable making their own decisions about mutual funds or other investments normally turn to a broker for help. Except in certain circumstances, such as the use of a dividend reinvestment plan and some companies that will sell directly, you cannot purchase stocks of individual companies or closed-end mutual funds—which trade on stock exchanges—without the services of a broker. Brokers can provide a number of other products and services as well. Many of these will not be suitable for the typical small investor, but in some cases they may be quite beneficial. In addition to helping with investment decisions, brokers can provide a variety of usually free information on stocks, mutual funds, bonds, and other items. Brokers come in essentially two varieties, **full service** and **discount.**

> **HOT spot** Eventually, many small investors are probably going to need a broker. They do not all need the same kind.

Discount brokers

The fees charged by discount brokers vary from one firm to another, but in virtually all cases, they will be well below those of full-service companies. If you feel comfortable and capable making your own investment decisions, seldom will you need a full-service broker. It is senseless to pay for services you do not need.

There is another reason why the small investor should give serious consideration to using a discounter. Most brokers do try to be helpful to all their clients. However, never lose sight of the fact that they are essentially sales people. Their living comes from their commissions. Brokers are only human. The clients who have the money to spend, spend frequently, and buy or sell in large quantities are more likely to get the broker's time, best advice, and special favors. Definitely not all, but some full-service brokers may not want to bother with the small investor at all. The same may be true of certain discounters. However, if you find a discounter willing to take your business, you need not worry about getting inferior advice or missing out on special opportunities. Discounters do not offer either. Discount brokers simply execute orders to buy and sell securities. Most will not bother you with phone calls soliciting your business either. In addition to placing your orders,

> *note* Small investors, because they are investing small amounts and will normally do only a minimum number of trades over the course of a year, do not generate much in the way of commissions.

discount houses will give you price quotations, will usually be able to serve as custodians for IRA accounts, and can often provide you with basic information on various companies and securities, although they will not suggest which ones are suitable for your individual needs. Most discount brokers have programs which enable customers to buy mutual funds; some funds can be acquired without a transaction fee. However, the minimum order for such mutual fund purchases may be too large to interest many small investors, and not all funds are available.

HINT If a company will not tell you its fees, most likely it is not a discounter.

Opening an account

HINT

If you decide that opening an account with a discount broker would be helpful, finding one is not difficult. Friends who are already investing may be able to offer suggestions. Check the advertisements in financial publications such as the *Wall Street Journal, Barron's, Money,* and others. Often these resources are available at your local library. Some discount companies also advertise in the financial section of daily newspapers and on the Internet. The yellow pages of your telephone directory are another source. Call, write, or e-mail brokerage houses that interest you, and request an application form to open an account along with information on what services are provided.

note

Be sure you meet the minimum requirements for opening an account. Some discount firms deal only in large-volume orders. Open only a cash account. Check to see that your account is insured, and be certain you know what kind of minimum cash balance you will be expected to maintain to keep it open or avoid service charges. Inquire about any fees that will be charged for such things as delivery of stock certificates, "inactive" accounts, or for closing out an account. Better yet, try to find a company that does not assess such fees. The policy toward IRA accounts varies. Some charge no maintenance fee. Others do, although in certain cases this may be waived if the account balance is greater than the required minimum.

CAUTION Small investors should not be buying on margin or dealing in options (see the chapter on the Four Horsemen).

There may be an advantage in dealing with a discount broker in your own community, if one is available. If nothing else, it is easier, quicker, and safer to deliver certificates to a local office when you want to sell securities. However, using a company in another city, even across the country, is almost as convenient. All have toll-free telephone lines for the benefit of their customers, and nearly all accept computer-placed orders with the bonus of a reduced commission charge. Some discount brokerage houses only accept orders made with a computer and the Internet. When selling, certificates can be delivered overnight or within a couple of days by insured mail, Express Mail, or private express companies.

> **CAUTION** The challenge is to find a broker who is not only willing to help but also knowledgeable. What you want to avoid is the recent graduate of training school who is often highly motivated but, unfortunately, inexperienced.

Although selecting a broker should be done carefully, if you find you are not happy with the one you have, it is not too difficult to make a change. In fact, the new company can usually arrange to have any assets in your old account transferred. All brokerage houses have procedures for the settlement of disputes with customers, usually through arbitration. It is unlikely you will ever need to use these, but it is a good idea to know what they are and be certain you understand them. For most small investors, most of the time, a discount broker should be able to get the job done. Still, there are times when you may need to consider using a full-service company. It will cost you more in commissions and fees, but it will be money well spent.

Full service brokers

Investors not comfortable making their own decisions may find full-service brokers almost indispensable. They can help select stocks, bonds, and mutual funds that meet your particular goals and needs. However, brokers are human. They have to learn and will make mistakes just like everybody else. You probably would prefer a surgeon who was not about to make you his very first patient. The same caution applies in seeking investment counsel.

> **HOT spot** Do be certain you are comfortable with and understand any investment proposals you are given.

Financial planner and author Gary Moore provides a useful approach. He suggests calling an office of the full-service firm you are considering and ask to speak with the secretary who has been there for the longest period of time. Then ask who in that office she would want to handle her account. That is the broker you want to approach about handling yours.

Most brokers try to be helpful, even when dealing with investors who will provide only occasional business. Do not be afraid to ask questions. Brokers who steer clients toward limited partnerships, new issues (initial public offerings), and frequent trading, probably have their interests at heart and not that of the small investor. Such activity generates good commissions for them, but is not likely to enrich you. Remember, all brokers are sales persons. Do not begrudge them their commissions. If they do their job correctly, they deserve them. However, it is the investor's job to consider all advice carefully. Ask to see any available financial reports or a copy of the prospectus for the suggested

> **note** Although they will charge a higher commission, full-service companies can normally place orders with all the larger foreign stock exchanges and perhaps the smaller ones as well.

investments. Read this material. Get clarifications of anything you do not understand before you give your final approval. Good brokers, rather than object, will be pleased. They will appreciate your interest and know that any assistance offered will be taken seriously.

Even investors who normally use discount brokers may find that, for certain services, they need a full-service company. Some discount companies offer only limited services for foreign securities not listed on a domestic or Canadian exchange. Many firms can also sell you a certificate of deposit with a more attractive rate than you may be able to get from your local bank. You may not need these or other services or be able to meet the minimum-investment amounts some of them require. However, it is good to know they are available in case they may be useful at some future time.

Banks and brokerage

Banks are now heavily into the brokerage business. They may offer discount or full-service assistance. If you want to do business with the brokerage branch of a bank, there is really neither an advantage or disadvantage. You should still compare fees and commissions with other alternatives, as well as make sure you select an individual broker with whom you are comfortable.

Unfortunately, some newer investors and, occasionally, others that have been around for awhile, think that investments purchased through a brokerage firm affiliated with a bank carry federal deposit insurance. This is absolutely incorrect in all instances. Every reputable brokerage company, whether full service or discount, insures accounts for such things as fraud and error on the part of the brokerage firm. No one will insure you against market risk. Most investments will fluctuate in price in response to market conditions. Some will do this more than others, but nearly all will do it to some extent. In the long run, financial markets reward those who are willing to absorb these risks.

Avoiding—and not avoiding—market risk

Persons who are totally or almost entirely risk adverse should limit themselves to those few investments such as certificates of deposit, money market accounts, bank savings plans, and United States Government Series EE, HH, and I bonds which retain a stable value. There is no other way to avoid financial market risk. Avoiding market risk has a price of its own, namely missing out on a variety of investment opportunities which over time should provide superior returns. The small investor does need to be cautious but also needs opportunities. Being willing to take on prudent, responsible market risk can furnish such opportunities.

> **HOT spot** Except in the most unusual of circumstances, one thing a stock market should enable you to do is buy and sell an investment quickly and at the present fair-market price.

Stock exchanges

There are several kinds of investments not traded on stock exchanges which are perfectly suitable for the typical small investor. These include mutual funds, bank certificates of deposit, savings and money-market accounts, and United States (Series EE and HH) Savings Bonds. Outside of these areas, sticking to investments traded on a recognized exchange will not guarantee you will be a successful investor, but it can help prevent some expensive mistakes. Especially to be avoided are limited partnerships, collectibles, cemetery lots, time shares, stocks not traded on an exchange or in the Nasdaq system, and any "investment" that someone tries to sell you through a radio or television program or by a telephone call. Some of these are legitimate (others are definitely not), but should you want or need to sell, you will find they are almost always highly illiquid. Either you will be forced to take a significant loss, possibly 50 percent or more, or you will find there are no buyers at any price.

Liquidity

Stock markets provide liquidity, and liquidity is always a desirable quality in an investment. Sometimes the investor may be willing to forego it if there are enough other positives, which may be the case with certain real estate investments. However, liquidity is always a factor which should be considered before making any investment.

The larger the stock market, generally the more liquidity you have. Where liquidity is limited, prices can become volatile, and you are more likely to pay too much or receive too little when buying or selling a security. This is especially a problem with some of the small, emerging stock markets in many of the developing countries. Still, even in these more risky economies, a stock traded on an exchange will usually be a better choice than one that is not.

The stock exchanges

In the United States, the *New York Stock Exchange*, because of the large number of companies listed and the sizeable volume of shares traded daily, does an outstanding job of providing liquidity. Shares can be bought or sold within minutes of when the order is placed. The much smaller *American Stock Exchange (Amex)* also does an adequate job, but stocks traded here can come under somewhat greater pressure if the volume of buy or sell orders begins to show a dramatic increase. Most stocks traded on the regional stock exchanges, such as the *Pacific Stock Exchange*, are also traded either on the New York Exchange or the Amex. Those few that are not, are seldom are good choices for small investors anyway.

Nasdaq

DEFINITION

The *Nasdaq* (National Association of Security Dealers Automatic Quotation System) technically is not a stock exchange, but it functions in a very similar fashion as far as the small investor is concerned. In reality, Nasdaq is a computerized network of security dealers who make a market (buy and sell) in securities not listed on an exchange. This used to be referred to as the **over-the-counter market,** although there never was an actual counter in the days before computers. Stocks listed for Nasdaq trading will in many cases have adequate liquidity, although not always as good as those on the New York Stock Exchange. In November 1998, the Nasdaq and the Amex merged into a single organization. They continue to operate and list securities separately.

> ⚠️ **CAUTION** Small exchanges which specialize in highly speculative or "penny" stocks should be avoided entirely.

When liquidity is lacking, things are more volatile and even relatively small orders may produce higher or lower prices than would otherwise be expected. In the past, the biggest problem the small investor possibly found with Nasdaq stocks was the "spread." Call brokers for the price of a Nasdaq-listed stock, and most likely they will give you two figures, the bid price and the asked price. The *asked price* is what market makers are willing to take as the selling price. The *bid figure* is what they are willing to pay if you have shares to sell. The difference between the two is the *spread*, and the spread is where they make much of their money. A large spread is an especially troublesome thing for small investors since their profit is often limited in the first place. They should always consider the spread and, as a general rule, avoid those stocks and bonds where the spread is large. Under pressure from the Securities and Exchange Commission and other concerned parties, the Nasdaq has undertaken measures to reduce spreads. These have had a degree of success, so the problem is no longer as great as it used to be. However, always be careful to determine what the spread is before buying or selling. Securities listed on the exchanges can also carry a spread, but these are usually small enough that they are not troublesome.

DEFINITION

Some Nasdaq-listed stocks are simply too speculative for the typical small investor. An example would be the controversial Arakis Energy Corporation, which announced plans to build an oil pipeline in the politically unstable

Republic of Sudan. The project was to be funded by an organization known as Arab Group International, headed by a Saudi Arabian. Various Saudis may have had the wealth to support such a venture (assuming they were willing to assume the extraordinary risk), but Arab Group evidently did not. Trading in Arakis shares was halted on the Vancouver Exchange, which has been home to some speculative excesses in the past. However, after a month's hiatus, the Nasdaq lifted its similar ban and allowed trading to resume. During that month, Arakis shares lost nearly two-thirds of their value. Certainly many Nasdaq companies are outstanding, including some of the country's major technology concerns, such as Microsoft and Intel. However, the need to always do your homework before purchasing any stock is especially true when considering a Nasdaq listing, and this is particularly the case if it is part of the special Nasdaq Small Cap Section.

> **HOT spot** Highly liquid stocks which have a large number of shares trading will generally have a small spread, but those of small companies, thinly traded, can have rather sizeable ones.

Other Nasdaq stocks

DEFINITION

While several thousand over-the-counter stocks are traded in the Nasdaq system, thousands more are not. They may be listed either on the Nasdaq Electronic Bulletin Board or in the so-called *pink sheets*, which are printed daily and in which dealers making a market in a particular security can list their bid and asked prices. In almost all cases, Bulletin-Board and pink-sheet stocks should be avoided by the small investor. Some of these companies are outstanding, but their stock is likely to be highly illiquid, and spreads for pink-sheet stocks can be considerable. The same word of caution goes for some small local company you may hear is selling stock in your community. It could be a good buy, but is there any market for it if you want to liquidate?

> **CAUTION** If it is not even listed in the pink sheets, you may actually have to locate a buyer yourself if you want to sell.

Another possible situation is "Cousin Fred," who could indeed have a great idea for a new business, and he is willing to let you have 1,000 shares at a bargain price. Chances are Cousin Fred cannot or will not buy them back if you need to get rid of them, and neither will anyone else.

Safety and the stock exchanges

There is one other thing that a listing on a major stock exchange or the Nasdaq can do for you, and that is provide a welcome degree of safety. No stock exchange can guarantee a profit or even assure you that you will not lose 100 percent of your investment. However, the major exchanges and the Nasdaq do screen new companies and funds before they will list them. They do have to meet certain financial requirements and agree to provide a considerable amount of information to investors. Companies that cannot continue to meet these requirements lose their listings. Occasionally, a "bad apple" does get through the system, but it does furnish some reassurance and keeps most, but not all, of the fraudulent operations out. This is not something of which you can be assured when buying an unlisted stock. Again, I especially like the New York Stock Exchange because of the high standards it expects from the companies it lists. However, do not expect any exchange to do your homework for you. Ultimately it is the investor's job to determine if an investment is right or not. No one, including the exchanges, will refund your money if you make the wrong decision.

Chapter 8

Dividend reinvestment plans

What you'll find in this chapter:

⟫ What is a real estate investment trust?

⟫ The main reasons to use cash purchase plans

⟫ About dividend reinvestment plans

⟫ How to deal with your brokerage company

⟫ How to dispose of your shares

Until rather recently, dividend reinvestment plans often seemed to be one of the world's best secrets, although they are certainly nothing new. Perhaps the reason for this is that while there was no conspiracy on the part of those who sell financial products, there was no incentive to bring up the subject either. However, gradually the word has spread, thanks in part to the efforts of several publications, and investors, large and small, in increasing numbers are discovering that these plans can be a very valuable tool. Let us take a look at what a dividend reinvestment plan actually is, and then explore why it may be especially suited to the needs of the small investor.

Dividends and reinvestment

Most companies that are profitable sooner or later will return a portion of those profits to their shareholders. In the case of American companies, this is normally quarterly. With foreign companies the situation may vary. How much per share you would receive depends on the decision of the board of directors. The dividend rate may remain steady for quite awhile. If profits increase, it may be raised and, if they decline, it could be decreased or the dividend omitted entirely. Occasionally, a special dividend may be declared, and sometimes companies will pay a dividend in additional shares of stock rather than in cash. Some companies, especially newer ones and those in emerging growth industries, may be quite profitable but pay little or no dividends, because they prefer to use their profits to expand their operations.

Assuming we are dealing with an American company paying cash dividends, stockholders would expect to receive a dividend check every three months. If investors enroll in a company-sponsored dividend reinvestment plan, their dividends will automatically be used to buy more shares of stock, including a partial or fractional share if there is not enough money to buy a whole one. There are several solid advantages for doing this.

 HINT The situation is undergoing some changes, but traditionally utilities have probably had the most generous payouts. Real estate investment trusts (REITS) also are noted for higher than average dividend rates.

In many cases, the new shares come free of any service charges or brokerage fees. If these are levied, the company may pay them for you. Even if this is not the case, dividend reinvestment plans are a convenient, nearly painless way to gradually increase your holdings. A few companies even throw in a bonus by providing you with the new shares at a discount of as much as 5 percent below the current market price.

Cash purchase plans

 DEFINITION As pleasant as this situation is, it is not the most important reason why dividend reinvestment plans are salvation for small investors. The vast majority are not only dividend reinvestment plans, but *cash purchase plans* as well. You may voluntarily send funds at periodic intervals which will be used to purchase additional shares of stock for your account. As in the case of dividends, often the new shares come without additional expenses of any kind. If a service charge is made, it is usually nominal, and any brokerage fees will be well below what you would pay if you went and purchased your shares through a stock broker, even a discount broker. If you are very fortunate, you may find that your company will give you a discount over the market price, but this is even less typical with cash purchases than it is with the reinvestment of dividends.

There are two major reasons for taking advantage of cash purchase plans:

1) ***The first is that they permit small investors to invest small sums of money.*** A stock broker is not happy when you come in the door and place an order for $25 worth of stock. Even if your order is accepted, the commission charged typically will be greater than the amount of your purchase. Many cash purchase plans will accept orders that small. Certain ones do have $50 or $100 minimums, but not many are higher than that. Generally there are also maximum order limits, but these need not concern small investors, as most likely they will be well above what they are planning to spend anyway.

A cash purchase plan permits you to place orders for a small amount of stock conveniently and economically.

2) ***A second factor is that cash purchase plans encourage you to dollar average.*** When you dollar average, you invest a similar amount of money in the same company at regular intervals. For example you might buy $50 worth of stock in the same company every month until you have one hundred shares. What dollar averaging will do for you is prevent you from making your one hundred share purchase at a time when the price is at a high, only to drop back later. Each month you invest the same amount, $50. If the price has risen, your money will buy fewer shares this time than last month, but if it has dropped it will buy more. Dollar averaging will not get you the absolute lowest price. What it will get you is a good price, probably an average price per share well below what you would have obtained if you had purchased all your shares at the same time.

Dividend reinvestment plans

Subject to certain limitations, and usually for a modest service charge, dividend reinvestment plans will, on request, sell any shares that you have accumulated and left in the plan. Brokerage charges for this service will be considerably less than you would pay elsewhere. If you prefer, the plan will issue you a certificate for all or a portion of the whole shares you have on deposit. These can then be sold when and where you please. You may continue to have your dividends reinvested and make cash purchases, or you may withdraw from the plan. Certificates are not issued for a fractional share, but you will receive its cash value if you are liquidating your plan holdings.

> ⚠️ **CAUTION** There is a growing tendency for brokerage companies to charge more fees and larger service charges, as well as raise the amount of the minimum investment, for dividend reinvestment plans. These tactics appear to be designed, in part, to discourage the small investor from participating.

Most dividend reinvestment plans accept voluntary cash purchases every month. You are, of course, never required to send money. Normally your money will be invested the first or the fifteenth of the month, but some plans may select another date. Some brokerage companies may permit participation twice a month, investing approximately every fifteen days. Others insist on a longer interval and buy stock for your account only every 45 days or even quarterly. Unfortunately, many closed-end funds, discussed extensively in the chapter on international investing, allow a voluntary cash purchase only twice a year or, in some cases, only once a year. However, even such limited opportunities are better than none at all.

So, what is the catch? There are actually several, but the plans are so valuable you should join them anyway, if at all possible. First of all, the company which interests you may not have a plan. Many do not. Those that have never paid dividends do not, and many growth companies, with minimal dividend payments, do not either. Others, for a variety of reasons, may decide not to establish one or may discontinue an existing plan. In a few cases it appears that the decision has been made because the company feels a plan attracts small investors who will hold only a few shares, but whose accounts cost as much to service as investors with thousands of shares. Occasionally, companies that continue their plans may encourage both plan participants and nonparticipants with fewer than one hundred shares to sell their holdings. They will do this by offering to sell their stock for them with no brokerage fees. That may make you feel unwanted, but of course you cannot be required to sell.

Probably the greatest concern that most people have about these plans is that participants have no control over time or price. Companies select the date on which shares for participants will be obtained. You get the price in effect at that time. Essentially, the same thing happens when you sell. If you wish to make use of the plan, there is absolutely no way to avoid this situation. The stock you wanted and would have bought three days ago if you could, may be selling for a dollar more per share by the time the plan buys it. You will have to pay the dollar. Plan participants in nearly all cases will feel it is worth it.

Occasionally, you may find a plan with some peculiarity all its own. There is one which does not permit ownership of a fractional share. When it pays a dividend, it first credits your account with one, only to several weeks later liquidate it and send you a new account statement along with a check for the proceeds.

 Even if you can afford one hundred shares, you may still find it more beneficial to look elsewhere.

That really does not make much sense, as even the largest investors would be entitled to a dividend that is unlikely to precisely equal the amount needed for an exact number of whole shares. You may find such oddities annoying, but do not let them keep you from joining.

 A few plans present you with a real problem. They will reinvest dividends for you, but they will not accept voluntary cash payments. Unless you can afford to buy at least one hundred shares of the company's stock, normally do not bother with them. They will not be worth the trouble.

Obtaining shares in a reinvestment plan

In order to participate in a plan you must be a shareholder, owning at least one full share. The question is how do you get that first share? There are actually several ways:

You could approach a sympathetic broker. While they are not in the business to fill one-share orders, some brokers may be quite understanding and supportive of what you are doing and why. After all, if you are successful at it, eventually they might just get some bigger business from you. So, they will accept your order for a few shares or even one. Some companies require more than one in order to participate, perhaps five or even as many as ten.

It is absolutely essential that the brokerage company issue you a stock certificate for your shares. If they are left in the brokerage company's name, so-called **street name**, you will not be able to use a reinvestment and cash purchase plan without considerable complications and, in many cases, not at all. Increasingly, brokerage houses are charging a fee to issue the certificate, and it will be at least several weeks before it arrives. Again, there is no way to avoid this. Once you are a registered stockholder you can contact the company for information on how to enroll in its plan. Plan agents in some cases, but not all, may automatically contact you about joining.

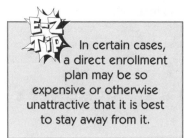

note Expect to pay the brokerage company's minimum commission, which in light of your minimal order will probably look substantial.

A growing number of companies make it very easy for their customers and other interested persons to become shareholders and join. Originally, these were mostly utility companies or banks, but many other types of businesses are now also participating. They can sell you directly, without a broker, the stock you need to get started and will see that you receive the necessary information to become a plan member. Some of these direct enrollment plans are excellent, but look at the details carefully. Others have much higher fees and other charges, plus higher minimum investment amounts than the traditional dividend reinvestment plans. Some employers may have a special investment plan for their employees. If you are eligible for any of these kinds of opportunities, they are certainly worth investigating.

In certain cases, a direct enrollment plan may be so expensive or otherwise unattractive that it is best to stay away from it.

Reinvestment resources

For the person with a serious interest in dividend reinvestment and cash purchase plans, two periodicals should prove especially helpful. These are *Better Investing*, published by the National Association of Investors

Corporation, and *The Moneypaper*. Both appear monthly. For a modest fee, and without a broker, both plans make it possible for you to obtain your first share and enroll in the plan in which you wish to participate. *Better Investing*'s fees are lower, but more companies are available through *The Moneypaper*. You must be a subscriber to use either plan. For information on *Better Investing* and the NAIC's *"Low Cost Investment Plan,"* contact the National Association of Investors Corporation at Post Office Box 220, Royal Oak, MI 48068. The telephone number is 810-583-6242. NAIC also does an outstanding job of investor education and providing assistance to investment clubs. It even has its own mutual fund. *The Moneypaper* also has a mutual fund and is published by The Moneypaper, Inc., 1010 Mamaroneck Avenue, Mamaroneck, NY 10543. Telephone: 914-381-5400 (web site: http://www.moneypaper.com).

The Moneypaper makes available to both subscribers and nonsubscribers a very informative guide to direct investment plans. It can be a useful tool in helping you select the plans which are of interest to you. The monthly publication selects certain companies it feels are worthy of consideration and offers these to subscribers at a discount from the regular fee charged. A second publication is also available from *The Moneypaper*. This is *The DRP Authority*, which appears quarterly and is devoted exclusively to providing information on dividend reinvestment plans. Subscription information can be obtained from the address above. In addition to *The Moneypaper*'s guide, several other guides on dividend reinvestment plans have been published. Check a local bookstore or your library to see what may be currently available.

> ⚠️ **CAUTION** Regardless of how you obtain that first share, if you own it in certificate form, you need to plan ahead for how you will dispose of it when you get ready to sell all your shares.

⚠️ **CAUTION** There are just a few more words of caution to note before leaving the subject of dividend reinvestment plans. Some companies will permit you to enroll in their plans through the programs provided by the NAIC or *The Moneypaper* without having a stock certificate issued for your first share. Others will not. It will not pay you to sell a single share through a broker. Probably the easiest thing to do is to have a certificate issued for some or all of your plan shares. These can then be sold along with your "orphan" share. For example, if the plan issues you a certificate for 99 shares, you would then have a round lot of 100 shares, which any broker will be happy to sell for you. Some plans will accept for safe keeping shares you currently hold in certificate form. At a later date, they can either sell your shares or issue you a certificate for up to as many shares as you have on deposit in the plan.

Traditionally, nearly all companies with dividend reinvestment plans have been sound, reliable ones. There are, of course, no guarantees that a company will make money, but most companies with such plans have, and this is especially important since these plans encourage long-term investing. Recently, the legal requirements for establishing a plan have been eased. It is possible that some companies which are not as financially sound may start plans as a convenient way to raise additional capital. Be alert. Just because a company has a dividend reinvestment plan, do not automatically assume it is worthy of your investment dollars. As always, do your homework. Check it out to be as certain as you can that it is a good investment value.

While dividend reinvestment and cash purchase plans are not perfect, they are one of the most valuable tools the small investor can use. Give them a chance, and chances are you will see your investments multiply. You can also use the same principle to add regularly to your mutual funds and to reinvest without fees any dividend or capital gains distributions made by these funds. Again, you will be dollar averaging, assuring yourself of good prices and a steady accumulation of capital. This is the way to build wealth on a firm and secure foundation. Why not give it a try! Probably the only regret you will have is that you did not start years sooner.

Chapter 9

Mutual funds— diversity for the small investor

If there is a type of investment which seems custom-made for the small investor, it is the mutual fund. Mutual funds offer choice, professional management, diversification, and liquidity—all at an affordable price.

There are some basic things about mutual funds that are not difficult to understand, but are helpful to know. A mutual fund sells shares to investors. The proceeds are then invested in stocks of individual companies, both corporate and government bonds, mortgage securities, and occasionally other things such as real estate and precious metals.

> **HOT spot** If you want to keep your entire investment effort simple but effective, you may never want to look at alternatives beyond the mutual fund. You really would not have to do so, either.

DEFINITION

- Funds sold directly to the public by the sponsoring companies are sold at their net-asset value, or the actual value of an individual share. They are known as *no-load funds*.

DEFINITION

- Those distributed through brokers and some financial planners are sold at their net-asset value plus a sales charge. They are *load funds*. Except under very unusual circumstances, both types may be redeemed at any time for their current net-asset value, which of course may be more or less than you originally paid for them.

- Some funds may charge a redemption fee when you cash in your shares. They are sometimes called *back-end load funds*.

- There is a type of fund which usually trades on a stock exchange and must be purchased or sold through a stock broker. These are *closed-end funds*, as opposed to the open-end funds we are exploring here. Closed-end funds are discussed in the chapter on international investing.

How mutual funds work

When you invest in a mutual fund, professional money-managers look after your money and put it to work. They decide what securities are to be purchased and which ones should be sold. Their services are not free, as each month they receive a small percentage of the fund's assets as a management fee. Since funds may hold numerous investments, in some cases stocks of over 100 different companies in a variety of industries, they provide diversity. Diversity offers you a degree

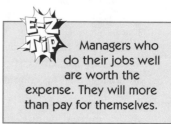

Managers who do their jobs well are worth the expense. They will more than pay for themselves.

of safety and stability, as even if one company should fail or go into a sharp decline, the others would not. If you are the kind of investor who finds it psychologically difficult to sell a stock, mutual funds take that burden off your hands. Management decides what and when to sell as well as what should be purchased for the portfolio.

Types of mutual funds

DEFINITION

Funds come in a variety of forms, each intended to do a somewhat different task. What follows is not intended to be either definitive or exhaustive, but it will give you some idea of what kinds are available and what they can do.

- A **stock or equity fund** will of course invest in the stocks of business corporations.

- **Growth funds** seek to uncover companies whose business and earnings are expected to show better than average increases in the years ahead.

- **Value funds** look for companies who for one reason or another are currently overlooked and thus underpriced.

- **Equity income funds** are normally conservative funds investing in companies with good records for paying high or increasing dividends. They may hold a portion of their assets in interest-paying bonds.

- Some may also buy **convertible bonds**, which pay interest and can be exchanged for shares of common stock should it be financially advantageous to do so.

- **Small-company funds** take somewhat more risk by investing in newer and smaller firms which may have the opportunity to grow at a higher percentage rate than older, more established businesses.

- **Sector or specialty funds** limit their investments to a particular segment of business, such as telecommunications or health care. Any of these might limit its activity to the American markets, or may include a few foreign companies as well.

- If a substantial amount of its assets is invested outside the United States, it will be known as a **global fund**. If no money is invested domestically, it is a **foreign** or **international fund**. We will look at global and foreign funds in the chapter on international investing.

 Should you desire a more detailed classification of both stock and bond funds, you will find an excellent one in the *Lipper Mutual Funds Quarterly,* which appears every three months in *Barron's*. This presently includes over 40 different classifications. However, the ones noted above are most likely those which will be of primary interest to small investors.

 Younger investors, in particular, may wish to give serious consideration to value and growth funds, although for the most part avoid those labeled "aggressive growth." Some of these aggressive growth funds have outstanding records, but the group as a whole has probably been too volatile for many small investors. Well-run growth and value funds over a period of years should produce nice annual returns for those who are patient.

> **HINT** Small investors who tend to buy and hold their funds will probably be more comfortable with value funds. Value funds may not do quite as well in bull markets, but will usually hold up much better in bear markets.

They can, of course, have losing as well as winning years. As a whole, of the two, value funds are probably the more conservative and apt to fluctuate in price somewhat less. The most attractive value funds may perform as well or even better than many growth funds.

> A small company fund probably should not be the first fund you own, but if you are able to diversify after you have taken a position in a couple of others, then this may be a good direction to explore.

Equity income funds are somewhat more stable and possibly attractive for older investors who cannot afford quite as much risk. They can be ideal for IRA accounts (see the chapter on retirement and taxes), since the dividend and interest income they generate can be tax deferred. Such funds are probably good choices for those of all ages who tend to be risk adverse, but are willing to have some stock-market exposure.

Small company and sector funds offer greater potential rewards, but with considerably more risk. Small companies have the potential to grow more rapidly than larger ones, but they also have a greater potential to fail. Sector funds by far come with the most risk. They are not for most investors. However, if you possess more than average knowledge about a particular area of business because of your employment or some other factor, then buying shares in a sector fund may make good sense. Hopefully you have adequate knowledge to know if conditions deteriorate to the point that you should sell. If not, then stay away.

Other types of mutual funds

Also available are **index funds**. Their portfolios will reflect the components of some popular stock-market index, most often the Standard & Poor's 500 or perhaps the Russell 3000. Index funds normally have very low management fees and other expenses, because there is little need for the fund to make changes in its holdings. Since index funds do not sell one stock to buy another very often, they also make very few capital gains distributions. As a result, investors avoid tax liabilities until they sell their own individual shares. Because of their low turnover and expenses, index funds often lead the pack during bull markets. It is difficult for most managed funds, with their greater expenses, to top their performance. However, in bear markets, index funds will probably suffer more pain than the managed type. Remember, with an index fund, you are essentially buying the market average.

HINT

Investors who are concerned about ethical investing may have a serious difficulty with index funds. When you buy an index fund, you get all the companies in the index. No substitutions are permitted. So, if you want to avoid investing in tobacco or some other industry, you will not be able to do so with the typical index fund.

note A few socially-responsible index funds have begun to appear on the market and, most likely, there will be more in the future.

Still another type of fund is the **balanced fund**. The typical balanced fund will have perhaps 60 percent of its holdings in stocks with the remainder in bonds, and perhaps a little cash. The rewards and risk for balanced funds tend to be less than for stock funds but greater than for bond funds. Some financial advisors do not like their "hybrid" nature, but for small investors, particularly if they are somewhat reluctant to move into investments with market risk, a balanced fund may make good sense, especially as an initial choice. Balanced funds give you exposure to stocks and bonds, and the opportunity to learn something about both. Related to balanced funds are **asset-allocation funds** where, depending on market conditions, the fund manager will increase or decrease the percentage in each category, but there will normally be a substantial position in both stocks and bonds.

Be wary of funds labeled as **capital appreciation funds**. Do not reject them entirely, as several are very solid performers with moderate investment strategies. Others, however, resort to rapid turnover in shares, leveraging, heavy use of options, and the acquisition of unregistered and thus illiquid shares. Before investing in a capital appreciation fund, always carefully read the prospectus. If it does frequently resort to these kinds of speculative techniques, look elsewhere for a more satisfactory investment.

Acquiring your funds

After you have decided on what particular kind or different kinds of funds would be best, the next step is to begin searching for the right fund to buy. The chapter on load and no-load funds and the one on doing your own research are starting points, which should yield some information which will help you get going. There is something to be said for companies that offer a family of funds. Should your investment objectives change, you can with a telephone call switch money from one type of fund to another either free or for a nominal charge. Just remember, if you do this, it is technically a sale of your shares and will result in taxation of any profits realized even though your money is immediately reinvested. Such an exchange within the shelter of an IRA account will, of course, be exempt.

> **HOT spot** Always instruct the fund to reinvest any dividends or capital gains distributions. This is how you get your money to earn additional money for you.

The amount of the initial investment you will need to make in order to open an account with a fund will depend on which fund you select. Typically, it has been $1,000, although serious effort may still uncover a steadily declining number that will accept less. Increasingly, it might be as much as $2,500 to $3,000, so you may have to do some saving before you make your first purchase. However, many funds do permit a considerably smaller first investment if it will be for an IRA account. They know there is a good possibility you will add to it regularly.

Once you open the account, additional investments can be made in lesser amounts. A typical minimum is $100, although it may be as little as $25. Many funds encourage regular periodic (usually monthly) investments through automatic deduction from your checking account. In order to make this attractive, they may offer a lower minimum, perhaps $50 or even less, than on investments you send directly to them. Such an investment plan is an excellent idea and becomes a regular habit, much like paying your monthly electric or telephone bill.

The prospectus

Regardless of whether you select your own funds or use professional help, such as a broker, always obtain and read the prospectus for any fund you are seriously considering. It may not be exciting reading, but if you read the prospectus carefully, it should prove rather enlightening and could help you avoid some expensive mistakes.

Many investors never take the time to review the prospectus. If later they suffer financial reverses, it is then that the investors may complain that they were not adequately informed. The information is usually there for those willing to make the effort to

> **HINT** Consistently high turnover (there could be a valid reason for it in an occasional year) can mean greater expenses and less favorable prices for the securities sold.

obtain it. Brokers and financial planners can supply a prospectus for any fund they sell. The publications in the research and resources chapter often provide telephone numbers and addresses of the mutual fund companies whose funds they rate or discuss. Also, do not overlook the numerous advertisements, although never buy a fund based solely on an advertisement. Simply use it as a way to contact a fund for more information.

Choosing wisely

One of the biggest mistakes made by large and small investors alike is to chase the "hottest" funds, those that have performed best over the past year or even the past quarter. Even those which are notorious "dogs" may have an occasional brilliant quarter. Last year's leader may be this year's also-ran. If possible, try to find out how the fund has done over the past ten years, or at least the last five. Also examine how it has made its money. Has it engaged in risky practices which may have been successful for a period of a couple of years, but could produce considerable reverses in the future? Some things to look for are:

- extensive buying and selling of options (a minimal amount of this is tolerable, even if not desirable)

- large quantities of securities which are not readily marketable or easily capable of being evaluated

- short selling

- heavy borrowing

- excessive turnover of the portfolio. If portfolio turnover is 100 percent, it means the fund on average sells its entire portfolio every year. Some funds have percentages much higher.

> If you do intend to hold a fund for more than a couple of years, a front-end load is preferable to a 12b-1 charge, which in effect is an annual load, rather than one paid only at the time of the initial purchase.

A careful examination of the fund's prospectus and latest report to shareholders should reveal all of this. Also look to see how the fund's expenses compare to similar funds. The lower the expense rate, the more assets remain for the fund's shareholders. As we note in the chapter on *load* versus *no-load* funds, do not automatically exclude a fund because there is a sales charge. Look at the fund's performance history. The fund may have done better than similar no-load funds. Some brokerage companies that previously sold only load funds to their clients will now also provide you with no-loads, while charging your account an annual fee or a brokerage fee at the time of purchase. Such a fee, in effect, is similar to either a load or a 12b-1 charge. If you need or want professional help in selecting your funds, it may be worth the cost. If you do not need the help, buy directly from the fund and invest the savings.

Things to remember

Once you select a fund, give it a fair chance to perform for you. Hopping from one fund to another usually will produce little more than increased tax liabilities. Unless the fund was sheltered in some sort of retirement account, any profits will be taxed at the appropriate rate. Of course, a capital loss might reduce your taxe, and may be a good reason for selling at a particular time. You should seldom, if ever, make the sale for tax reasons alone, but if you feel that remaining in the fund is not a good idea for the long term, then certainly sell it and take any tax advantages this might provide.

 note When you sell a fund, even if the proceeds are rolled over into another fund, you have a taxable event.

Unless only a small amount of money is involved, such as a regular monthly investment through an automatic deduction from your checking account, be careful not to make fund purchases just before the fund makes a distribution of capital gains and dividends. In order to retain their tax-exempt status, mutual funds (both open and closed-ended, and also real estate investment trusts) must distribute to their shareholders nearly all the income they generate. Many will do this annually, near the end of the year. Some may do it several times a year. If you purchase shares, even just a day before the date of record for shareholders who are to receive the dividend, you will be liable for taxes on the entire distribution, even though you owned the shares for only a single day. If you have any questions about when the next distribution will be made, it would be a good idea to call the company and inquire about this matter. If the fund is sheltered in a retirement account, then there is no problem. All taxes are deferred until you begin to withdraw funds from the account. For nonsheltered accounts, funds with low portfolio turnover become particularly attractive, as they tend to hold stocks that appreciate rather than sell them. As a result, their capital gains distributions are usually smaller, and so is the shareholder's tax bill.

If you want to keep things simple and yet relatively safe, then for the portion of your investments which will be in common stocks, mutual funds may be all you need to know. They provide flexibility, diversity, and professional management at a reasonable price and offer the opportunity for solid profits in the hands of patient investors, large and small alike.

Mutual funds are also ideal for the small investor looking at the bond market. We turn to that subject shortly.

To load or not to load?

DEFINITION

A *load* charged when you purchase mutual fund shares is essentially a sales charge. Today loads usually run from 1 percent up to 5.75 percent. Loads come in several varieties:

- Most common is the **front-end load** which is assessed when you buy the shares.

> **HOT spot** Obviously, the more you pay in loads, the less of your investment remains to work for you.

- A **back-end load** or **redemption fee** is paid when you cash them, although some back-end fees are reduced or eliminated entirely if you hold the shares for at least a certain minimum period of time.

- If a fund charges a 12b-1 fee, it is really a **small load** which fund holders bear annually. Money from 12b-1 fees goes to cover the expenses of marketing the fund. If you are a long-term investor and holding your shares for many years,such fees can ultimately cost you more than the front-end or back-end load, which is paid only once. Some funds may charge either a front-end or back-end load plus an annual 12b-1 fee. This is particularly important for small investors to remember, since their "grub stake" may not be that large at the start of things.

note If brokers or financial planners select the load funds for you, quite probably, in the past, those funds may have outperformed many no-load funds even when you take the sales charges into account.

Based on the above, conventional wisdom says wise investors never buy load funds. As in numerous other instances, conventional wisdom may be correct in many cases, but completely wrong in others. If you compare two mutual funds and everything else is identical except that one charges a load and the other does not, then obviously the no-load fund is the only way to go. But, there are those times when selecting a load fund makes good sense. In a world where there are literally thousands of funds to choose from, and they come in all kinds of varieties, it is not surprising that some investors may feel they need professional help in making the right choices. Free advice is often worth exactly what you paid for it. If you are seeking competent, reasonable, objective assistance from brokers or financial planners, then do not be shocked when they suggest load funds. This is how they get paid for their services. Just make sure you understand and are comfortable with the suggested funds. Should the selections turn out to be good ones the fees will be more than justified. Consider them a form of "insurance" designed to help you minimize making investment mistakes.

If you feel comfortable in doing your own research and making your own investment decisions, then by all means consider no-load funds. The money you save puts more money to work for you. That is your reward for doing your own homework. However, in the course of investigating your possibilities, should you come across a load fund that despite the load looks as if it may outperform the no-load alternatives, then give it fair consideration. Total performance is what counts in the end. In a sense, a load fund is like a race horse who starts behind the rest of the field. It is going to have to run longer and harder to win. Some horses have that ability. Small investors should not try to run short races. You are in this for the long term, and the 12b-1 charges mount up over the years. However, do not reject a fund for the sole reason that it levies a 12b-1 fee. It may have virtues that make it worth your while to endure this irritation.

> **E-Z TIP** All other factors being equal, if you decide to go with a load fund, one with a front or back-end load is usually preferable to those with a 12b-1 charge.

What the small investor needs to remember is that loads are a critical factor to consider when determining which mutual funds you may want to purchase. However, they are not the only factor.

Chapter 10

Bond mutual funds—more small investor power

Not every small investor will be interested in the bond market. Some will feel they have adequate diversification by holding stock, mutual funds which buy stocks, and low-risk investments such as certificates of deposit. In many instances, they are probably correct. Yet, it would be a sad thing to pass up possible opportunities in bonds, simply because they were overlooked or forgotten. Bonds do have some advantages which neither stocks nor cash possess.

When you buy stock in a company directly through the purchase of shares on an exchange, or indirectly through acquiring shares in a mutual fund, you in effect become a part owner of the company. Many people may have some familiarity with United States Series EE Savings Bonds. In fact, these are discussed at length in another chapter. If you have ever owned one of these bonds, then part of the national debt we have heard so much about in past years is actually owed to you! The federal government has promised to eventually pay you back the cost of

> *note* When you buy bonds you are not an owner. You become a lender.

the bond and, in the meantime, to make interest payments until it does. While there are some unique features pertaining to Savings Bonds, essentially all bonds share these basic characteristics. Someone promises to pay you back and will pay you interest either until they do or until you sell your bond to a third party.

Bonds and the federal government

Obviously, the federal government is a major seller in the bond market. This is how it must finance a portion of its activities, since tax revenues and fees are not adequate to pay the entire bill. While foreigners do buy part of this debt, numerous Americans (ironically in some cases those who have been most fearful of the budget deficit!) are especially attracted to it, because of its advantageous tax treatment. Interest paid on federal bonds is subject to federal income taxation, but it is exempt from state and local income

| HINT | Federal bonds are also purchased for their safety. |

taxes. This can be a critical factor in those states with very high rates and becomes even more attractive if there is a municipal income tax as well. While a budget gridlock between the President and Congress could cause the government to default on its debt, at the very worst this would be a temporary state of affairs. It would so upset financial markets that both branches of the government would be most reluctant to have to take responsibility for it. As long as Congress is willing to raise the federal debt limit, the legal power of the federal government to borrow money, even if it is to refinance older debt,

| **HOT** spot If inflation went to 5 percent in a year, a $10,000 bond would now have a redemption value of $10,500. |

is virtually unlimited. Thus a permanent default or failure of federal bonds is almost unthinkable. This is not the case with states or local governments, whose borrowing powers are limited and who must, in most cases, operate with a balanced budget.

Because of the high degree of safety, federal debt normally carries a lower interest rate than similar bonds issued by corporations, which of course can default. Markets reward risk, and the debt of the federal government is low-risk debt.

Other bonds, bills, and funds

Federal debt comes in three basic types. **Treasury bills** have a life of one year or less. After that, they mature and are redeemed for their face value, having originally been sold at a discount whose size depends on the current interest rate. **Treasury notes** will mature in not less than two years nor more than ten. They are sold at face value and pay interest semiannually. **Bonds** have a maturity of more than ten years. Currently the maximum length is thirty years.

In 1997, the federal government began to issue bonds whose interest rate was linked to the rate of inflation. If inflation rises, so will payments to the bond holders. These bonds may be attractive to those looking for an investment with less risk than stocks, but one whose yield cannot be ravaged by inflation. The redemption value of the bond would also rise. However, these bonds are not without their problems. An article in the May 20, 1996, issue of *Barron's* noted that similar bonds issued in Britain and Canada have been volatile and not done as well as the rest of the bond market. Unless the bonds are held inside a tax-deferred retirement plan, those issued by the federal government are subject to taxation each year on the increase in the redemption value. If this sort of inflation protection does appeal to you, consider a bond fund limited to this kind of investment and one you can hold in a tax-deferred plan.

> *note* Some municipal bonds and bond funds are privately (not by the federal government) insured against default, although this does not mean their market price cannot decline.

note **Municipal bonds** include not only those issued by cities but also states, counties, school districts, and other local governments. The interest on these bonds is free of all federal income taxes regardless of how much other income the tax payer may have. Bonds issued by various governments within a particular state are also exempt from that state's income taxes.

As a result, municipal bonds are particularly attractive to those in the highest tax brackets. These investors often discover that, although the bonds may carry a lower rate of interest than they could earn elsewhere, they will receive a higher rate of return, because they get to keep all of it. Occasionally, municipal bonds can also be good investments for others who have more modest incomes.

CAUTION

There are times, however, when municipal bonds can give you a tax liability. If you buy the bond at one price and then are able to sell it later at a higher price, you have a capital gain, not interest income. Capital gains on the sale of municipal bonds are subject to the normal state and federal income tax rates.

Business corporations also issue bonds as a way to raise capital. Some of this debt is traded on stock exchanges in much the same manner as the shares of the same corporations. Most of it trades in the so-called **over the counter market**. Bonds are rated according to their financial safety by three companies: Moody's, Standard & Poor's, and Fitch. A high rating permits the borrowers to sell their debt at a lower interest rate, since those buying it take on less risk. The rating companies also evaluate municipal bonds.

DEFINITION

Small investors who want to invest in bonds will often find the most convenient way to purchase them is through **mutual funds**. With this method, investors can acquire diversification and the safety it provides. Buying additional shares in the fund also provides a convenient, low-cost way to add to your holdings. By using funds, you also avoid concerns over the *callability* of a bond, which is the right of the issuer to redeem it at a date before maturity. You also need not worry whether a bond is a **debenture**, backed only by the general credit of the issuer, or whether it has a greater claim on the issuer's assets.

Probably the chief factors to consider with bond funds is whether the bonds in the fund portfolio are *corporate* or *government* (federal or municipal), and what is the average time to maturity of the bonds. Short-

Most small investors will do best by staying with short- and medium-term funds.

term funds normally have an average maturity of up to three years. Intermediate funds range from three to ten years. Long-term ones will be at least ten and could be as high as fifteen or even twenty.

As a rule, the longer the term the higher the interest rate earned, but there is a price to be paid for this. Bond prices normally drop when interest rates rise. The prices of long-term bonds will tend to fall much more dramatically than those of short or even intermediate-term ones. What was gained in somewhat higher interest yields could evaporate in a capital loss, if you sold your shares at such a time. Some funds may try to take advantage of the stability of shorter maturity times and the greater yields of longer ones by holding a mixed portfolio of both. They may have success with such a strategy, but it is not the easiest thing to accomplish. A short-term bond fund can even function as an alternative for some funds that might be held in bank certificates of deposit.

Stay away from so-called **high-yield bond funds,** whether corporate or municipal. These purchase "junk bonds," bonds which must pay a higher than average interest rate because the borrowers have a lower credit rating. In good times they can appear attractive, especially since conventional rates may appear to be rather low. However, they are speculative, and should the economy worsen these bonds and the funds that buy them, you could be in for considerable trouble. It has happened before; it could happen again. Some otherwise good bond funds may state in their prospectus that they are permitted to purchase a small percentage, usually 10 to 20 percent, of less than investment-grade bonds and bonds that have not been rated. This is tolerable, even if it is not desirable. Also avoid funds using extensive leverage and derivatives to boost yield.

> **HINT** A careful examination of the fund's prospectus and annual report should provide sufficient information to determine if it is able to keep its expenses at a low rate.

As a rule, you will find less difference in the performance of different bond funds with similar objectives (long, medium, or short-term) than in the various stock funds available. This means a bond fund's **expense ratio** is very important. The lower the expenses the more profits are left for the shareholders. Load funds which invest in bonds are at an obvious disadvantage, much greater than those which buy stocks. However, do not ignore them when considering a bond fund. Despite the odds against them, some are able to out perform their no-load counterparts.

When selecting bond funds, the same rule applies that is in effect for stock funds. Make certain you are comparing apples with apples, not with oranges. Do not compare a conservative utility stock fund with one which invests primarily in small capitalization (small company) stocks. If what you want is a short-term bond fund, compare the performance of one you may be considering with other short-term funds, not an intermediate or long-term fund. Different kinds of funds are obviously intended to do different things, and their records will reflect this fact.

Also available are **international bond funds** and **global bond funds**, which invest both in the United States and abroad. Foreign bonds offer diversification along with the possibility of a higher yield, as interest rates in other countries at times may be falling when ours are rising, or falling at a faster rate than at home. However, currency exchange rates can complicate matters. Foreign bonds may be yielding higher interest, but if the dollar is rising in value against foreign currencies, you could realize substantially less than the domestic

> **HOT spot** Expect foreign bond funds to have much higher portfolio turnover than domestic ones, and also higher expense ratios.

rate. Of course, when the dollar is falling a foreign bond fund can offer some protection. Foreign bonds may also be subject to more market risk. The market price of all bonds tends to fall when interest rates rise, just as it tends to rise when rates fall. With some foreign bonds these fluctuations could be significant, although bond funds should moderate this somewhat through their diversification.

DEFINITION

Convertible bonds are bonds that, at the owner's option, may be exchanged for shares of the issuing company's common stock at a predetermined price. This appears to offer the best of all possible worlds. As long as you hold the securities in the form of bonds, you are entitled to the interest. If the common stock rises in value, the bonds can be converted into stock (the company could also force this by calling the bond) and then sold for a capital gain, or held for possible future additional appreciation. Sometimes it does work out exactly this way. However, remember in investing there really is no free lunch. If someone offers you something, there is probably a good reason why.

As a rule, convertible bonds pay a lower rate of interest than a conventional bond would. This is the price you pay for the possibility of a future capital gain, and the reason why companies issue them in the first place. If the stock price rises and the bonds are converted, they also benefit by having the debt entirely wiped out. In addition, there are occasional instances where companies may resort to convertible bonds because either their financial situation is not as good as they would like it to be, or their performance has been below par. The two factors are closely related. In order to get investors to buy their bonds at a reasonable rate of interest, they have to offer something additional: the convertible feature. Such bonds often are not necessarily "junk," but they may involve somewhat more risk than is readily apparent.

Small investors interested in convertible bonds need the security of diversity, and the only practical way to get that is to buy mutual funds which invest in convertible securities. Both the usual open-end funds plus the closed-end type, which trade on stock exchanges, are available. A number of convertible funds have produced a nice rate of return.

Preferred stocks, as their name indicates, are not bonds, but they tend to function much like bonds, so we discuss them here. Preferred stock pays a fixed dividend, one normally above that of the company's common stock. Like bond interest, this dividend is neither lowered nor raised, and preferred stock will tend to have its market price rise and fall with interest rates. As in the case of bonds, preferred stock does best when rates are falling, since newer issues would be expected to pay a lower rate than those issued when rates were higher. If rates rise, the market price declines in order to compensate the purchaser for the lower rate of return received compared to that on a new issue.

 note Preferred stocks issued by American companies also resemble bonds in that they have no regular voting rights.

 Companies which find themselves in financial difficulty have the legal right to suspend payment of dividends on preferred stock. However, all omitted dividends would have to be paid before any future dividends could be declared on the common stock. Should the company decide to go out of business, preferred stockholders have a higher claim on any remaining assets than do the common stockholders.

Corporations often buy preferred stock because most of the dividends will be exempt from federal income taxes. This advantage is not available to individuals. As a result, preferred stocks are usually not the best investment for the small investor, unless you have a convertible securities fund, which may have some in its portfolio along with its bonds. Small investors normally do best with open-end mutual funds. With open-end mutual funds, you get diversification, professional management, and the opportunity to regularly add to your account without spending a large sum of money.

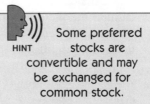 HINT Some preferred stocks are convertible and may be exchanged for common stock.

DEFINITION

If you are interested in bonds for very long, you will probably come across the term *unit trust*. Unit trusts are portfolios of bonds put together by professional money managers and then marketed to the public. In some ways, unit trusts appear to resemble a mutual fund, but there are differences: Unit trusts are purchased by big investors and typically would not be available to the small investor, who is better off with mutual funds anyway.

Things to keep in mind

During the summer of 1998, the Treasury Department announced changes in policy, and these enable many small investors to buy Treasury notes, bills, and bonds directly from the government rather than through a mutual fund. The minimum investment has been lowered to $1,000. Funds still offer the advantage of permitting you to add to your account with amounts of less than $1,000 once the account has been opened with the required initial minimum investment. Treasuries are, for all practical purposes, free of risk of default (but not market risk if sold before maturity) and buying them directly eliminates the need to pay fund expenses or possible sales loads. Treasuries can even be purchased over the Internet at the Bureau of the Public Debt's web site (http://www.publicdebt.treas.gov). Sales are also made in person, by mail, and telephone.

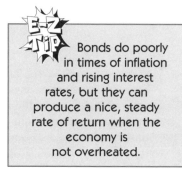

E-Z TIP
Bonds do poorly in times of inflation and rising interest rates, but they can produce a nice, steady rate of return when the economy is not overheated.

Who should consider investments in bonds? Those who want diversification beyond stocks and money-market instruments may wish to consider them. If your need is current income, bonds are worthy of consideration. When stock markets go into steep decline, bonds can help cushion the blow to your portfolio. Such declines are often followed by a lowering of interest rates in order to help stimulate the economy. Except in times of great inflation, they probably subject the investor to less risk, but at the price of less reward in the long run. Putting some of the investment funds you do not want in stocks into bonds, rather than cash and cash equivalents, is probably for many small investors prudent risk and potentially rewarding.

Chapter 11

Mortgage-based securities and real estate investments

What you'll find in this chapter:

- ⟶ Why you should explore pools of mortgages
- ⟶ Ginnie Maes, Fannie Maes, and Freddie Macs
- ⟶ When to use pass-through securities
- ⟶ The benefits of real estate investing
- ⟶ The liquid real estate investment trust

HOT spot

Small investors usually think of paying their mortgage. It may surprise them that they can invest in mortgages also! One of the great things about doing this is that not only may you obtain a nice rate of return, but you can do a good thing with your investment dollars. You can help someone—who otherwise might not be able to do so—buy a decent place in which to live.

DEFINITION

The kinds of mortgages we are discussing are actually *pools of mortgages* which are made by private lending institutions, such as banks, but are partially subsidized to provide a lower interest rate for the borrower and guaranteed against default by various agencies of the United States government. Most common are those known as **Ginnie Maes**, which are backed by the Government National Mortgage Association, but the **Fannie Maes** of the Federal National Mortgage Association, and the Federal Home Loan Mortgage Corporation's **Freddie Macs** are also available.

Pass-through securities

There are several characteristics about these mortgage-based, or pass-through, securities that make them attractive to investors. What is passed through to the investor are the principal and interest payments made on the underlying mortgages. They produce a nice stream of income, and should the borrower default, the federal government guarantees timely payment of the unpaid portion of the principal which was borrowed.

> In mortgage-based or pass-through securities, there is a degree of safety not found with corporate bonds and uninsured municipal bonds.

Another attractive factor is that these securities tend to be about a third less volatile than bonds with a similar length of time to maturity. When interest rates rise, their market price will decline, but not as drastically as bonds. However, the reverse is true. They will not do as well as bonds when rates fall, because people will pay off their old loans and refinance at the lower rate. Nevertheless, in times of falling interest rates they should produce a decent rate of return, and their performance in all kinds of conditions is more stable than that of bonds.

If mortgage securities have their advantages, they also have disadvantages. Ironically, probably the greatest disadvantage is one of their strengths, namely their federal guarantee. Unfortunately, many people who have purchased mortgage securities believed that they were buying something like a bank *certificate of deposit* or a bank *money-market fund.* They could happily collect interest and never worry about loss of their principal, since they believed that was insured. In reality, all the federal guarantee covers is default by the borrower. You are not insured for loss in market value. While the price of pass-through securities will fluctuate less than that of bonds, as we noted, it does fluctuate. Should you wish to sell your security, it is quite possible you would receive less than you paid. In fact you should expect this if interest rates have risen since the time of your purchase.

There is another difficulty, but fortunately there is an easy solution for this one. When you buy mortgaged-based securities, you are a lender. However, unlike bond lenders who receive interest payments from the borrower and get their original principal back in a lump sum, should they hold the bonds until maturity, mortgage lenders receive both principal and interest with each payment made to them. The lender then has the challenge of reinvesting these partial returns of principal. This would be extremely difficult, especially for the small investor, if it were not for mutual funds. Buy your Ginnie Maes and other pass-through securities by holding shares in a mutual fund, and the fund will automatically do the reinvesting for you. You are still subject to market risk, because the fund is subject to it.

CAUTION Pass-through securities can be an excellent value and an opportunity to do something really constructive with your money, but the same rules apply here as elsewhere. Know what it is you are buying. Know what risks you are taking.

Because of the typically high price for Ginnie Maes and similar securities, plus the complications of reinvesting the principal payments, mutual funds are the only practical way for small investors to hold mortgage-based securities. Many fund families will have a fund that specializes in these. A few also have funds that invest primarily in adjustable-rate mortgages, which might provide less volatility at the price of an average lower yield. Regardless of which type of fund you select, you will be getting both diversity and the opportunity to add to your account with modest additional payments. You can dollar average (see the chapter on dividend reinvestment plans) on a regular basis, if you wish. Be careful to compare fund expenses, and look for a fund which has done well over a period of time, not just in the last year. Avoid those which try to improve their performance through frequent use of high-risk derivative investments, which are based on

HOT spot After we do our homework, many of us may feel a Ginnie Mae fund is an ideal place for some of our investment dollars.

mortgage-securities but are not the same thing. A limited degree of this may have to be endured. Examination of the fund prospectus and its most recent annual report should reveal to what extent such tactics are used.

Of homes and castles

There is an old Wall Street saying which warns, "never invest in anything which eats or needs repairs." That may be an overly pessimistic start to the subject of real estate for the small investor. It may also be an appropriate and cautious approach which helps us avoid some of the pitfalls that lurk out there. Forget those television infomercials and books that are going to make you a real-estate millionaire in your spare time, with no money down. It is not impossible for that to happen, but it is not probable.

For a number of small investors sound, nonspeculative real estate investing does present some particular problems which are not found with other kinds of investments. That does not mean real estate should be avoided entirely. For some people it may even offer better than average opportunities. So, it is time to look at what basic factors have to be considered if you want to be a real-estate investor.

Many financial experts do not consider the home you live in to be an investment in the strict sense of the word. You have to live somewhere. If you sell your home to raise money, where do you go? Of course, there are options such as replacing it with a smaller home, renting a residence, or refinancing the home rather than selling it. This last step would enable you to obtain some of the equity you have accumulated if you have owned the home for a number of years. Homeowners can also obtain **home equity loans** which give them a source of funds and tax-deductible interest (as would the interest be on the original mortgage or a refinanced one). There are no restrictions on how the money may be used, but it could be designated for such worthy things as financing a child's education, adding an addition to the home, or paying medical expenses not covered by insurance. For the interest to qualify as a tax deduction, you must be able to itemize your deductions on Schedule A of your federal income tax return. Other restrictions also apply, but these normally will be of no concern to the small investor.

Another major factor that makes home ownership attractive from an investment standpoint is that, for any home sold after May 6, 1997, all capital gains up to $250,000 for a single person and $500,000 for a married couple are free of federal income taxes. There are certain exceptions, but in most instances

> ⚠ **CAUTION** Decline loans being offered for more than your equity, as this is a quick way to become financially overextended.

you or your spouse must have lived in the home at least two of the five years before the date of the sale. This means the small investor normally will have no federal tax liability on the sale of a residence.

What may be the best reason for purchasing a home has nothing to do with investing at all. Many people simply get a great deal of satisfaction and security out of home ownership. If you are one of these, then buying a home is something to seriously consider.

Still other matters can add to the attractiveness of a home of your own. For many persons, a mortgage is their largest expense, but in part it is also a forced form of savings. A portion of each payment goes to reduce the principal of your original loan and to increase your equity in the home. People who find it difficult to save money will do it this way in spite of themselves! To cut interest expenses dramatically and accelerate savings, take out a mortgage for as short a time period as you can reasonably handle. At the time of financing, if interest rates are currently well below the average, a fixed-rate loan is most likely best. If the interest rates are unusually high, consider an adjustable rate.

The rates probably would not go much higher, and there is a good possibility that, in time, the rates will decline.

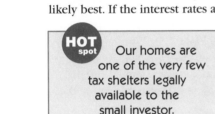

HOT spot Our homes are one of the very few tax shelters legally available to the small investor.

Most real estate also provides a nice inflation hedge. When prices are on the rise, real estate usually sees solid increases in value. During relatively high periods of inflation, as in the late 1970s, it has often been especially attractive.

Before you call that real estate agent or go house hunting on your own, you should also look at the negatives in home ownership and most other kinds of real estate investment. Probably the most serious of these is the fact that real estate can be a very nonliquid investment. It may take months or even years to sell a piece of property. Unless you want to go to the time and trouble (which could be extensive) of selling the property yourself, expect to pay a substantial commission when you do obtain a buyer. On raw land this may be as much as 10 percent, although it will be less on a home.

Until you do sell your home or other real estate, there will be certain inevitable expenses which must be met. These include taxes and insurance, which should always include adequate liability insurance to protect in case of a lawsuit against you (you need liability insurance even if you do not own a home). Buildings will require maintenance and repairs. Some of these, such as a new roof, may be substantial. Undeveloped land may need to be cleared and mowed from time to time, or possibly fenced.

Some people have also made the mistake in believing that, since the legendary humorist Will Rogers was correct when it came to land that, "they aren't making any more of it," this meant you could never lose money in real estate. The Florida land bubble of the 1920s and the more recent California recession of the early 1990s, to cite just two examples, demonstrate how dangerous that assumption may be. As previously noted, real estate does quite well in holding or increasing its value in times of inflation. In times of recession or depression, the opposite may occur. Further, there may be no buyers at almost any price. Meanwhile your expenses continue.

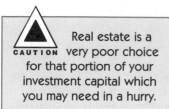 Real estate is a CAUTION very poor choice for that portion of your investment capital which you may need in a hurry.

Still other problems can affect your real estate investment. The home you live in and now want to sell may have been in a very attractive neighborhood thirty years ago when you bought it. However, gradually over the years the neighborhood has declined. Thanks to inflation, you should still make a profit over the original price, but it may be far less than you previously thought.

Rental property

Investment strategies pertaining to rental property can fill an entire book by themselves. What follows here must be limited to a basic introduction to the subject. Again, it is aimed at the small investor who, at most, may have the financial capability to consider one or possibly two modest rental properties.

Among the major advantages of rental property are those pertaining to taxes. Because you can deduct all expenses related to your rental property plus depreciate it, you may often show a taxable loss, although the property has been rented much or all of the year. Your mortgage interest also becomes deductible as an expense even though you might not be in a position to itemize and take a mortgage deduction on Schedule A of Form 1040, if this were a personal residence.

note In the short-term, rental property is in this delightful situation of producing some income while possibly actually reducing your taxes.

There is, of course, a catch, one that is often overlooked when rental property is considered. What the Internal Revenue Service gives with one hand it takes away with the other. When the property is finally sold, the depreciation which has been taken (the IRS requires you to depreciate) will be "recaptured." This means you must reduce your basis, the amount you have invested in the property, by the amount of depreciation taken. For example, if you had paid $50,000 for a rental property, taken $25,000 in depreciation, and then sold it for $100,000, you have a fully taxable profit of $75,000, not $50,000. That can come as a shock, especially if the profits have already been spent by the time the tax bill comes due.

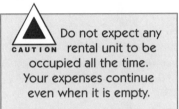

There are numerous other problems with becoming a landlord. If you must obtain a mortgage in order to purchase your rental, you may find that the rent you collect will be less than your mortgage payments plus expenses for taxes, insurance, maintenance, and repairs. To be sure, your loss is tax-deductible. You may also show a nice profit later when you do sell the property, but in the meantime the money invested will not be in a position to help produce monthly income, if that is what you really need. Further, you will have to find the money for a down payment to purchase the property even if you are willing to take a mortgage to finance the balance.

Other problems may appear. You may have problems with tenants who fail to pay their rent or who call you at the most inconvenient times about needed repairs. There is also the difficulty and expense of finding suitable tenants in the first place. Some of these headaches can be avoided by enlisting the services of a property manager. Many real estate offices will have a rental department. However, expect to pay a commission, typically half a month's rent, when the property manager does find you a tenant. The monthly management fee, which includes collecting rents and handling necessary repairs, is normally 10 percent of the rent collected. In the case of vacation property with short-term rentals, commissions and fees may total as much as 40 percent of rent paid.

If you have some spare time to manage your own property, and especially if you are handy at making various repairs, you may actually find you enjoy being a landlord. By doing most of the work yourself you keep your expenses down, it may also be a profitable enterprise. Should you be able to acquire a piece of rental property without a mortgage, it might turn a modest profit even if you decide it is best to be an "absentee" landlord and use a property manager. Certainly, rental property can also help you diversify your investments and thus increase your financial safety. However, consider carefully what is involved before you decide to become a real-estate baron. It is considerably more complex than the delight you may have felt some years ago while playing Monopoly and collecting rent when someone landed

>
> HINT As with any real estate, remember that rental property is not a liquid investment. You may have a long wait for a buyer when you do want to sell.

on your property. In fact, maybe you remember even then it could sometimes be quite painful if you drew a Chance or Community Chest card and were called upon to pay the bill for "general repairs on all your property" or for that street repair assessment.

Condominiums and time-shares

Condominiums and time-shares as investments have virtually all the problems mentioned above plus a few of their own. With a condominium you will have a monthly maintenance fee to pay, and this will be due on rental property whether the unit is occupied or not. Also remember that condominium associations have the authority to issue rules and regulations. If you do not like these you may have little recourse other than to sell your property. Should the association be required to do some sort of major renovation, such as a new roof, for which it does not have adequate reserves, expect a special assessment, which may be quite sizeable.

DEFINITION

Time-shares also levy maintenance fees. Such units are often very difficult to resell and sometimes bring only a fraction of their original purchase price. As investments they leave much to be desired. Time-shares come in two basic forms: *deeded*, where you have an ownership interest in the property, or *nondeeded* which permits you to use the property for a specific amount of time each year for a certain number of years.

If you truly expect to use a time share as a personal vacation place, its purchase may be desirable. However, consider buying one on the secondary market from an individual owner or a firm that specializes in resales. This can save up to 50 percent or even more. You may also want to:

- Check to see if your contract has "non-disturbance" and "non-performance" clauses, which protect your access and use of the property if the builder or manager encounters financial difficulties.

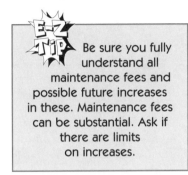
Be sure you fully understand all maintenance fees and possible future increases in these. Maintenance fees can be substantial. Ask if there are limits on increases.

- Get complete information on available exchange programs, including their conditions and limitations.

- Visit the property to see how well it is managed before you purchase it.

- Check on the records of the builder and manager.

- Talk with other owners, if possible.

- Compare time-share costs with your traditional vacation expenses to determine if there actually would be any savings.

A condominium can make an ideal residence, especially if you like the convenience of having your outside maintenance done for you and want access to recreational facilities such as swimming pools and tennis courts, which often are provided. The right condominium may even be suitable as rental property and may be expected

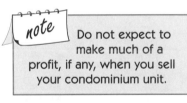
Do not expect to make much of a profit, if any, when you sell your condominium unit.

HINT

to appreciate in value. However, whether it be for rental purposes or as a residence, be sure you are aware of all regulations and restrictions and have a complete understanding of all regular fees plus possible special assessments.

Real estate investment trust

For many small investors there probably is little point in discussing the advantages and disadvantages of investing in real estate. With the possible exception of a personal residence, the amount needed for a down payment to purchase a piece of property will simply be too high. Some investors may also be reluctant to take the plunge because monthly mortgage payments must be made even if the property remains unrented. However, there is one type of real estate investment, often overlooked by the small investor, which has none of these liabilities. Furthermore, unlike real estate in general, it is highly liquid. This is the *real estate investment trust*, or REIT, (pronounced "reet") as it is commonly called.

In some ways a REIT looks much like a mutual fund, especially the closed-end variety. Many REITs, like closed-end funds, are listed on the stock exchanges. It is no more difficult to buy or sell shares in them than in any listed stock. A number of these same REITs also have dividend reinvestment and cash purchase plans, a situation which can make them especially attractive to the small investor. It is possible to increase one's holding over a period of time and without committing a large amount of money at any time.

> **CAUTION** Some REITs also invest in mortgages, but mortgage REITs often invest heavily in high-risk derivatives, making them very speculative and not suitable for small investors. Financial professionals refer to them as "toxic waste."

Like nearly all mutual funds, REITs are structured under the tax code in such a manner that they pass along a minimum of 95 percent of their income. As a result, REITs do not normally pay taxes on their earnings and usually yield attractive rates of return. Shareholders are responsible for any tax liability they may encounter by receiving dividends or capital gains from REIT investments, but at least earnings are not subject to double taxation, as is the case with corporate profits.

REITs invest in property. Some may own a variety of holdings including apartment complexes, shopping centers, and office buildings. Others specialize in a single type of property. Various REITs own mobile home parks, parking garages, and health-care facilities. Many REITs are intended to be permanent organizations, while others are designed with a limited life in mind. The latter will have their assets distributed among their investors when they do expire.

Various financial experts do not think REITs are suitable investments for the small investor. Opponents of REITs do have some powerful ammunition. During certain time periods they have not done well, underperforming both the stock and general real estate markets. Claims are also made that some REITs also inflate the value of their real estate holdings. The problems with REITs are true, but the conveniences for the small investor who otherwise might have few or no opportunities in real estate are also there.

Like any other investment, it is best to do your homework before you go shopping. However, if you are willing to do this, REITs may offer a reasonable way to invest in real estate, diversify one's investments, and earn an attractive rate of return with reasonable risk. REITs do tend to resemble stocks and mutual funds more than they do typical real estate investments. As such, those who purchase them must be willing to accept not only market risk but also frequent, sometimes daily, fluctuations in the value of their shares.

If you decide to invest in REITs, there are several factors the small investor should consider. Invest in REITs that are intended to be permanent entities rather than those with a limited life. Make sure the REIT is listed on a major stock exchange or the NASDAQ. In this way you will have no difficulty disposing of your shares should you decide to do so. Unless you can afford to buy at least a round lot of 100 shares, you probably should consider only those REITs with dividend

> *note*
>
> REITs are more volatile than real estate in general, but probably no more so than many stocks and mutual funds.

reinvestment and cash purchase plans. These will enable you to accumulate enough stock to give you a meaningful investment without straining your budget in the process.

There is one important factor about REITs that needs some explanation. REITs normally base their dividends on what is termed **funds from operations**. Funds from operations are not the same thing as cash flow and often are significantly larger than net income, since they do not take into account such factors as depreciation. As a result, REITs often pay out

> HINT
>
> REITs which do not try to deliver the moon are also more likely to avoid serious financial difficulties and debt burdens which become too heavy to carry.

considerably more than their net income. If this goes on too long the REIT may have to borrow funds or pay investors by partially returning some of their capital. Because of the peculiarities of real estate and its tendency to appreciate, some REITs can go on indefinitely paying more than net income. However, it is probably best for the small investor to

limit REIT purchases to those with conservative payouts, where the dividends do not exceed net income by an excessive amount. In this way you can have some assurance that the dividend rate will not undergo drastic cuts, unless, of course, profits should decline.

Always do your homework before investing in anything. With REITs this is even more the case. Effort and determination can help you find REITs with solid, conservative management and realistic payout policies. Take a careful look at the annual report, not just the size of the dividend payout. Read all mailings from management carefully. Look for evaluations of individual REITs, when available, in the publications of the financial advisory services. Several of these are discussed elsewhere in this book. All else being equal, a REIT with a dividend reinvestment and cash purchase plan is a better choice than one without. Regular use of it lessens the danger

Develop the habit of reading what financial analysts in Barron's and other publications say about the REIT market as a whole.

that the bulk of your investment will be made at the least advantageous time. If you are willing to make the necessary effort, you may be able to find a REIT quite suitable for you.

For those who like some of the conveniences of the REIT, but are not completely comfortable with the concept, there are several mutual funds which invest in real estate, REITs, and companies serving the real estate industry. These may be a very attractive alternative or supplement to the REIT. Some of the large mutual fund families offer funds of this type, as do other companies.

In summary

For small investors, buying your own home does make sense. It can provide a sense of security and comfort as well as a tax shelter to help with the retirement years. REITs and real estate-related mutual funds are also worth considering. Beyond this how much you should or can do with real estate will depend to a considerable degree on your own particular situation. Can you afford a down payment? Do you have the time and knowledge that some real estate investments require? Is the money to be invested funds that would not be required in an emergency? These and other questions that will come to mind should be carefully and honestly answered before investing in real estate. Real estate can be an excellent investment, but for numerous small investors there are possibly better opportunities.

Chapter 12

All that glitters: precious metals

What you'll find in this chapter:

➠ How much gold should you invest in?

➠ The future of gold investments

➠ The best way to invest in precious metals

➠ Selecting the right precious metals

➠ How valuable is your jewelry?

The gold bug

Through the centuries, gold has made people do strange and foolish things. There is something about the precious metal that must encourage those who would otherwise be quite normal to take leave of their senses. It certainly has had that impact on many a would-be investor. In fact, within the investing realm it has created a whole new species of insect—namely, the gold bug. The most ferocious form of this creature is absolutely certain Western civilization as we know it is going down the tube, and everything but gold (well, possibly a few other precious metals) is going with it. Less dangerous subspecies merely feel that for one reason or another (usually some "fun" thing such as hyperinflation or another Great Depression) gold will reach fantastic new price levels approaching something like $3,000 an ounce.

What many gold bugs have in common is that they totally ignore one of the basic rules for successful investing, namely *diversification*. There may well be a place for gold in the plans of the small investor, but it certainly should not be at the expense of everything else. It is also good to occasionally remind oneself that predicting the direction of gold prices is about as easy as predicting the direction of interest rates or the Dow. In short, on a day to day basis it is futile, and even over the long run it can be quite difficult.

Investing in gold

So, why should the small investor even bother with the stuff? Gold might be looked upon to some extent as a "misery investment." It often tends to do best when everything else is doing poorly. Traditionally, gold has been valued as a hedge against both inflation and political uncertainty. When currencies are under attack, gold has also been seen as a safe haven. Gold usually does

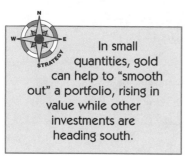

In small quantities, gold can help to "smooth out" a portfolio, rising in value while other investments are heading south.

poorly when inflation is low or in times of moderate deflation. However, in extreme deflation, such as during the Great Depression of the 1930s, it may do very well. If the unimaginable does happen, and the survivalists turn out to be correct after all, gold might be seen as the final refuge.

Quite possibly gold may continue in the future to play its past role as insurance against inflation and currency fluctuation. However, this is by no means certain. In recent years, international crises have failed to budge gold prices much. Instead, investors at such times seem to do what they do in the face of a currency crisis. They merely switch to a strong currency. A somewhat similar situation exists in regard to inflation. Many investors now hedge against it by purchasing options and futures contracts linked to interest rates rather than gold.

While gold may have lost some of its past luster, it still does have some attributes which are commendable. In developing countries where financial markets may be less complex and offer fewer alternatives, gold may well remain for some time the inflation and currency hedge of choice. Such possible demands for gold can boost its price in all markets. Rising affluence, especially in Asia, may be an additional favorable impact. More gold is being purchased in China and Japan simply because residents of those countries can afford to do so. Some of it is jewelry, while the remainder is probably sought as financial insurance. India is another highly-populated Asian nation where demand for gold may increase as that country appears poised for stronger future economic growth.

Gold's characteristics are more or less true for other precious metals, namely silver, platinum, and palladium. These also have industrial uses which can affect the demand for them and in turn their market prices. Normally, platinum sells at a premium to gold, although occasional exceptions do occur. Since much of the world's platinum and gold supply come from South Africa, political events in that country can also impact precious metal prices. A South African crisis, which could at least potentially affect production, will normally cause prices

> *note* In the future, precious metals experts believe major gold-producing areas will eventually be South America and West Africa, as well as Indonesia and other nearby islands.

to rise. Other significant gold sources are Canada, the United States, Australia, and Russia (which produces most of the palladium), with some other highly productive mines scattered elsewhere throughout the world.

Small investors can comfortably ignore gold entirely if they wish to do so. If they feel tempted to undergo metamorphosis and be transformed into gold bugs, they probably are best advised to avoid precious metals investing completely. Gold has been the ruin of more than one would-be small investor.

Some financial advisors who stress socially responsible investing feel gold should be avoided for another reason. They feel gold investors are nothing more than hoarders. As such, they do nothing to contribute to economic growth and prosperity. If you feel this is the case, then again it would probably be better to invest in things other than precious metals. No investors should invest in things that make them uncomfortable.

> HINT To a certain extent, precious metals can still serve as a hedge for small investors who lack access to some of the more sophisticated hedging instruments available to institutional and other large investors.

On the other hand, a case can be made for precious metals and the small investor. As noted, precious metals can help to smooth out an investment portfolio, since they often rise in value when most other things decline. This may continue to be true especially in times of high inflation and political turmoil. These metals do have some industrial uses as well as value to the jewelry business, so investing in them does not always have to be mere hoarding. As long as only a small percentage of one's holdings is in precious metals investments, the risk of becoming a gold bug and engaging in the irrational behavior that species often exhibits seems minimal.

What to do if you invest

Probably, the small investor should limit precious metals investments to no more than 5 percent of total assets, with perhaps 7 or 8 percent being an absolute maximum. To some extent, such investments should be looked upon partially as a form of insurance (although it comes with no guarantee!) designed to help protect you under certain adverse financial situations. That way, you will be less tempted to see them as some sort of speculation or be overly disappointed if they produce little in the way of dividends or capital gains.

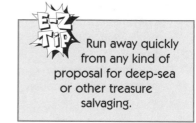

Run away quickly from any kind of proposal for deep-sea or other treasure salvaging.

If you decide to make some investments in gold, it is important to make the right ones, as the opportunity for poor ones unfortunately is great. Normally, small investors should not attempt to purchase bullion either in the form of coins or bars. The reason is simple: The dealer or mint markup you pay makes it extremely difficult to make a profit. You will probably have to take less than the market price when you sell, and there are also the problems and associated costs of storage and insurance. If you enjoy collecting coins for the sake of collecting and learning that is fine, but for the small investor coins are usually not a good investment.

If you decide on stocks of individual mining companies, confine your choices to those traded either on the New York or American exchanges. Too many things presented to the public as mining companies are little more than cow pasture. Outright frauds also occur, as the 1997 collapse of Bre-X Minerals ably demonstrated. This Canadian company claimed to have a huge, rich ore discovery in Indonesia. Unfortunately, the test samples had been salted. Bre-X stock went to zero. Under no circumstances buy shares traded only on small regional stock exchanges. Some of these companies are fine, but the small investor does not have the means to determine which are and are not. Above all, never buy into companies offered to you by an unsolicited telephone call or through the mail. That same warning also holds true for bullion or for coins advertised primarily as an investment.

HINT

While South African mines often pay the best dividends, the small investor probably should limit consideration to companies headquartered in either the United States, Canada, or Australia, although they may have operations in various developing countries. Such companies are more likely to be well established, adequately funded, and sufficiently diversified than those strictly limited to one emerging market or another.

For most small investors desiring some sort of position in gold and other precious metals, a *mutual fund* probably makes the most sense. For one thing, it offers the protection of diversity, and this is more important than usual when dealing with mining companies. Since the fund will own shares in a variety of companies, the potential damage caused by a collapsing mine, fire, or labor unrest is minimized. Many funds will also have holdings in several countries, including South Africa. This lessens political risk in otherwise attractive markets.

Some funds own only mining shares. Others will hold both stock and bullion. The latter will tend to be less volatile since, as a rule, the price of gold fluctuates less than the shares of many of the companies that mine it. Funds that do buy bullion may limit themselves strictly to gold. Various ones, however, also take positions in the other precious metals. Central Fund of Canada, a closed-end fund, traded on the American Exchange, is virtually a pure bullion play, as this fund purchases little else.

HOT spot Another plus for silver is that it has far more extensive industrial uses than does gold. Although there is no guarantee, future industrial demand could increase.

The small investor who wants some exposure to precious metals may be best served by the mutual fund which invests in shares of mining companies in several countries and also bullion. This will give you added diversity and less volatility. If the potential for gain is lessened, so is that for loss. Several of the large mutual fund families have gold or precious metal funds. These offer the convenience of switching to another type of investment if after a time you decide, as have many others, that precious metals are not necessary for your investment strategy. For those who decide to stay they also provide the opportunity to dollar average and thus cut your costs per share by making, regular, periodic investments over several years or even longer.

Going for the silver

Some believe the much smaller silver market may have far more potential than gold. Undoubtedly Warren Buffett's extensive purchases in 1998 helped to create renewed interest. Silver prices underwent severe depression during most of the 1980s and early 1990s, after spiking upward in the first few years of the 1980s. As a result, mines closed, and others cut back on their silver production. This means less silver is coming on the market.

For the small investor, investing in silver is far more challenging than gold. Some of the precious metal funds may hold silver bullion or stock in companies that mine silver. However, in the past these have usually been a rather small percentage of their holdings.

The situation with mining stocks is not a lot better. Much of the silver coming to market these days is a byproduct of gold or other mining operations, so it is difficult to buy shares in a company oriented toward silver. Two possibilities are Coeur d'Alene Mines and Hecla Mining,

> **E-Z TIP** Small investors should always avoid options and futures when considering any kind of precious metals investment.

which trade on the New York Stock Exchange. In addition to gold, they mine significant amounts of silver and, in all probability, would increase silver production as prices improve. Sunshine Mining and Refining Company, also listed on the New York Exchange, is nearly a pure silver play, but the company's near total dependence on silver and financial difficulties in past years make this a somewhat speculative consideration—but possibly one that should not be forgotten. Silver bullion coins of the United States, Canada, and Mexico are available at modest cost, but the retail markup on these plus the much lower prices dealers pay to repurchase the coins, mean silver would have to rise dramatically before you would have a profit. There is also the problem of proper preservation and storage until you do sell. Silver numismatic or collector coins are best left to those who have a degree of knowledge about this area.

Gems and other precious metals

In regard to platinum, palladium, and gem stones, things are even more difficult. Some funds will hold platinum (a very few may also buy palladium) bullion and stock in a few companies, especially South African, that mine platinum. Again, these are likely to be only a small percentage of their portfolio. Direct purchase of platinum mining stocks, for a variety of reasons, will not normally be practical for the small investor. A few platinum bullion coins are available, but they are more expensive and have all the problems of gold and silver ones.

HINT There are those who believe DeBeers, in the years ahead, could lose its near monopoly on the gem diamond market, with a sharp decline in the price of the stones being the result.

Shares of diamond producer and distributor DeBeers Consolidated Mines and also its parent organization, the Anglo-American Company, do trade in American Depository Receipt form on the Nasdaq and can be easily obtained through any broker. These have to be considered speculative. Shares in companies mining or exploring for diamonds in northern Canada are extremely speculative, unless possibly a company has other mining interests. These usually should be avoided.

Jewelry and other items crafted from precious metals should be purchased only because you enjoy owning and using them. Generally, they perform very poorly as investments. This is probably especially true of so-called modern "limited editions" which are produced for the collectibles market.

If you have Internet access and want to learn more about gold as an industry, you can visit the London-based World Gold Council's web site (http://www.gold.org). Remember, the Council's purpose is not only to inform, but to promote gold usage and sales. A small investment in precious metals may or may not be appropriate for you, depending on a variety of circumstances.

Chapter 13

Asset allocation and the small investor

What you'll find in this chapter:

➠ Do you have enough to diversify?

➠ How long to hold on

➠ The best strategy for diversification

➠ Which bonds are best for asset allocation

➠ Determining your investment style

Some students of financial markets advocate a policy of putting all your eggs in one basket and then watching that basket very closely. That approach can work, but it is not really a suitable one for small investors, who must limit their risk. It probably is not even the best method for most big investors, since studies indicate that how you distribute your money among various kinds of investments is probably more critical to your ultimate success than the particular stocks, bonds, or mutual funds you finally select for these investments. If this is the case, then what percentage of their money should small investors allocate to the variety of investments available?

The road to diversification

As a starting point, we examine a basic formula advocated by financial advisor and writer Gary Moore in his book *Ten Golden Rules for Financial Success*. Moore suggests taking your age and subtracting it from one hundred. The sum you get is the percentage of your investments which can be in those kinds of investments which generally produce greater rewards but also are subject to fluctuations and greater risk. These include stocks, longer-term bonds, many mutual funds, and real estate. The percentage represented by your age is invested in more stable investments such as certificates of deposit, savings bonds, annuities, shorter-term bonds, money market funds, and other cash savings. Note what this formula does. The younger you are the more risk it encourages you to take, and that is a sound approach. Should some reversals come your way, you have more time to recover from them.

note Generally, the longer any investment is held the less volatile its record will look.

You may find the above formula ideal. If you are not comfortable with it, do not worry. It is important to know your own personal tolerance for risk. If a particular investment makes you nervous for more than a brief period of time, you probably should not own it.

Especially when you first begin investing, you may want to start with a degree of caution. Perhaps no more than 10 or 20 percent of your savings might be in stocks or mutual funds. As you get more familiar with this kind of investing, you can gradually increase the percentage. Many small investors may want to limit that percentage to no more than 50 percent, no matter what their age, since potential losses can be more devastating to them than to larger investors who may have more flexibility and a greater ability to recover. However, if you are still rather young, or you have a greater tolerance for risk, you may find that a somewhat higher percentage does not disturb you. In the end no one can really give you a magic figure. Periodically, depending on your circumstances, you may need to change your percentages.

note

The beginning investor might rightfully ask, why is it necessary to diversify anyway? The answer is really quite logical. Different types of investments do not all fluctuate up and down at the same rate and at the same time. By diversifying, you may lose some profits, assuming you are

STRATEGY You need to consider not only your age and ability to accept risk but what financial responsibilities you may have, such as dependents who rely on you for support or a home mortgage.

near perfect at investment selection, but you will also lose considerable volatility, and that may add to your ability to sleep at night.

If all of this seems complicated, it can be, but it does not have to be. You probably would do a reasonably decent job of diversification if half of your investments were in federally insured certificates of deposit and United States EE bonds, while the other half was in a proven, conservatively managed global mutual fund, such as the Templeton Growth Fund. Half of your principle would not be subject to market fluctuations, but would earn interest, while being about as safe as investments possibly can be. The other half, in many years, would be able to achieve capital gains in excess of typical interest rates while being diversified in stock markets in the United States and around the world. It is an approach possibly worth considering for both its simplicity as well as its safety.

HOT spot If you diversify, some of your investments should be doing reasonably well at almost any time, even if others are not.

However, the more adventuresome may seek other combinations of investments. These will not only provide diversification, but should, if you are interested, help teach you about the characteristics of the various kinds of investments available. You can then decide which are best for you.

Your diversification plan

Many diversification plans would contain three basic kinds of investments:

1) cash and cash equivalents

2) bonds

3) stocks and other investments

Stocks

Within these categories, still more diversification is possible. We already mentioned the stocks above, so let us first turn in that direction. Once you decide what percentage of your investments will go into stocks, you can further diversify between stocks of larger companies and those of smaller ones. The smaller ones offer more potential for growth, but also a great deal more risk. You might want to consider a mutual fund that specializes in small capitalization companies for this part of your portfolio. Mutual funds themselves, since they hold stocks in a number of companies, offer excellent diversification and some, perhaps all, of your stock investments may be in the form of mutual funds. You can also diversify between American companies and those in other countries. Foreign stocks include those in more established and less risky markets, such as Britain and Germany, to those potentially very rewarding, but also highly volatile newer emerging markets of the developing countries.

E-Z TIP

Mutual funds may be the easiest way to invest beyond America's borders.

It is not necessary, and probably not even possible, for you to have your stock investments spread across all of these different kinds. Here we are just taking a look at what is available and what you might wish to consider. Obviously as your investments grow in size, more diversification is realistic should you feel it is worthwhile.

Cash investments

We also previously mentioned the cash portion of our investments, so let us turn to that next. Certainly money you expect to need over the next three to five years should be invested here. You would not have time to recover from a market decline should one occur, and they do. Reasonably liquid and safe assets also need to be kept on hand to handle those inevitable emergencies and simply to provide a feeling of security, which in turn helps give you the confidence to make your less conservative investments. These funds can be held in a basic savings account, certificates of deposit, EE bonds, and money-market funds. Bank money-market funds are federally insured. Those available through mutual fund companies or stock brokers are not, but they normally pay a higher rate of interest and have had an excellent—but not perfect—safety record. They are certainly worthy or your consideration. So are short-term bond funds available through certain mutual fund companies. These hold bonds generally no more than three years from maturity, so price fluctuation does occur but is rather minimal. Interest rates are often higher than what you receive on a certificate of deposit, and you can obtain your money at any time without penalty. There is no federal insurance. For this type of fund, it is especially important to compare management fees and other expense charges, so be certain to read the fund's prospectus. Funds that are sold with a load or sale charge are worth the cost in some instances, but the actual performance of many short-term bond funds is likely to be quite similar. Therefore, you may do better with a *no-load*, or at least a *low-load*, fund with low expenses. Consider putting some of your certificate money into a short-term bond fund.

You could be reasonably diversified with the above two components—stocks and mutual funds on the one hand, and cash equivalents and short-term bonds on the other. However, you can add to your diversification by including other

Small investors should not try to buy individual bonds. Purchase shares in a short-term bond fund.

bonds. Bonds fluctuate in value, but normally not as much as stocks or mutual funds holding stocks. At times, bonds may go up in value when stocks are declining. At other times, bonds may move in the same direction as the stock markets. Normally, look for bonds to rise in value when interest rates decline, but to do poorly when rates increase and in inflationary periods. The longer the period until the bonds mature, the more volatility their market prices will have. Longer-term bonds normally reward you for this volatility by paying a higher interest rate. So, you can further diversify by holding bonds of various maturities.

Bonds

HINT

Additional diversification can be obtained by considering bonds issued by states, municipalities, and other local governments. The interest earned on these, but not any possible capital gains, is free of federal income tax and income taxes of the state where they are issued.

The bond component of your portfolio could also include an international bond fund or possibly a global money fund. Interest rates in other countries can sometimes be more attractive than at home, but this is not always the case. Still further diversification can be obtained by including mortgage-related securities (most often Ginnie Maes), which are guaranteed against default (but not decline in market price) by the federal government. Normally these will fluctuate less in value than will bonds of comparable length of time to maturity.

note   State and municipal bonds normally pay a lower rate of interest, so they are primarily attractive to investors in the higher tax brackets. However, there are times when the small investor may find it wise to consider them.

Small investors should seldom, if ever, try to buy individual bonds or mortgage securities. It is usually both costly and complicated. Instead, purchase mutual funds. It is critical that you buy those with a low expense rate and preferably no load, because as a rule there is less difference in the performance of bond funds than with stock funds. So, the expenses become a key factor. However, there are indeed some low-load bond funds, usually also with a lower than average portfolio turnover rate, that are excellent performers and worthy of your consideration. Do not buy so-called high-yield funds that hold high-risk junk bonds. They may give you a higher return in the short term, but in the long run they could hurt you badly.

Real estate

Still other ways to add diversification could be to include real estate and real estate investment trusts (REITs), which trade much like stocks. Perhaps 5 to no more than 7 or 8 percent of a diversified portfolio might be in mutual funds investing in precious metals and mining stocks, although this is strictly an optional choice.

More help

 Should you wish to make a more in-depth study of asset allocation and what it can accomplish, you may want to take a look at *Asset Allocation: Balancing Financial Risk,* by Roger C. Gibson and published by Irwin Professional Publishing. Although written for professional money managers, the book should prove helpful for many who can or must handle their own financial affairs. Among other things, Gibson provides three model portfolios. While intended for persons with substantial assets, all three can serve as guides to creating your own, and all three take a rather conservative approach. His lower-risk model allots 55 percent to short-term debt instruments, 15 percent to long-term debt instruments, and 30 percent to equity (stocks, real estate, and precious

> **HOT spot** Used carefully and in consideration of your own needs and ability to tolerate risk, asset allocation can be a very valuable tool. It should help you sleep better at nights and weather any financial storms which may come your way.

metals) investments. For the medium-risk portfolio, the percentages are 37, 18, and 45 percent; and for the higher risk model they are 15, 20, and 65. Each of the three basic categories is then further divided into various sub-categories. In his lower-risk model, precious metals and similar investments are only 3 percent. Stocks include both large and small companies. Both stock and debt instruments have domestic and international components.

note

Regardless of what percentages you finally decide are best for you, asset allocation, if it is to work to the fullest, from time to time will require you to shift some assets to restore your target percentages. This takes willpower. For example, it calls you to take some profits and reduce your exposure in the very areas where you have recently been most successful. However, in so doing, you are probably reducing risk in those markets where there currently is the least value and future price declines are most likely.

Chapter 14

Finding out: research and the small investor

What you'll find in this chapter:

➡ Where to get information on investments

➡ What performance ratings really indicate

➡ Television, software, and Internet resources

➡ Who should join an investment club

➡ The upside of dollar averaging

There are very few specific stock or mutual fund recommendations in this volume. That is no oversight. The book is intended to serve as a helpful guide and reference work for a considerable period of time. When you need clarification on some aspect of investing for the small investor, hopefully you will come back to it and find the assistance you want. Any list of stocks and mutual funds which you should buy or sell would be out of date and almost useless within a few months or even weeks. Financial markets are dynamic, not static. The change is constant. Although this work stresses the need to have a long-term investment horizon, and for small investors to be real investors rather than traders, it is essential to have a good idea of what current conditions are before investing. This means doing some research of your own and then making your own decisions. That requires some work, but nothing the average person is not capable of doing. After doing it awhile, you may discover it can be quite educational and even entertaining.

> **note**
> Even if a recommendation made by someone else recently or in the past is a good one, it is important to determine if it is a good one for you.

Wading through the information river

Actually, more financial information is readily available than most people can use. There is always the danger of becoming so immersed in material that you tend to become paralyzed and do not know what to do. One way to avoid this is to start by concentrating on a few good sources. See if these provide what you need. If they do not, you can try others. Later, you can add additional ones if you wish.

Libraries

A good place to begin is to make a trip to your local library and do some sampling there. Subscribing to many of the resources you might find helpful can be quite expensive. Most libraries will have at least some of them, and you can explore them freely before deciding if any are so essential that you do want your own subscription. You can also buy single copies of some at various stores and newsstands.

> **E-Z TIP**
>
> After you determine what you want to read on a regular basis, a subscription or two might be convenient and beneficial.

Publications

Readily available, and probably one of the most useful places to look, is the *Wall Street Journal*, published daily, Monday through Friday, except holidays. The *Journal* is an outstanding source for both business and general news. There will also be very thorough coverage of the previous day's results in the various financial markets. The *Journal* is not intended to give you specific recommendations on what you should do. It will give you specific information on what is happening in particular companies, industries, and countries. Using this and other material you have gathered, you will then be better equipped to decide

> **HOT spot**
>
> Somewhat similar to the Journal, but with its own style and features, is *Investor's Business Daily*. You can decide which you prefer, or whether you want to make use of both.

what is best for you. Serious *Journal* readers will benefit from taking a look at Michael B. Lehmann's excellent book on how to use the *Wall Street Journal*.

Published by Dow Jones, which also is responsible for the *Journal*, is *Barron's*. It appears every Saturday. There is probably no better readily obtainable source of financial data than this. The statistical section will provide you with current price information on virtually any stock or mutual fund you may be following. There is also solid coverage of foreign stocks and other financial markets. Columns in *Barron's* cover a considerable variety of topics including interest rates, commodities, international markets, and real estate. A periodic column looks at computer resources for the investor. Feature articles are timely and often include specific recommendations by some of the country's best known financial experts. It can be an extremely versatile tool for the serious investor.

At this point, however, a major word of caution is in order. *Barron's*, and most other financial publications, are not written for the small investor who is struggling to invest $50, $100, or a few more dollars a month. Much of its readership comes from the

> **HINT** Get leads and insights from your reading, but make certain your decisions fit your situation.

higher-income brackets and from people who manage other people's money as their career. Such readers, when they invest, usually invest large sums of money, and in many cases their time horizons are quite short. They are also able and sometimes willing to take financial risks that others should not. As a result, anything you read in a publication such as this must be weighed very carefully, or the results could be rather unpleasant should you decide to act on it. Small investors should not be traders, constantly moving money around. The vast majority who try it will be losers. Whether or not the big folks should do this, they frequently (in many cases usually) do. Consequently, suggestions and insights intended for them are often highly inappropriate for others. Look over their shoulders all you want, but do not attempt to play their cards. Play your own.

Three key players

Several publications will prove particularly helpful to investors, large and small, who want information about individual stocks and mutual funds. These are *Value Line, Morningstar,* and the stock guides published by Standard & Poor's. Subscribing to any of these services is very expensive, so take a look at your library, if at all possible. *Value Line*'s service provides basic coverage of a wide variety of stocks and closed-end funds traded on the exchanges. In addition to statistical information, a report is included on what the company has been doing and its future plans. Companies are also rated in terms of their

financial safety and timeliness, or how likely their stock will increase in value in the not too distant future. Small investors may actually find it beneficial to pick stocks rated highly for their safety, but which are out of favor as far as timeliness is concerned. These can then be accumulated gradually through dollar averaging and cash purchase plans (see the chapter on

Condensed versions of the Standard & Poor's guides are available at reasonable prices, and in some cases free of charge from a brokerage service.

dividend reinvestment plans). In addition to stocks, in recent years *Value Line* has also provided a service which evaluates mutual funds.

Morningstar specializes in examining mutual funds. A five-star rating from *Morningstar* is highly coveted in the mutual-fund business and is difficult to earn. Information is given on fund characteristics and performance for a period of ten years. This makes it possible to see if a fund has had a consistent record, rather than just an occasional spectacular quarter. There are also special editions of *Morningstar* which cover closed-end funds and foreign stocks which trade on domestic exchanges in American depository receipt (ADR) form.

Standard & Poor's in its guides provides information on individual stocks. While this may not always be as thorough as the coverage in *Value Line*, every listing on the New York and American exchanges is included, and there is extensive coverage of Nasdaq stocks. A rating is given for most companies, based on their earnings and dividends.

Small investors who become familiar with the above three services should be able to gather sufficient information on almost any individual stock or mutual fund that might interest them. Addresses and telephone numbers are provided which will make it convenient to contact the fund or company for more information, including annual reports and, in the case of mutual funds, a prospectus.

Other publications

Although not as readily available, and again too expensive for most small investors to consider subscribing, if you can gain access to *Grant's Interest*

HINT

Rate Observer, spend some time with it. Editor James Grant is a brilliant student of the financial markets. While sometimes more bearish than most others, Grant's insights can prove very helpful. If you have Internet access, you can sample *Grant's Interest Rate Observer* and its related publications (http://www.grantspub.com) and also connect to various other interesting and useful financial sites.

Some new investors may find the resources we discussed so far a bit on the "heavy" side. Actually, with just a little exposure to them, you will soon find your comfort level rising dramatically. However, there are other publications which should prove easier to use, and yet contain much which is of value. Two which are of particular interest are *The Moneypaper* and the National Association of Investors Corporation's *Better Investing*. Both contain plenty of investment help which is readily understandable by the beginning investor, while still being of value to the experienced. What makes these two publications particularly valuable, however, is that they can be your entrance to various company dividend reinvestment and cash purchase plans which, as previously mentioned, enable you to conveniently accumulate stock in small, affordable increments. See the chapter on dividend reinvestment plans for more information and how to contact both publications.

The Moneypaper and *Better Investing* are excellent and highly useful publications. Their primary focus is on individual stocks rather than mutual funds. You may find that some of the widely circulated financial publications will prove helpful in exploring what the mutual funds have to offer as well as providing insight on other financial topics. Again, your library may be a

> **HINT** Be especially careful in using performance rankings of mutual funds. The funds rated as the best may have received that rating because of a strong year or even past quarter.

good place to discover some of these, although you should also find several at various stores and newsstands. Among those you may find useful are *Forbes*, *Kiplinger's Personal Finance Magazine*, *Money*, *Fortune*, *Worth*, and *Business Week*. Also useful are *Bloomberg Personal* and the *Wall Street Journal's* magazine *Smart Money*. Most likely you will find others as well. For general economic news with a global outlook, *The Economist* does an outstanding job. If you have access to a university or college library, you may be able to obtain The *Far Eastern Economic Review*. It is one of the very best sources of news about Asia and contains a wealth of information on Asian and Pacific markets which is not easily obtainable elsewhere. That same university library (or a very good newsstand) may also have *The Financial Times,* which quite properly calls itself "The World Business Newspaper." Based in London and published around the world, it does an outstanding job of covering Europe while not neglecting the other continents. The American Association of Individual Investors is a nonprofit organization which publishes a journal ten times per year, plus an annual mutual fund guide, and provides additional services which may be of benefit to the small investor. They can be contacted at 625 North Michigan Avenue, Chicago, IL 60611-3110 (312-280-0170).

Remember the small investor

As noted, while all of these sources are ones you may wish to consider, remember they are often not written with the small investor in mind. Some funds outperform in bull markets, but do worse than the average in bear markets. Some funds may have a strong year or two because they take aggressive risks you would not want to take. If the rating covers a ten year period, or at least five, it is more likely to give you an accurate picture of that particular fund's normal results. In comparing funds, compare one with similar objectives. For example, a global stock fund's performance should not be measured against that of a municipal bond fund. They are designed to do two quite different things. Also keep in mind that most readers of financial publications may have more money at their disposal than you. They may be able to take risks you should not. Unfortunately, many of them may also have a trader rather than an investor mentality as well.

Other resources

Subscribe to some of the above or do any investing through a mutual fund company or a broker, and there is a good chance that eventually you will find your mail box is the home of a fair number of advertisements for various financial newsletters. Some of these may specialize, for example, in stocks of small companies or mutual funds. Others are of a more general nature. Generally, financial newsletters are rather expensive, often costing several hundred dollars per year, although a cheaper trial subscription is usually offered. It is doubtful that any of these can do you more good than the more widely circulated, and far cheaper, publications. Some may lead you astray, predicting all kinds of dire catastrophes (bad news seems to sell better than good) which never happen. Beware of claims of fantastic past profits. These are often theoretical, based on what would have happened had the publication's philosophy been applied at a particular time. They may also ignore the impact of commissions and the need for near split-second timing to duplicate the claim.

Various television programs can provide you with considerable financial information. They may also give you leads on stocks or funds that you may wish to further investigate. Generally, it is not a good idea to buy one of these stocks or funds simply because someone suggested or mentioned it. Always do your own homework before acting. If the opportunity is genuine, it is unlikely to disappear overnight. About the oldest and best known program is Louis Rukeyser's "Wall $treet Week," which is aired on PBS stations, usually on Friday evenings. Rukeyser also has a monthly financial publication, *Louis Rukeyser's Wall Street*, which may be of interest. Many of the contributors are frequent guests on his show and are prominent names in financial circles. A program which is one of my personal favorites is another PBS effort, "The Nightly Business Report." It provides a nice variety of domestic and international financial news for a half-hour ever week night. The shorter fifteen-minute "Morning Business Report" is also worthwhile.

> **E-Z TIP**
> If you absolutely insist on subscribing to a newsletter, then you probably should consistently follow its advice. To do so only half the time is almost to guarantee you will not get satisfactory results.

You might want to start out your mornings with CNN's excellent "Business Day." The program is an hour in length, but the basic information is presented each half-hour, so that is adequate if your time is limited. CNN's evening half-hour program, "Moneyline," is also worth viewing.

> **HOT spot**
> What may be fine for traders and speculators may not be suitable for long-term investors.

Real financial news junkies will sooner or later discover entire cable networks devoted to their addiction. CNBC and CNNFN are two that are widely carried throughout the country. A number of stations also air at various times Bloomberg Television. All three of these sources carry a wide variety of quality financial programming and furnish an extensive amount of information and commentary. Much of this is excellent. Just remember, much of it is not oriented either toward the small investor or those with a long-term view of investing. As a result, be very careful to evaluate what you view before you seriously consider acting on it.

As in the case of the publications, you do not need all of these programs. Look around, discover the ones you enjoy and find interesting, and concentrate on those. Do some exploring, and come up with others you might like, such as "Adam Smith's Money Game," which is still another PBS offering.

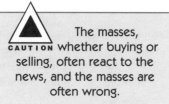

The masses, **CAUTION** whether buying or selling, often react to the news, and the masses are often wrong.

Watch and read more for general information and orientation toward the financial markets rather than for specific recommendations. Be somewhat cautious about what you are told, and always check out its accuracy as much as possible should you decide to act on it. This seems obvious, but is far too often ignored. Finally, always remember that by the time you read about something or hear about it, so have numerous other people, some of whom have been in a position to act and thus already change the situation. The old Wall Street saying about "buy on the rumor; sell on the news" is not normally the best advice for the small investor, but it does contain some truth.

Investing and the Internet

Recent years have seen a tremendous growth in interest in computers as a source for obtaining news and as tools for financial analysis by investors. Both the American Association of Individual Investors and the National Association of Investors Corporation provide services to computer users. Among the financial software which is readily available, Microsoft's *Money* and Intuit's *Quicken* are two of the best known, and should not prove difficult for most people to use. Computer software can help you keep track of your financial investments and their value. It can also assist you in balancing your checkbook and analyzing your mortgage and other loans. Increasingly, much of it is sophisticated enough to help you make investment decisions. What none

Do not expect software to be a miracle worker and, yes, read the instruction book and use any available tutorial before putting any program to work.

of the software can do is think for you. The assistance software provides will be only as good as the data you feed it. Use software carefully and wisely, and the programs can be beneficial tools.

Anything said about the Internet is likely to be obsolete before it can be read. However, if you are among that rapidly growing segment of the population that does have Internet access, then a few basic comments may be helpful. By using an Internet portal or search engine, such as *Lycos, Yahoo!, Excite,* and others, you can find quantities of information on almost any financial subject you desire. Just one example is the Finance and Investment section of Yahoo's Business area (http://www.yahoo.com). There is also the specialized search engine *FinanceWise* (http://www.financewise.com), which is exclusively intended for financial research and reference. Portals can take you to much valuable and highly useful information, but be careful. The Internet is everywhere yet nowhere. As a result, it is virtually impossible to regulate. Various financial scams turn up on the Internet. Chat rooms sometimes hype stocks which, even if they have some merit (and some never did), are now vastly overpriced as a result of all the attention they are getting. The Internet has also been used to market **initial public offerings** (IPOs). A few of these may have been all right, but many have been financial minefields, and the typical investor has no way of telling which is which. There is also much Internet financial information which may be quite legitimate but not suitable for the small investor. Many of the better sources of help are not free and will charge a monthly fee. Only the potential user can determine if the cost is worth it.

Two basic Internet sites that are worth visiting are CNNFN's (http://www.cnnfn.com) and *Bloomberg's* (http://www.bloomberg.com). Both provide a nice selection of domestic and international information on a variety of financial markets. CNNFN's is also linked to *Quicken's* helpful site. Both are free. Mutual-fund investors may wish to visit *Morningstar's* location (http://www.morningstar.net). Many of the other publications and programs discussed in this chapter also have web sites where you can thoroughly digest or at least preview their contents. Any search engine should conveniently take you to the ones of your choice. The same tactic will enable you to reach the web sites of the various corporations and mutual fund companies. These vary in quality and information provided but can be helpful.

Many people, especially those rather new to computing, may use a service such as *America Online* or *CompuServe.* These do provide financial assistance. For a monthly fee, they will furnish you with stock quotations, mutual fund data, and a variety of financial and business news plus access to the entire Internet. Generally, you can obtain free software (new computers will already have it) and a free limited-time trial. Check the advertisements in computer publications, or possibly a friend who already is on-line can assist. If you have been reluctant to try a computer, this is a good way to see if it might be something that could be beneficial in the future.

> **note** Using the Internet for financial research probably requires more discrimination and a greater sense of caution than when using any other approach.

Still another use of the computer is for on-line brokerage accounts. Typically, commissions are as low as you will find anywhere, but there are drawbacks. At times, especially when market activity is heavy, you might find it difficult to place an order. If you want a stock certificate there will be a service charge. Also, there have been complaints that executions, especially on Nasdaq-listed stocks, are not always at the best price. Many do provide some financial news and other information, but that is not their primary purpose. They do not make specific recommendations. You can obtain further information about on-line discount brokers in financial publications and on the Internet itself. Some regularly advertise there.

Other helpful books

> **CAUTION** Almost always, avoid books sounding alarms about pending economic doom and those promising big financial rewards with little effort or risk. Save your money.

You will find an annotated bibliography of books that may be helpful or even essential at the end of this guide. Several titles are also mentioned at various times when they may be particularly pertinent to what is being discussed. It may also be a rewarding pastime to occasionally browse the financial section of a local bookstore for new works, but be a discriminating consumer. Separate the wheat from the chaff. An excellent source for good financial books, many classics and almost unobtainable elsewhere, is Fraser Publishing. You can request their catalogs by writing to Box 494, Burlington, VT 05402 or calling 800-253-0900. Of particular interest is their *The Contrary Opinion Library* catalog. It is a gold mine of hard-to-find books, many of which were written decades ago, yet still provide rare insight into the present and future. Useful statistical publications and computer software can be purchased at reasonable prices from *Chase Global Data & Research,* 73 Junction Square, Concord, MA 01742 (telephone 800-639-9494). Chase's material is helpful for determining how different types of investments have performed over a period of years.

> **HINT** When investing and making other financial decisions, knowledge often is power.

It certainly is not necessary to utilize all the sources mentioned in this chapter. In fact, too much information may result in confusion rather than useful knowledge. Take your time. Sample among the suggestions. Seek out others on your own. Eventually you may find one or more that are particularly to your liking. If it is a publication, you may want to consider subscribing, so that you will have complete, uninterrupted access. In any case, refer to the resources you do find helpful regularly.

Investment clubs—some thoughts for the new investor

With the publication of the best-selling *Beardstown Ladies' Common Sense Investment Guide,* people who previously had never heard of investment clubs began to express interest in them. An investment club may be an ideal place for many small investors to begin, but they have certain limitations as well as quite a few assets. Let us first look at the benefit side of things.

> *note*
> If your chief interest is mutual funds (and for certain small investors it probably should be), clubs cannot offer you much help with this segment of your investing.

The benefits

If you join an existing investment club or help start a new one, you are pooling both your knowledge and money with other persons who share a common goal, namely making more money. The typical club probably has about fifteen to twenty-five members. Much less than that, and it will not have enough funds to invest. Much more, and things begin to get unwieldy. Members usually meet monthly, and each contributes an agreed amount of funds. In many clubs this sum is a modest one, but there are some that do require more. Club members research stocks which are of interest and report on their findings. The membership votes on what companies will be purchased and if any current holdings are to be sold. Should you decide to withdraw as a member, you may do so at anytime, and you will receive your fair share of the assets.

DEFINITION

As a result of the above, clubs enable the small investor to participate in stocks which might normally be too expensive for them to own as individuals. Clubs also encourage the critical habit of investing consistently and regularly. In effect they produce a form of *dollar averaging*, where when market prices are low more shares are obtained, and when they are high fewer are secured. One of the major benefits clubs provide is a good financial education. Newer investors can learn from the more experienced ones, and everyone has access to the research which is done before buy and sell decisions are made. Clubs also give you the opportunity to make new friendships or enrich old ones. Many have achieved outstanding results with their investments and, in fact, most which have been around for a while tend to show at least some profit. Small investors may want to give serious consideration to becoming a member.

While clubs provide numerous benefits, there are certain factors to consider before joining. Although there is nothing to prevent them from investing in mutual funds, most clubs do not or, at most, make funds a small portion of their portfolio. Clubs, by investing in a variety of companies, really produce the kind of diversification which you would expect from a mutual fund, so they really have little incentive to purchase the funds themselves.

If you are thinking about joining an existing club, it is just as vital that your objectives are similar to those of the present membership. If they are not, look for another club.

Another factor which needs to be closely examined is the club's investment objectives. About the worst possible situation is if members have contradictory goals. If some are oriented toward short-term trading or volatile stocks, while others have a long-term orientation, at best results are likely to be very disappointing. It is vital that members agree on what it is they want to accomplish and how they want to accomplish it.

Some clubs may be ideal in every way except one—they are simply too expensive. Do not commit to make a monthly investment to a club which is greater than you can comfortably afford. It will hurt you, and if you fail to make timely contributions, you will hurt the club. Find one that is within your budget. If you cannot find one that is affordable enough to leave you some money for investing on your own, then you might want to consider postponing membership. Clubs can teach you a lot, but some of the most important investing lessons you will learn will come out of your own personal experiences. Besides, even the best of clubs probably cannot help you meet all your investment objectives.

> **note** Investment clubs are not for everyone. Some people will do better and find it more enjoyable flying solo. However, a well-run investment club can give you the equivalent of a Ph.D. in investment education.

If you are considering helping to organize a new club, keep in mind that a considerable amount of work is involved. Good bookkeeping is absolutely essential, and so is insurance in case the bookkeeper and treasurer turn out to be less than honest. You will also need to select a broker whom the group likes and trusts. The Beardstown (Illinois) Ladies' club is a member of the National Association of Investors Corporation. Your club should be also. Although NAIC accepts individual members, it provides a number of services especially designed for investment clubs, and undoubtedly many of its member clubs consider it absolutely essential. You can write to the NAIC at Post Office Box 220, Royal Oak, MI 48068, or telephone 810-583-6242. Most NAIC-affiliated clubs who follow the organization's sound, value-oriented investing principles should do fine. The Beardstown Ladies received a shock and some unfavorable publicity when they discovered their profits had been miscalculated, and actual gains were smaller than first thought. Still, they have not done badly and most likely better than some of their critics believe.

Chapter 15

Proverbs for pondering

Do any investing for a period of time, and you are likely to come across some proverbial gems that you may have wished you had heard before you ever started. Well, if you have not started, here is your chance. If you have, perhaps you will find some that are new. In any case, a bit of review may prove beneficial. They can help you avoid many a potential financial swamp.

"If it sounds too good to be true, it probably is."

Every investor needs to have this one posted within sight of the telephone. When that unsolicited call comes urging you to "invest" in wireless cable or some sort of oil royalty scheme, you will be well equipped to "just say no." It is also a good one to have around when watching real estate infomercials on television or listening to celebrities pitch commodity futures on the radio.

"If it is such a good thing, why are they letting me in on it?"

Keep this alongside the one above. It also explains why the small investor should almost never buy an initial public offering, more commonly called an IPO, or simply a new issue. Many brokers get a lot of these to offer to their clients, and perhaps at a reduced or no commission. Some of them are not good things. They are superb, almost guaranteed to go up in price once they begin to trade on the secondary market. The trouble is, you will never see any of these. Brokers have to eat. Good IPOs go to their good clients, their best clients. Those are the big boys and girls, never the small investor. Get offered an IPO and you can almost be certain it is a dog, something the brokerage house is desperate to unload. Do not feel insulted. The big boys get offered plenty of these, too. To get their cake and ice cream they have to eat their brussels sprouts.

HINT

Under very unusual circumstances you may happen across a good IPO and even have the chance to buy it. If that does occur, it most likely will not be because somebody called you, but because you uncovered something on your own and managed against all odds to find someone who would sell it to you at the offering price. Should you be so fortunate, go ahead and congratulate yourself after you have made the purchase. Although it could, do not expect it to happen again. "Lightning seldom strikes twice," says another old cliche.

"A bull can make money. A bear can make money. A pig seldom does."

This one contains at least some truth for the small investor. Although the road sometimes seems more like a roller coaster, in the long run, stock markets tend to rise. Small investors who do not borrow money to purchase their stock or buy on margin have all the odds in their favor if they are patient enough. This is true in many cases even if they bought when prices were too high.

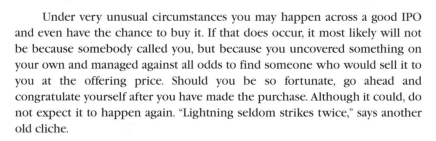

HINT Long-term bulls have usually been adequately rewarded for their patience and perseverance.

Since small investors should avoid short selling and options, it is more difficult for them to take a bearish approach. Remember, especially for the small investor, it is virtually impossible to determine if any financial market is about to go up or down. Having said this, a certain amount of bearishness can help provide protection. It can keep you from becoming overly optimistic and thus overly extended. The bear knows markets can decline as well as rise. Small investors need some vanilla-flavored investments, such as insured bank certificates of deposit, which are about as safe as an investment can be. They need the stability these provide for their financial security and mental peace of mind.

Having the bear by your side can also make you more sensitive to the prices you pay for the stocks and other investments you purchase. Knowing prices can fall, you will want to look for those things which are already at bargain levels and avoid any which have been bid up beyond what the prudent investor would be willing to pay.

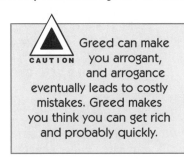

Greed can make you arrogant, and arrogance eventually leads to costly mistakes. Greed makes you think you can get rich and probably quickly.

The part about the pig is absolutely correct. Pigs have a reputation, whether deserved or not, for being greedy animals. Greed kills investors large and small. Greed makes you do silly things, even dangerous things. Greed makes you buy stock in companies with "laser" in their name which are selling for one-hundred times their annual earnings, if they have any earnings at all. If you are going to let greed make your financial decisions for you, why not go to some casino instead? At least there you can have a little fun while you are losing your money.

"Bulls make money. Bears make money. Chickens get plucked!"

The Pure Fundamentalist, a financial newsletter, used this as an advertising slogan. You already know the part about the bull and the bear. All you need to know now is about the chicken. Refuse to take some reasonable risk and you will get plucked. Usually the chicken plucker will be inflation. What little you can earn on the lowest-risk investments will be taken away from you by inflation and taxes. Sometimes inflation will demand even more than that, cutting into your principle. It is a point ably made over the years by one of the greatest investment counselors of all time, John Marks Templeton, founder of the Templeton Mutual Funds. Chickens will also pass up excellent opportunities with both potential rewards and reasonable levels of risk.

"Buy high. Sell low."

This one is obviously true. It is also one of the most difficult things in the world to do. Fear and greed along with other human emotions are the chief culprits. How do you find the courage to buy when everybody else is absolutely convinced that Chicken Little was right after all? How do you sell when the same crowd becomes convinced this really is the best of all possible worlds?

"This time it's different."

Just to make sure you are paying attention, we are including some that are totally false. NASA used to send astronauts to the moon, and probably

> **E-Z TIP**
>
> It is probably sound advice to say stay out of crowds. You can pick up all kinds of dangerous things from them. They are harmful to your financial health.

will again someday. Not much else goes there, especially financial investments. At some unknown moment, what went up most certainly will come down. It has always been that way in the past, and there is absolutely no reason to think it will not be that way in the future. Do not try to market-time, but do look for value when you buy. On those occasions when prices get so high they are almost laughable, you may wish to consider disposing of some things, even though you normally are a long-term investor who sells only when a better buy comes along. When prices are that high, one probably is about to come along.

HINT

"Beware the permanent trend."

This is the opposite of Number 6, and it is true. As we already noted, investment prices never go up forever. Sometimes people also forget that, unless a company goes bankrupt, they do not go to zero either. As we said before, patience in investing is usually rewarded.

"In the long run we are all dead."

These words of wisdom were supposedly first uttered by the brilliant British economist John Maynard Keynes. They serve as a thoughtful warning. Throughout this book we stressed investing for the long term, buying value, and forgetting about market timing and quick profits. Yet, we should remember infinity is not a realistic goal. We do need to know what our investing goals are and when we have reached them. When it becomes time to take a profit, it should be taken. In the meantime, we do not want to become so obsessed with saving and investing that we become misers. King Midas discovered what a tragedy it was to have everything he touched turn to gold. You will not live forever. Enjoy life and find meaning in it while you still can. Investing is the means to the end, not the end itself.

> **note** If you have shopped carefully and not bought at inflated prices, in time you should reap a reasonable profit, even if for a while prices do drop.

"Cash is trash."

This is another of the false ones, especially for the small investor. Your diversification plan should always include some stable, low-risk investments, such as EE savings bonds, bank certificates of deposit, and other types of insured bank accounts. We simply cannot assume as much risk as those with greater assets, and this becomes even more true as we become older. There is then less time to recover from a serious financial reversal. Holding low-risk investments provides the kind of security the small investor needs in order to assume greater risk with the remaining assets.

"Buy the dips."

There is partial truth in this one. Often a stock or bond market decline does offer some tempting buying opportunities to those who are not faint-hearted. These should definitely not be overlooked. Mutual fund investors can take advantage of them also. However, beware of a potential trap. In a true bear market, the dip may be followed by a rise which in turn may be followed by an even greater dip; what was a bargain one month has become, in an ironic sense, even a

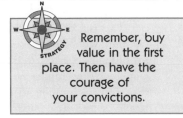

Remember, buy value in the first place. Then have the courage of your convictions.

bigger one the next. That can be troubling, but need not prove fatal if you do not panic. Bear markets are no more eternal than are bull markets.

"If you don't know who you are, the stock market is an expensive place to find out."

This profound bit of wisdom from Adam Smith's *The Money Game* has been mentioned elsewhere. It will not hurt to mention it here, because it is vital truth. Investors who do not know themselves may assume too much risk, or too little. They become very vulnerable to those nasty and dangerous demons, namely fear and greed, who are out to possess all investors. Such persons will probably not enjoy what they are doing and most likely will not be very successful at it. They could find themselves making the same mistakes over and over again and losing a great deal of money while doing this. If you have not done so already, get to know who you really are and, if necessary, make peace with yourself before taking on the challenges of investing.

"The stock doesn't know you own it."

This gem comes from financial writer Andrew Tobias. Love is a wonderful and necessary thing for all of us. Love people, animals, and trees, not your investments or stock certificates. Fall in love with your investments or the fancy pieces of paper that symbolize them, and again your judgment gets cloudy. Be slow to part with an investment. Be an investor, not a trader or speculator.

> ⚠ **CAUTION** Realize that there are times when an investment should be sold. Fall in love with it and you may refuse the necessary divorce. That will cost you money.

"You are buying a stock, not a company."

This is another one from Adam Smith. There is some truth in it. Keeping it in mind will help lead you to the same conclusions as Number 12 above. Few investments are likely to be forever. On the other hand, if you remember that your stock does represent partial ownership of a company, it will help you to treat your investments as investments rather than as casino chips. For many people, shares in companies and mutual funds are often little more than lottery tickets and the dream of big bucks as quickly as possible. We already talked about the probability of winning the lottery.

"The more things change, the more they remain the same."

This French proverb can be found in Benjamin Graham's *The Intelligent Investor*, a book probably every person should read before ever starting to invest. There is much truth, both explicit and implicit, in these words. Financial markets never precisely repeat their history. People who forget this may fall into the trap of thinking one theory or another can be used to successfully time markets. However, over an extended period of years we can see certain patterns in these same markets, and these can serve as warnings and guides.

> **note**
> For making financial decisions, history is never enough—and yet sometimes it is all we have.

"If you're in a game and don't know who the fool is, it's probably you."

This one is noted by Andrew Bary in an article he wrote for *Barron's*. Heeding its eternal truth can be powerful protection against highly speculative "investments" and outright confidence schemes.

"Things are seldom as good or as bad as they seem."

If you keep this one in mind, it may be quite profitable. Generally, investors overreact to both positive and negative events. Refusing to follow in their footsteps, while making your own careful decisions, should help save your capital and enable you to increase it.

"If riding the roller coaster makes you sick, don't buy a ticket."

I wrote this one, so take it for whatever you think it is worth. It applies to investing in emerging markets such as Mexico, Brazil, China, Russia, or Indonesia, to name a few. Such places have great potential, and markets in the long run will reward the investor for taking risks. But, that is just the point. If the potential reward is great so is the actual risk. Expect tremendous volatility in such places. That is what you get paid for accepting. If watching 50 percent or more of your capital go into temporary melt-down leaves you nauseated, then you might be happier putting your money to work in more stable environments. There are plenty of such alternatives.

"To get nowhere, follow the crowd."

This one came from a church bulletin board, and whoever was responsible for it probably was not thinking about investments at the time.

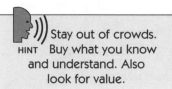
Stay out of crowds. HINT Buy what you know and understand. Also look for value.

Nonetheless, it is solid financial advice, in addition to whatever other virtues it may have. When investing, it usually does not pay to do what everybody else is doing. The crowd will be chasing the latest fad and buying it too late at inflated prices, if it was ever worth buying at all. When the crowd wants what you own, it may be time to sell it to them.

"The trend is your friend."

A variation of this one, which originated when stock prices were still printed by ticker-tape machines rather than computers, is "don't fight the tape." Both versions at first glance seem to contradict what we previously said. Given the peculiarities of financial markets, they really do not. Following the herd should naturally be avoided, but many an investor has bought into a nasty bear market and then been horrified to see prices decline still further, sometimes much further. Likewise, if you sell, just because you are certain we are at a bull market top, you may see the market continue upward, running away from you.

Market timing is extremely difficult and downright impossible for most of us. Buy when you see value. Sell if you find a better opportunity or really need the money. Stick to such an approach, and you will seldom follow either the crowd or buck the trend.

"You don't cancel the fire insurance because the house did not burn down."

A fund manager who had invested heavily in gold-mining shares provided this insight at a time when gold was selling at distressed prices. You can be over insured, but a certain amount of defensive investments can be a good idea. A small investment in precious metals and mining companies can help balance a portfolio. So can reasonable amounts of cash and other very conservative investments.

"Buy straw hats in winter."

This old adage is timeless, tested advice. Even the best investments are better at those moments when they are out of favor and nobody wants them. They will be on sale, genuine bargains ready to be snapped up by the smart investment shopper.

"The purpose of bear markets is to return money to its rightful owners."

James Grant quotes this cynical old piece of Wall Street wisdom in his brilliant work *The Trouble With Prosperity.* It may be cynical, but it contains some painful truth. Bull markets bring not only prosperity but greed and arrogance, which ultimately lead to unreasonable speculation and over-extension of credit. Bear markets wring this excess out of the system and pave the way for the next advance. Without the bears, ultimately there would be no bulls.

"More is never enough."

Andrew Tobias furnishes this timely warning. Even when we are successful, we have a tendency to want more. Maybe even "all of it" is not sufficient. Greed has an insidious way of infecting any investor. Be ever on the lookout for it. Greed can kill our sense of judgment and destroy the very essence of our being.

"Buy to the sound of cannons. Sell to the sound of trumpets."

John Rothchild refers to this nineteenth century adage in his potential classic *The Bear Book: Survive and Profit in Ferocious Markets.* Rothchild notes it was first uttered by another Rothchild, who was no relation, and who got things completely backwards. The statement is false. Peace is almost always bullish. War is usually very bearish.

"Don't fight the Fed."

This is another one from Rothchild's book. He claims to have gotten it from Marty Zweig. Normally, it is good advice. When the Federal Reserve Board lowers interest rates the results are usually good for both stocks and bonds. When it raises them, it is bad for bonds and ultimately will also be for stocks, although it will probably take more than one increase before stocks respond.

"Dead cats sometimes bounce."

My wife absolutely hates it when I make this observation. Ugly as it is, there is some truth in it. Sometimes after a big and possibly sudden drop in a market, it will bounce partly back up again. The difficulty is in knowing whether the bounce is the start of better days ahead, as in the case of the 1987 stock market crash, or if it is simply a sucker rally, as was true after the 1929 crash and the 1997 Asian market decline. However, to be on the safe side, it may not hurt to at least consider the possibility that the cat is giving you a possible selling opportunity.

"Buy when there is blood in the streets."

Supposedly Bernard Baruch, investor, speculator, short seller, and advisor to Franklin Roosevelt, liked this one. There is some truth to it, if not carried to an extreme. Beat-up markets can be bargains. Often it is a case of the more beat-up the better. Just make sure you have the stomach for them, because they will require you to stick with them through some most unpleasant days and nights.

> **HOT spot** In hindsight, 1932 was a great time to buy stocks. But at the time, most people could not even contemplate the possibility.

"Treat markets much like hurricanes. Evacuate if you get a warning, but be prepared to ride out the storm."

I admit authorship of this one. Sometimes, you may discover a market is in trouble. Do not try to time it, but you can see it is highly overvalued. Head for the exits. However, if you do not make it, above all do not panic. Assuming you have not bought junk, bought on margin, or in some other way borrowed, you should survive with minimal damage. There will be opportunities to rebuild. People who panic in storms sometimes get killed.

"Unfortunately, you've got to get the generals shot before the market can march on ahead."

Financial authority Vince Farrell offered this profound insight one morning on CNNFN. It is similar to the San Juan Hill theory of Marc Faber, editor of the *Gloom, Boom, and Doom Report*. The generals are the large, powerful stocks. They may continue to advance up the hill for quite a few months after the ordinary troops, the smaller stocks, have already begun to retreat. Often it is only after the generals have finally fallen that many investors realize we have already been in a bear market. The good news is that once the generals have been slain, the bottom possibly may be not too far away.

"You never know who has been swimming naked until the tide goes out."

This was Warren Buffett's response upon hearing about the near collapse of Long-Term Capital Management, a hedge fund which, in the fall of 1998, had leveraged itself into a very dangerous position, not only for its investors but for the entire financial system. Government intervention helped arrange massive private loans, and the fund survived, along with the country's markets. Still the warning remains. Be ever vigilant, stay diversified, and as debt-free as possible. If the unexpected happens again, the resulting mischief could be much more serious.

"Don't confuse brains market with a bull market."

Here is another cynical old Wall Street saying with much wisdom. In bull markets, most everyone seems to be making money and also thinking how smart they are. Bull markets are not infinite. Their end has a way of separating the intelligent investor from those that merely follow the herd.

"Some forest fires you stay and fight. With others, you have to walk away."

I learned these words from my old friend Bob Burns, who had a long career in the National Park Service. Bob was a real outdoorsman, who loved to go in and help put out a raging forest fire. But he knew some fires were too dangerous to fight. You better get out while you still have the chance. The same is true with certain investments. With some you need patience. With others take your losses as soon as possible and walk away. It also takes study and experience to know at any particular time whether you are dealing with one or the other.

 Over the years, you may find it helpful to add to this list as you discover the great pleasure of uncovering your own gems of investment insight. Be on the lookout for additions to your collection. You never quite know exactly where the next one may be hiding, just waiting to be found.

Chapter 16

The woman investor

This chapter is written especially for women who want to explore investment possibilities. Men are welcome to read it also. When it comes to investing, research shows there are gender differences. Knowing what these are helps all of us to understand ourselves better. That makes us better investors. However, when it comes to investing women face some special challenges that men usually do not. They may also have a few advantages. So, let us look at investing from a woman's perspective.

The Cinderella complex

A problem for some women investors that still shows up more than one might expect these days is the so-called *Cinderella complex*. Eventually, Prince Charming will come along, sweep me off my feet, and take care of me for the rest of my life. Women, unfortunately, have often been socialized to believe that dealing with money matters is a man's job. Leave all that to your husband, go shopping, and do not worry yourself further about it. The trouble is, even if Prince Charming does come along he may be a fine fellow, but he may also

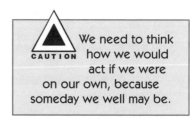

possess about as much financial knowledge as Cinderella. Early in this book, we noted that achieving financial success is best done when it is a family affair. We really need everyone's knowledge and skill and everyone striving to achieve common financial goals, rather than seeking those which may be in potential conflict.

However, there are other reasons why the Cinderella complex is such a dangerous one. In an ideal world, Cinderella and Prince Charming "live happily ever after." This is not an ideal world. Divorce and death of a spouse are real, everyday tragedies faced by both women and men. In some cases, a spouse may never come along at all. It means simply this: A woman ultimately is responsible for her own financial security, just as she is responsible for all the other aspects of her life. That is true of everyone, regardless of gender.

> **E-Z TIP**
>
> Most likely, Cinderella and Prince Charming will do far better financially if they form a partnership of equals. That probably will help the rest of the marriage as well.

Divorce or death may leave a woman with few or almost no financial resources. Even where there is a property settlement or life insurance, the question of what to do with the money must be faced. Too many women have had little or no education that will help them meet such a challenge, especially if it comes rather unexpectedly.

There is yet another factor that women encounter. There are many exceptions, but most women can expect to outlive their husbands. If he was several years older at the time of the marriage, then the period of widowhood could be lengthy. You could count on children to help. That could also be something of a disaster, since with the assistance comes a potential loss of personal independence and, possibly, the

> **CAUTION**
>
> We need to think how we would act if we were on our own, because someday we well may be.

children do not have their own financial houses in order. You may love them dearly, but you may not be able to rely on them to do what you need to do for yourself anyway. It would not hurt men readers to remember this as well. In the end, all of this returns us to the reality that we alone are responsible for our own financial well-being.

Men vs. women investors

Once this fact has been accepted, a roadmap of sorts has to be drawn in order to determine how we are going to get where we need to be. Studies indicate that women and men often have different investment styles. In certain instances, women do possess an advantage over men. Men are far more likely to go out and "bet the family farm." They may make what they think are investments, but what are really speculations. Worse yet, in certain cases they may do it with borrowed money. The usual results are quite painful and, in some instances, lead to true disasters, such as loss of the family residence.

note The now-famous Beardstown Ladies have shown that, when it comes to investing, anything a man can do a woman can also.

Women are less likely to speculate than men, but on a whole they are less likely to save. When they do save, too often they simply "squirrel it away," fearful of taking even prudent risk. Part of the reason for this situation is the difference in what money means to women and men. Men often see it as power. Money can free you from those things you do not want to do and enables you to do those you wish to do. Women may see it as security, something that protects you from adversity. Of course money, to a certain extent, can actually do both.

Learning smart investing

Keeping several factors in mind can help anyone develop an "investing style" which will be beneficial. Women, even that large number who never thought they were Cinderella, are sometimes reluctant to take on more risk in their investments because they feel they do not know what to do. Acquiring a solid investment education does take a little time, but it need not be difficult. This guide alone will lead you to a number of excellent sources of information. With a little effort and exploration, anyone can find plenty more. Another excellent way to educate yourself is to join an investment club. Some of these are exclusively for women. See the chapter on investment clubs for more information on this approach.

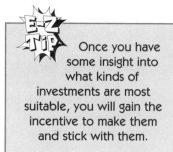

Once you have some insight into what kinds of investments are most suitable, you will gain the incentive to make them and stick with them.

It definitely helps to have investment goals in mind. Everyone needs to know for what purposes they are investing. In nearly all cases, invest for the long term and diversify. With diversification comes safety, and with safety comes the ability to handle more prudent risk. It is also important to know who you truly are. Many women should take on more risk in their investments. Financial markets reward risk, especially over the long run. However, do not take on more risk until you are really ready. When you are ready will be the time when you are comfortable with it and confident you can handle it. With experience this will come, so it is important to get started, even if it is with the most conservative of investments.

Online resources

Women with access to America Online can make use of an excellent tool. Among other things, AOL's financial channel will connect you to the on-line version of "The Nightly Business Report," seen on PBS. "The Nightly Business Report's" on-line resources include a special section for women investors. It is extremely well done and should prove quite helpful. Also, check your local library and bookstore. A growing number of books devoted to a woman's financial and investment needs are now available. For those who do not have AOL but can access the Internet, "The Nightly Business Report's" web site can be easily reached (http://www.nightlybusiness.org/index.html), and this should provide at least some of the above information.

If sound investing is something almost any man can do, then so can almost any woman. Time can be an important ally. The important thing is to get started now.

The family assets

Beyond determining what to do with your money, there are other financial matters the prudent woman will not ignore. If you are married, there

DEFINITION

is the question of how the family assets should be held. Some wealthy persons may be exceptions, but for small investors in most instances *joint tenancy* with right of survivorship is best. What this means is that real estate, stocks, mutual funds, and other things of value are held in ownership by both husband and wife. Neither may dispose of them without the other's permission. When one dies, the other automatically acquires full ownership without going through probate or without a legal trust agreement. In the event of a divorce, a fair property settlement for both parties is more likely. This type of ownership does not guarantee, but can help to develop trust, full disclosure, and a genuine working partnership. For persons with large estates it can have some unfavorable tax consequences, but, again, few readers of this volume will have to worry about that.

Remember, there are various kinds of joint tenancy. The one that will be advantageous in most instances is joint tenancy with right of survivorship.

There are always exceptions. If either husband or wife inherits assets from a family member, there may be the feeling that this property should not be placed in joint tenancy, especially if the marriage is experiencing difficulties or has in the past. If there is need to provide for children from a previous marriage, there may also be sound reasons for some other kind of arrangement. Basically, joint tenancy works best where the assets were acquired in partnership, even if only one spouse made most of the money. A wife who had little or no income because she stayed home to raise children has a right to a fair share of what her husband earned. Joint tenancy can help to insure that right. It can also help minimize the expenses of probate when either spouse dies.

Life insurance

Does a woman need life insurance? It depends on the situation. Remember that this book treats life insurance as protection, not as a savings or investment plan. A woman with no dependents who is either single or married to a working spouse probably needs none. If her income is lost, her spouse still has his own. However, a married couple where both spouses' incomes are essential to meet long-term obligations may need to insure each. For example, home mortgage payments continue even if one income is lost.

There are times when a woman with little or no income also needs life insurance because, if she were not there, additional family expenses would occur. This is most likely where there are small children and a surviving husband would have to arrange child care while he is working. If the woman heads a single-

> **HOT spot** Since women tend to live longer, it is essential that they plan for all phases of their life, both now and for retirement.

parent family, then some life insurance protection may be even more critical. As the chapter on insurance notes, usually term insurance will provide the most protection for the least money. When it is no longer needed, the policy can easily be dropped without complications.

In the final analysis, the kind of financial planning a woman needs to do is really rather similar to that of a man. Careful and realistic planning will do much to help maintain both dignity and independence.

Chapter 17

Destructive demons and four horsemen

The monsters greed and fear

Greed and fear are the two most powerful forces that move financial markets, it has been said—that happens to be true. No investor can completely eliminate these two highly destructive demons. You can check and contain them, but the minute you let down your guard, no matter how slightly, they rise up to strike again and again. The investor who forgets this will learn some painful and expensive lessons.

Of the two, greed is probably the more dangerous, because it is the one that we are least likely to recognize or admit dwells in our inner being. However, fear is, for the most part, little more than the mirror image of greed. Where one dwells the other most likely be found slumbering nearby.

The weapons of fear and greed are strikingly similar and equally lethal. They attack the investor's sense of rationality. Logic, good judgment, and common sense all perish as a result. Only after the damage has been done do we realize that once again we are the victim of these demons we thought he had exorcised forever. In the end, the best defense that you can muster against fear and greed is to realize how vulnerable we are to their cunning ploys and to understand we are not quite as wise or virtuous as we would like to think.

Greed

HINT

There is no absolute litmus test to determine if these monsters are present, but there are some indicators that can act as warning signs. When all kinds of bank accounts are held in complete disdain, when "cash is trash," be certain that greed is on the loose. No investor, not even the small investor, need have every investment in bank products or money-market

> *note* We may scorn a certificate of deposit paying 5 percent a year until a bear market pummels the stock market, and securities decline 20 percent or more in value. Suddenly 5 percent looks rather attractive.

CAUTION

mutual funds. To do so is to lose most of the opportunity that investing offers. However, small investors, in part because they are small investors able to take only limited risk, should probably always have some of their holdings in such cash equivalents.

Another way greed strikes is to cause us to compare our investments with those made by others. Perhaps we were proud of that stock that increased 15 percent in value over the course of a year until we heard of others doubling their money in six months! Now a "mere" 15 percent looks like nothing at all, and we are tempted to make what for us may well be the worst possible investment at precisely the worst possible time, when it is likely to be vastly over priced.

HINT If folks start discussing the need to take a "more aggressive" approach, it may be time for someone to remove the punch bowl. Greed is making usually sober persons drunk with envy.

Greed has numerous other tactics at its disposal. Some people constantly chase last quarter's or last year's best performing mutual fund. Others are desperate to get the last tenth of a percentage point on a bond yield. When we resort to these kinds of approaches we forget all our goals, choose investments that do not suit our needs or objectives, and take risks we have no business taking. Also, be cautious when you hear people who normally do not invest in stocks or mutual funds start talking about "getting into the market."

We mentioned the old saying on Wall Street: "A bull can make money. A bear can make money. A pig seldom does." Some old sayings contain much wisdom. This is one of them. Do not let greed swallow you up. Stick to the road you have chosen. Stay the course. Finish the race. Above all, be vigilant.

Fear

While fear may be somewhat more recognizable, it claims just as many victims as greed. When fear strikes, panic follows. Investors are certain their net worth is about to tumble to zero. Without thinking they begin to sell, often just when prices are about at their lowest, and they have already taken the loss that frightened them in the first place. If you are selling just because everybody else seems to be selling, fear has won.

How to exorcise the demons

While not magic cure-alls, two nineteenth century books can serve as effective medicines to help banish both fear and greed. If anything, they may be more timely now than when they were written. The first is Charles Mackay's 1841 classic, *Extraordinary Popular Delusions and the Madness of Crowds*. The late financial wizard Bernard Baruch claimed this book saved him millions of dollars. Mackay skillfully explores such popular manias as the London South Sea bubble and the Dutch Tulip mania, among others.

Gustave Le Bon's, *The Crowd: A Study of the Popular Mind*, first appeared in the late nineteenth century. It is a brilliant treatment of mass psychology. Anyone reading it will become more sensitive to how psychological factors impact financial markets, sometimes in seemingly irrational ways. Both this work and that of Mackay are still in print and readily obtainable. Both should be considered must reading.

> Above all, diversify. Having all your eggs in one basket is risky indeed. In the world of investing you never quite know when someone might drop the basket.

There are other ways to protect yourself against the demons of fear and greed. Some of these are discussed elsewhere in this book, but are worth at least brief mention here. Avoid buying stocks on margin or otherwise borrowing to pay for securities. That way you will never have to fear the inability to meet a margin call or panic that you will have to raise more cash to pay for investments now worth less. Should financial markets decline, if you wish you can rather safely ride out the storm until calmer seas again prevail.

HINT

Make sure you have a good idea of what you want to accomplish through your investment program and how you intend to accomplish it. If stormy weather sets in, you will feel more secure if you are on a firm foundation.

Finally, examine yourself carefully. Get to know how much risk you can honestly live with and assume no more. If you are losing sleep nights worrying over your investments, take it as a good sign you are trying to handle too much risk. Lighten up to the sleeping point. Work hard at getting to know your psychological make-up and what you want out of life. As Adam Smith says in his classic *The Money Game*, "If you don't know who you are, the stock market is an expensive place to find out."

The four horsemen of the Apocalypse

In the Biblical book of Revelation, also known as the Apocalypse, four frightening characters appear wielding death, woe, and destruction. They represent war, famine, pestilence, and devastation by wild beasts. The small investor, even one faced with a market crash, is not likely to meet up with characters as terrifying as these. Still, there are some potentially destructive horsemen who may offer you a ride which is best declined. Yes, they will call out to you that others have mastered their fiery steeds and been handsomely rewarded for their efforts. Their words are true, but they fail to warn you of the perils that lie ahead. It is better to travel more slowly and certainly a lot more safely. In addition, you may find yourself sleeping a bit more securely by not having to deal with some difficult ethical questions which these more speculative investment strategies can raise.

> *note* Such legendary investors as Sir John Templeton, Peter Lynch, and Warren Buffett admit they cannot predict the direction of stock-market prices. Perhaps a few folks can. It is unlikely they are you and I.

Horseman #1: The short seller

DEFINITION

Sooner or later you may hear someone talking about *short selling*. This is the practice of selling stock you do not own, but borrow, with the help of a broker, from someone who does. Short sellers expect the price of the borrowed stock to eventually drop. They can then buy at a lower price, replace the loaned shares, and retain a profit.

Typically, investors have been warned that in short selling they risk unlimited losses. Buy a stock and even if it tanks all the way to zero the most you can lose is your original cost (the same is true of most but not all other investments). Short sell, so the tradition goes, and the sky is the limit. Theoretically, there is no stopping a stock you sold from rising indefinitely, along with your loss.

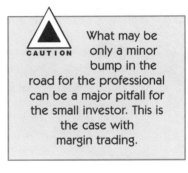

What may be only a minor bump in the road for the professional can be a major pitfall for the small investor. This is the case with margin trading.

That may be the theory, but it is seldom reality. Yes, there have been some celebrated cases of investors losing huge sums in short selling, particularly when speculators would get wind of the short sell and attempt to buy up as many shares as possible in order to drive up the price, and make liquidating the short painfully expensive. However, this is not what happens in most instances. Martin Zweig, in his book, *Winning on Wall Street*, quite ably demonstrates that the proper use of a *stop-loss order* (a device whereby a broker is told in advance to buy stock and cover the short when the stock reaches a certain price) for all practical purposes eliminates the danger of unlimited losses or losses greater than the original investment.

DEFINITION

So what is the problem? For the professional investor with detailed knowledge of a company, there may be none. For small investors, the danger is that when they try to short sell they are very likely to cease being investors and attempt to be market timers–market timers with a short time horizon. The results may turn out to be what market timing usually produces–losses. Short sellers are also responsible for making the dividend payments on the stock they borrowed and sold. Short selling should be avoided.

Horseman #2: Buying on margin

DEFINITION

When considering buying on margin, the best advice is "yield not to temptation." *Investing* or *buying on margin* is really quite simple. It is nothing more complicated than borrowing a portion of the funds needed. At times, nearly all of us have had legitimate reasons to borrow money, perhaps to help finance an education, home, or a car. When buying stocks on margin, a broker loans you a percentage, typically 50 percent, of what you need to complete the trade. Not only does this enable you to purchase twice as much stock, but margin loans usually come with a favorable rate of interest, far better than most persons could obtain through a bank, assuming the bank is willing to make "an investment loan" in the first place.

> **HOT spot** You may have felt that the stock's decline was only temporary, but with margin trading, unless you are willing to meet margin calls, you will not get the chance to find out.

The attractive thing about such margin purchases is they permit *leverage.* If what you purchased increases in value, your profit is double what it otherwise would have been. Since the value of your stock holdings has now increased, your broker will normally be willing to loan you even more money for additional purchases, thus giving you still more leverage and still greater potential profits. Certainly, sizeable sums of money have been made with margin accounts. Should your credit be decent and you are reasonably solvent, you can probably find a broker who will be willing to open one for you, especially if you have previously done business with the firm on a strictly cash basis. *Resist the urge.*

CAUTION

Leverage works both ways; all too often this is forgotten. It can help to create large profits. Just as easily it can bring about horrendous losses which may prove fatal for the small investor. As we said before, stick to the basics, and even in the worst of investments the most you can possibly lose is the original amount of that investment, plus of course what it might have earned in some nice, safe, federally insured certificate of deposit. Buy on margin, and you have the potential to lose not only your money but somebody else's as well. The real problem in losing other people's money is, unfortunately, they expect to be paid back.

Should the value of your stocks begin to decline, you would receive what is known as a "margin call" from your broker. You would need to provide enough additional funds to increase your equity in the stocks in your account back up to the required minimal percentage. If you cannot meet a margin call because you do not have the necessary funds, or for any reason decline to do so, your broker will go ahead without further warning and liquidate your stock holdings. In emergency situations, if your broker is unable to make contact with you, your securities may be sold without any notice at all. The losses are, of course, your responsibility.

There is a psychological problem with margin trading as well. If you are heavily margined, there may be the tendency for your investing judgment to be clouded. Under such strain we may be tempted to succumb to those old demons, greed and fear. They are constantly seeking to lure the unwary investor, and if they get their way, we will usually buy when prices are at their highest and sell at their lowest. We do the wrong thing at the worst possible time. In addition, it is wise to remember there is no such thing as a free lunch. Margin loans do bear a lower rate of interest, but they still have their cost. Investors free of debt in both their personal and investing life are investors much more likely to be in command of what they are doing. That is the type of investor who is more likely to show a healthy profit. The small investor should not buy on margin.

Horseman #3: Stock options

DEFINITION

Stock options may seem like a safer path to follow. In reality they are not. When you purchase a *stock option* you have obtained the right to buy or sell a stock within a limited period of time at an agreed price. Options should not be confused with either stock rights or warrants, which are quite different things, although at first glance there is some similarity. If you obtain an option to buy stock, you have acquired what is known as a "call." You have the right to call away the stock from the person who sold you the option. An option to sell stock is a "put." You can "put it" to the option seller by forcing him to buy stock at a price he really does not want to pay. The price you pay for either the put or call option is known as the "premium." All options have expiration dates. An option not exercised by that time becomes worthless, and the purchasers have lost their premiums.

CAUTION

Options have some legitimate uses by institutional and other major investors to help them hedge portfolios and thus protect gains and minimize losses. Such uses need not concern us here, except to serve as a reminder that what may be acceptable under certain circumstances can be highly dangerous for that investor learning to go beyond "paycheck to paycheck" living. The real danger for the small investor (who typically buys a *call* rather than a *put*) is that there is that lure of big profits at relatively little cost. If you buy an option to purchase 100 shares of a stock you can, in effect, control those shares for a fraction of what it would cost you to buy them outright. Your only expenses are the premium and the broker's commission on the premium. You are, of course, betting against the seller (writer) of the option. If you purchase a call to buy a stock currently selling for $45 per share at a price within the option period of $50 per share, the actual market price must rise above $50 before you have a profit. The seller is betting that will

note Strip all the mystique from options and what you may find is that they are in many ways nothing more than a sophisticated form of gambling.

DEFINITION

not happen. The longer the option period and the less spread or difference between market price and the price at which the option can be exercised (what is known as the *striking price*) the greater the premium you will pay.

Puts work essentially the same way. Now you are betting that the market price will drop before the option expires. If this happens, you can buy the shares you need in the open market and then sell them to the option writer at the previously agreed upon higher price.

None of this sounds particularly risky. In fact, it may sound safer than most investments. After all, your loss is not the total value of the stock involved, but simply the premium paid if you fail to exercise the option before expiration. Actually, it is not quite that simple. In a typical stock market purchase, it is possible for both parties to win. The seller of the stock may have bought it previously at a lower price and is now selling because he needs or wants the money for some other purpose. Perhaps he may have found some other investment which he feels is even more attractive, or maybe he is about to make some sort of major purchase, such as an automobile. You, as the buyer, will in turn eventually sell, and hopefully also at a profit. Both of you are quite happy with the results.

It never works that way with options. If you buy a call you are betting the price of the underlying stock will rise. The call writer is betting it will not. You both cannot be correct. Either you will lose your premium or he will at least lose part of his potential profit. To be sure he may have written the call to protect a profit already made in the rise of the stock, but were he confident it would continue to rise he would not have bothered. If it is a **naked call** (as opposed to a **covered one**), and the option writer does not already own the stock, then it is as much a gamble on the option writer's part as that of the purchaser. In options, one party wins; the other loses.

> **HINT** Because losing is incremental it may take time to see what is happening.

Playing the options game may raise ethical questions. Are options good for our financial markets? Are options good for America and its economy? Even if we decide the ethical damage is slight, there are other good reasons for not playing this game. The highly respected investor John Templeton noted that success comes in part by learning from others. We can learn both what others do well, and we can also learn from their mistakes. In this instance, the focus has to be on the mistakes.

The basic fact is that most investors who purchase options lose money. Since losses are limited to the premiums paid, they may seem relatively small (although to the beginning investor even this may not be correct). However, over a period of time those losses mount. It is much like feeding quarters into a slot machine. Sometimes you win, but the odds greatly favor the house. Small investors are not the house. They lose. Most option writers are professionals. They would love to play this game with you. Walk away from the gaming table before you are invited to play. You will definitely miss out on some exciting action, but your wallet or purse will still be intact.

Horseman #4: Commodity futures

What has been said about options is even more true of commodity futures. Probably few small investors will have the funds necessary to trade commodities, so the temptation may not be there. However, it never hurts to know at least a little about the countless ways devised to separate investors from their money. In fact, it may be absolutely vital, since at least on occasion celebrities have been enlisted to do radio commercials pitching futures to the unwary. Although they cannot expire unexercised,

> **CAUTION** Either the price of a commodity goes up, or it goes down. You cannot have it both ways.

futures contracts in some ways resemble options (but there are options to purchase futures!)

DEFINITION

When you purchase a *commodity future*, you purchase the right to buy or sell a specific amount of some commodity at a later date at the previously agreed upon price. Futures can be obtained for a variety of products including soybeans, wheat, lumber, coffee, precious metals, and currencies.

Commodity futures do have a legitimate role to play for producers. The farmer raising soy beans can purchase futures and be guaranteed a particular price for his crop once it is harvested. He no longer has to worry about market fluctuations. Currency futures help world traders stabilize their transactions by removing the uncertainty about changing exchange rates.

> **HOT spot** Dealing in commodity futures is one of the few ways possible to lose more than you invested.

There can be no quarrel when futures are used for such hedging techniques. However, to buy and sell futures as a form of speculation is one of the most dangerous games the small investor can possibly play. As in the case of options, both sides cannot win. The small investor purchasing a future contract is up against professionals who know the particular commodity thoroughly and are keenly aware of the slightest movements in its price.

CAUTION

Adding to the risk is the fact that the commodities game is a highly leveraged one. Contracts are obtained for a rather small percentage of the total price involved. If the market moves against you, losses can mount rapidly. Should you want to take your loss by liquidating your position, you may find you are unable to do so. Commodity prices are permitted to fluctuate only within a limited range per day. When a particular commodity hits the lower limit of that day's range, then trading for all practical purposes shuts down. The frantic trader could find this happening several days in succession. Meanwhile, losses continue to mount. There are ways to hedge your bets, but this is a game best avoided in the first place. A higher percentage of commodity "investors" lose money than those in options, where the percentage, as we have previously remarked, is substantial.

Friends of the horsemen

Limited partnerships

The "four horsemen" have some fellow travelers who might be briefly mentioned before moving on to other matters. While some limited partnerships are good investments, it is practically impossible for the small investor to identify these. A couple of thousand dollars is enough to get into many, and brokers love to sell them because the commissions are usually much higher than what they would be for a stock purchase involving the same amount of money.

DEFINITION

Limited partnerships are business entities where two or more people (or organizations) legally join together for such purposes as acquiring real estate and leasing equipment. They are "limited" because the investor has no financial obligation

> **note** An old proverb notes that, originally, the limited partners have all the money and the general partner the experience. In the end, the limited partners have the experience and the general partner all the money. There is much truth in it.

beyond the original investment and does not take an active role in managing the business. Unfortunately, some are put together by people with little or no knowledge of the industry involved, and quite often fees paid to this general partner are rather high. Normally, limited partnerships are a poor choice for the small investor. They also create another problem for all investors. Many are not very liquid, and selling them without a substantial loss can be challenging.

> HINT The exchanges and the Nasdaq cannot guarantee you a profit or safety, but they do screen the companies they accept for listing, and this means they will at least have to meet basic minimal standards.

Certain limited partnerships have been around longer, but recent years have brought an explosion of exotic financial products based on mortgages, bonds, and options. Some of these involve taking the original investment and dividing it up into various derivative products. Others are hedges in one form or another. Usually such things are sold with the promise of higher than average yields. What is not stated is that with these yields also comes greater risk, sometimes far greater. For the most part, all such investments can be dismissed with the simple warning that if you do not fully understand them they should be avoided. There are enough good, basic investments around that the small investor has little to gain and much to lose by getting involved in these sort of things.

Penny stocks

Some of the small regional stock exchanges, such as Denver and the now defunct Salt Lake City and Spokane exchanges, have been havens for so-called "penny stocks" which sell for anywhere from a few cents to a couple of dollars a share. Many are mining companies. Others may claim to have a new concept which will be a tremendous technological breakthrough once it is developed. Occasionally, these blossom into solid companies, and those who bought their shares early reap nice financial rewards. Again, the problem is that the small investor has no safe way to evaluate their prospects. Most penny stocks go nowhere. Some are outright frauds. Compounding the problem is that sometimes penny stocks are sold over the telephone by unscrupulous operations known as "boilershops." If a stock is not listed on the New York or American Exchanges, or traded in the Nasdaq system, in all probability it should not be purchased by the small investor.

Market-neutral funds

New products which appear promising, but could "blow up" in the hands of the unsuspecting, seem to appear all the time. Recently, a new form of mutual fund, based on the hedge funds marketed to wealthy investors, has been sold. Known as a market-neutral fund, the managers are buying some stocks and other investments while selling short still others. These funds are usually highly leveraged. They have the potential to make a lot of money quickly, whether markets go up or down. They have perhaps even more potential to lose it quickly if the fund manager bets wrong on his selections. Small investors simply do not need this sort of "opportunity," or numerous other ones which will undoubtedly come along in the future.

Day trading

Finally, note must be taken of the rapidly growing mania of day trading. Day traders make their profits through small but rapid increases or declines in the price of a particular security. Actually, day trading is nothing new. Day traders have been around for years, but the traditional breed were largely seasoned veterans, with much experience in dealing with financial markets. These are still around, but their numbers have been swamped by vast hordes of novices who have discovered how quickly, easily, and cheaply day trading can be done through the Internet by using on-line brokerage companies.

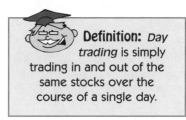

Definition: *Day trading* is simply trading in and out of the same stocks over the course of a single day.

Internet day traders are not investors but simply speculators, caring nothing about the companies they buy and sell, and in some cases are "owners" for but a few minutes. Often they compound the speculation by leveraging, borrowing from their brokers to add to their positions.

Does the modern day trader make money? Certainly some do. Most are not so fortunate. One study indicated that 50 percent "blow up" or lose their entire "investment" within six months of starting to trade. Others probably just need more time to reach a similar end. Of those that do make money, in many cases their profits are quite modest at best. I once knew a professional sports writer whose specialty was covering horse racing. He was a frequent small better and admitted to a slight profit over the years. However, in one of his columns, he confessed that it was extremely hard work which brought minimal returns for the effort. Further, he was certain that virtually all amateur horse bettors would ultimately turn out to be losers. Much the same thing could be said about day trading.

Investing need not be some sort of complicated, mysterious process but, like most other things, there is a right way and a wrong way to go about it. Avoiding being trampled by the "four horsemen" and their allies certainly helps to keep us out of harm's way.

Chapter 18

Thoughts on market timing

The perils of market timing

If we were searching for the most common mistake made by both large and small investors, most likely faulty market timing would win the prize. I confess that my own costliest errors were attempts to time the market. The reason is not hard to discover—accurate market timing is nearly impossible to do. Perhaps three of the greatest investors of the second half of the twentieth century—John Templeton, Warren Buffett, and Peter Lynch—are in that category because they had the wisdom to admit they could not determine the directions markets would go, and did not make such a determination part of their investment strategy.

HOT spot If it is a terrible feeling to watch the bear maul your profits, it is even more awful to watch the raging bull run right by you while you stand helplessly, unable to move rapidly enough to catch it.

Despite the sage wisdom of this "Investment Trinity," theories on how to time the rise and fall of financial markets will always have their legion of followers. Some may actually be successful for a while, but the longer you attempt to time the markets the more difficult it becomes. Part of the reason for this is frequently forgotten. Market timers usually have better success predicting bear or declining

Seldom do you make money following the crowd.

markets. They may have moved safely to the sidelines well ahead of the impending day of doom. However, that is only half of the job, and probably the easier. Timers need to know when to get back into the market. Studies indicate most big stock market gains occur over relatively short periods of time. These are almost impossible to predict in advance. Miss them, and your profits will be minimal even though you may have also missed some heart-wrenching declines. This situation is certainly true for the American market. It is even more so for most foreign markets, especially the highly volatile emerging ones.

There is another factor which makes timing about as easy as climbing Mount Everest. If someone actually discovers a way to do it, the approach works only because everybody else is not doing it. However, as soon as the success of the system is discovered, everybody will follow, and any ability it may have had to take advantage of market inefficiencies will have been lost.

Small investors who try to time markets are especially vulnerable because, as a rule, they have to pay a higher commission percentage than large investors when they buy or sell stocks, and they could run into sales commissions (loads) and redemption fees on some of their mutual funds. Timing can encourage a short-term mentality and frequent trading. The results are not only the potential for market loses, but greater investment expenses. While you might avoid the latter by sticking with no-load mutual

HOT spot Actually, some timers will be successful over the next few days, weeks, months, or even years, but it may not be for the reasons we might normally think.

funds, these companies, as a rule, frown on those who trade in and out of their funds. You may discover a no-load fund whose prospectus indicates management reserves the right to close out your account if such a pattern develops.

If you have done any reading on financial matters or watched some of the programs on television it may be logical to be skeptical. After all, there seems to be such an abundance of market timers around. A few years ago, I remember one of the country's most respected financial publications carrying a story authored by a well-known timer and newsletter writer who has been around for years. He was predicting a 1929-type crash within the next six weeks. I did not rush to sell anything, but I suppose if he had been correct, I should have take this chapter out of the book. However, although he was very wrong, can they all be wrong?

One helpful reference

If there is a modern classic among the books written on financial markets, it is Burton G. Malkiel's *A Random Walk Down Wall Street.* Before ever buying a single share of stock in a company or a mutual fund, this is a book which should be read. Malkiel's work has been attacked, and even he finds places where it will not always apply, but the book, first published in 1973, has gone through several editions and stood the test of both time and critics. Professor Malkiel argues that regardless of whether one uses fundamental (looking at a company's "nuts and bolts") or technical (past and current market trends and characteristics) analysis or both, virtually everything knowable about a stock is already factored into its current price. Stock markets are so efficient at absorbing this information that their direction cannot be predicted, since the price of a stock has already taken it into consideration. Certainly some things would affect prices. Among these are various natural disasters, but no one can know these until after they occur, and at that point "everyone" knows. True, if you possess genuine inside information you could benefit. You would also be committing a serious violation of the law if you acted on it.

It is beyond what we can do here, but Malkiel, in as nontechnical language as possible, carefully explains to the reader why his very thorough research indicates this is the case. Malkiel claims that a simple policy of buying and holding is likely to do one far more good than the nearly impossible attempt to predict the future of financial markets.

Random walk vs. skilled timing

Of course, as noted, some people are successful at market timing. The random walk theory would argue that is not surprising, nor does it disprove the theory. Should 1,000 people flip a coin and call it heads or tails, from a statistical point of view, we should expect approximately half to call it correctly. If these 500 then repeat the exercise, about 250 should be correct a second time. After the third round there will be 125, and after the fourth about 72 or 73. A few more rounds, and we will be down to a small number who appear to be geniuses at predicting coin flips. Gather together enough market timers (a rather easy task!) and you get, more or less, the same results. Those fortunate enough to survive to the end will probably accumulate great wealth selling their system. You and I probably cannot duplicate their results. However, if enough of us try, statistically we know a few of us will. That will serve to verify its accuracy, and another market-timing genius will have been born.

> **note**
> Elaine Garzarelli became the first woman "guru" of Wall Street by successfully getting her clients out of the stock market before the big crash of 1987.

It would be unfair to say that all successful market timing is the result of statistical good fortune. Some market timers have had a degree of success and are quite skilled at what they do. Charles Allmon, who has long been known for success in selecting potential growth stocks, was sitting on the sidelines, mostly in cash, when the 1987crash came. His former closed-end fund, Growth Stock Outlook Trust, was a rarity at the time the Dow-Jones average made its record decline. Other than some gold mining companies, it was one of only a handful of stocks that actually rose that grim day in October. Martin Zweig, successful fund manager, former newsletter publisher, and frequent guest on PBS television's "Wall $treet Week," earned a deserved reputation as an astute student of market history and one who can apply his findings to gain insight into the future. Zweig has made money for his clients in years when most other advisors have not. During much of the 1980s, from his office in Gainesville, Georgia, Robert Prechter applied the *Elliot Wave Principle*, developed by R. N. Elliott in the 1930s and 1940s, to gain strikingly accurate insight into the direction of the financial markets. There is much to be learned in paying attention to what these folks have to say. They have carefully studied the markets, and they can give you considerable insight into how they have worked in the past, and sometimes why.

> **note**

However, the big problem with even the best of the timers is they cannot get on base every time they come to the plate. After the crash, Garzarelli managed a mutual fund for several years. Its results did not attract rave reviews. Allmon continued to stay out of the market, looking for a yet deeper decline that never happened. Meanwhile, the Dow has risen thousands of points since that fateful day. Prechter had great success predicting the bull market of the 1980s, but he had less luck with the 1990s.

Martin Zweig's outstanding book *Winning on Wall Street* has an excellent chapter on seasonal indicators.

While he was now predicting a drastic decline, his followers lost opportunities as the bull continued thundering onward. Zweig has probably been the most consistently successful, but some of his advice required frequent trading and near split-second timing, which at least the small investor would find nearly impossible to achieve.

Lessons you can learn from market patterns

Yes, you can learn valuable lessons from some of the market timers and from the technical analysis on which market timing is based. These will give you insight into those times when markets are obviously over-bought or over-sold. This knowledge, in turn, will help you move cautiously when the financial scene looks more like a minefield. You can also learn about other things that do seem to have a certain consistency about them, such as *the January effect,* the pattern of small-company stocks to outperform the rest of the market in that month in most years. There are the Santa Claus rally, the presidential-election cycle, and other patterns you may find helpful to know. However, in the end, the small investor will nearly always do best to buy value and hold until either the money is needed or a better value comes along. That is essentially how our Investment Trinity, mentioned at the start of this chapter, made their fortunes and made fortunes for their clients.

More hints for the small investor

note Warren Buffett has been quoted as saying his favorite holding period for an investment is, "forever."

Warren Buffett was a student of the legendary Benjamin Graham, who literally wrote the book on value investing. Before attempting to play the frequently fatal game of timing the market, invest some time in reading Graham's classic, *The Intelligent Investor.* While some parts may now be dated, there is still much sage advice here. Follow Graham's approach and you will buy undervalued companies that have solid opportunities to eventually be recognized and rise in value. It does take some work, but if you do not want to do it yourself, you can still find some mutual-fund managers who will. Look in the fund's reports for the rate at which it turns over its portfolio. If the figure is 100 percent, it theoretically means the entire portfolio, on average, is bought and sold in a single year. If it is 20 percent, then it means the typical stock is held five years. Some funds have rates well over 100 percent year after year. If you find one where the rate is consistently below 50 percent you may have a value player who, at least to some extent, takes a buy and hold approach.

Market-timing is an extremely difficult game. Some nimble-footed players may be able to do it. Small investors almost never can. Peter Lynch, who managed one of the all-time most successful mutual funds, Fidelity's Magellan fund, commented that more than half the people who invested in it lost money. That is what market timing can do to you. An editorial in the August 1994 issue of *Better Investing* notes that a study by professors P. R. Chandy and William Reichenstein found that all of the market advance between 1926 and 1987 came in a mere 6.7 percent of the time.

Being a value investor

Bull markets and bear markets are both inevitable. As unpleasant as bear markets are, they help to drain speculative excess out of the economic system and pave the way for the next bear market. Thus, both market tops and market bottoms are real, but they are also close to impossible to sense until you are essentially in the midst of one. Rather than try, it is best to make your buying and selling decisions on the basis of value. If an alternative investment offers better value (and there are those moments when that may be cash or something else rather

> **HOT spot** Do keep in mind that market timing and a value approach to investing are not the same thing, although it can be easy to confuse the two.

dull but safe) than the one you hold, a change may be in order. If not, then do not fix that which is not broken.

The value investor is patient. Value investors understand that any kind of financial market can remain over- or undervalued for a long period of time. However, in the long run, those who buy value and sell investments which have become overpriced should do well. They may even appear to be timing the market, but in fact they are not. All they are doing is understanding that ultimately markets which are overbought or oversold return to more reasonable levels.

 If you are still not convinced of the futility of market timing, then try the following for several months, or at least several weeks: Be sure to carefully study the "Market Watch" column which appears every week in *Barron's*, one of the country's leading financial publications. In this column, the editors do an extremely skillful job of sampling the opinions of the leading market watchers in the country, most of whom are seeking to time the markets. In virtually every issue, some will be inclined toward a bullish position, while others will be equally bearish. These are all professional experts, with access to the best data. Despite this, they cannot agree on what direction stock and bond prices are heading. If, inevitably, many of them are going to be incorrect, then why should those of us who have not made this our career think we can do better? As we said above, the small investor almost never can.

Familiarity breeds all kinds of things

In his highly acclaimed book *One Up on Wall Street*, Peter Lynch notes that the individual investor can sometimes have an advantage over the mutual fund managers and other large institutional investors. Buying or selling on inside information, or information that would not normally be available to the public, is illegal. However, using information available to, but not yet encountered by, most of the public certainly is not. By virtue of the fact that small investors work in a particular industry or live in a particular community, they may occasionally come across just that kind of opportunity.

A small company, but one with a chance to dominate a growing market, may decide to establish itself in your town. This is no excuse to ignore your homework, but if you do find out as much as you possibly can, and the company still looks as good or better than when you started, it may be time to seriously consider purchasing some of its stock. Do not let the fact that it is a local operation scare you away. Familiarity should not always breed contempt. Eventually, the financial advisors and big investors will discover it.

However, be sure your investment is liquid. If the company's stock is traded on a major exchange or the Nasdaq, then there is no problem. You can sell anytime you desire. If it is not so traded, then it may be better to stay away. Should things go wrong, at a later date, you very well could be stuck.

The above suggestions also hold true for possibilities that may arise out of your work. Perhaps you may see a new technology introduced that will drastically change things in a certain business or industry. Maybe you sense there will be a solid demand for a new product about to be marketed or rapidly increasing orders for one already established. Again, these can be incentives to do a little research and see if any investment opportunity may be present.

> **E-Z TIP:** Before you invest your money, determine there is more there than just some sort of psychological frenzy that may soon fade away to stark reality.

On the other hand, if there is the danger of familiarity breeding contempt, there is also the problem of it breeding unrealistic enthusiasm. Sometimes a new company may receive more publicity in the local media than its future warrants. I once invested in a local company which received much favorable coverage in the press because it was local and had a unique service to offer. Fortunately, I was able to drive by its plant on a number of occasions and observe the lack of activity there. It was obvious it was not living up to its press clippings. While its service was unique, no one wanted it. I was able to sell with a small loss before the stock dropped considerably further. Sadly, one area business that did carve out a solid niche market and rose dramatically in value I ignored until it was too late. I thought something that close to home just could not be that good. It was. Next time I will pay closer attention to Peter Lynch. He did not become one of America's celebrated money managers by doing the wrong thing.

The unexpected opportunity

Experiences such as these have encouraged me to keep my eyes and ears open no matter where I might be. There is always the possibility that you might uncover an excellent investment opportunity, even if that was not your primary objective. In the summer of 1995, my wife and I made a trip to Canada's Prince Edward Island. The Canadian Confederation was really born at

Charlottetown on Prince Edward Island, and researching the history and the political system that came out of meetings that gave birth to the country was my reason for going there. Not only is the island historic ground, it is a place of great beauty and tranquility. Like numerous other travelers, we soon fell in love with it. We even came across one family that, after a visit, found that a part of them could never leave. They bought a home and now spend their summers on the island.

Undoubtedly, part of the reason why Prince Edward Island remains such a serene spot is precisely because it is an island. It has not been inundated by more tourists than it can handle or over-zealous development. In the summer, it might take nearly an entire day to get on or off, as the lines of cars and trucks backed up waiting for the first available ferry. The only other way to get in or out was to take one of the rather limited number of available commercial flights or fly on your own plane. At least this was the way it was until mid-1997.

> **HOT spot** Even Peter Lynch did not bat "a thousand." All of us can learn from our mistakes and go on from there.

If Canada's smallest province has been an island of calmness and beauty, it has also been one of restricted economic opportunity. Many of its young people talk with enthusiasm about their island home, but they go elsewhere for their advanced education and the careers they hope will follow. So, it is not surprising that quite a few residents applauded the controversial step that linked the island to the mainland with a causeway to New Brunswick across the Northumberland Straight. This was no small undertaking, but was a reality by June 1997.

By the time of our arrival, construction was already underway. We drove to the sight, which was adjacent to the ferry landing and the long lines of vehicles patiently waiting for an available boat. It was, from the start, a controversial project. Some feel it will destroy not only the tranquility, but also the traditional farming and fishing industries. Others feel just as strongly that without it the province has a dim future. One looking at and hearing all of this cannot help but feel some sadness. The change is probably inevitable, but there will be a price to pay for its benefits.

In the United States, I have seen other islands dramatically altered by new or improved links to the mainland. In some ways, they were quite different, being much smaller and usually oriented strongly toward a tourist or resort economy. However, there also seemed to be a parallel to the Prince Edward

Island I saw awaiting the opening of its causeway to the Canadian mainland. Once these places became readily accessible, they grew with rapidity. They lost some of their peacefulness along with their isolation, but there was no turning back. There does not seem to be any reason to believe Prince Edward Island will be an exception.

In October 1995, among investors there was much pessimism about Canada. There was a good possibility that Quebec would vote to leave the country, and both the federal government and several of the provinces were struggling to put their financial houses in order. To a contrarian investor, it seemed like the perfect time to buy Canadian, and the ideal choice appeared to be Island Telephone, the largest provider of communication services on Prince Edward Island. It was a company which definitely seemed certain to see a dramatic increase in its business once the causeway was completed. Now looked like the perfect time to invest in it. Although it would appear to have little to lose even if Quebec did depart then or later from the Canadian Confederation, the share price, like that of many other Canadian companies and the Canadian dollar, had experienced some decline as a result of the referendum on Quebec's secession. Trading only on the Toronto and Montreal Stock Exchanges, it was easy to buy or sell, but it was largely ignored by American and even most Canadian investors. The company's financial picture was sound, solid profits with a good, but not overly generous, dividend, which most likely could be maintained even if business did decline.

> **HINT** At home or when away, be alert and observant. In time you will probably find a company of your own.

In short, late October 1995 seemed like the ideal moment for a small investor to take advantage of what he had been able to see. I bought a modest amount of Island Telephone Company shares, and as soon as possible enrolled in the company's dividend reinvestment and cash purchase plan. It was open to Americans, although at the time I made my investment there were very few of us who wanted to bother. Only a little over 1 percent of the company's stock was owned by non-Canadians. In fact, 45 percent of it was in the hands of Prince Edward Islanders, despite the province's rather small population.

DEFINITION It may be much too optimistic to think I have one of Peter Lynch's celebrated *ten baggers*, a stock that increases in value ten fold or even more. Maybe it will not even be a more modest "four" or "five bagger." It is hard to say, but I am willing to wait to find out. I do not expect to be disappointed on this one. In the meantime, the share price has seen a very healthy increase and, thanks to the dividend reinvestment plan, I now have more shares than when I started. The worst case scenario would appear to be a reasonable profit. Also boosting my enthusiasm for the future is the fact that in May, 1999, Island Telephone merged with three other telecommunications companies operating in Atlantic Canada to form a new company known as Aliant, which now trades on the Toronto Stock Exchange. Aliant should be able to operate more effectively and efficiently than any of its four parent companies could expect to do.

If I am ever fortunate enough to return to Prince Edward Island, I doubt I will find that magic isle I discovered on my first journey. It will have changed, and I may not be so happy about some of the changes. However, if I need to call home, I will be pleased to do so using the facilities of my telephone company which, as a result of its merger, also changed, but hopefully to find even greater opportunities.

Chapter 19

The world is your oyster: investing globally

The times are changing—rapidly. Not too many years ago, investing outside the United States was something few people considered. Now, many investors would think it essential, and hardly because they feel America's future is limited. Rather, it is simply a case that there are too many opportunities beyond our borders that should not be overlooked.

HOT spot There is no reason at all why small investors cannot have their share of this fascinating "global pie."

In some cases, global investing may actually be almost impossible to avoid, even if investors are totally unaware of it. Many pension and mutual funds, while keeping most of their assets here at home, will invest a modest portion of their money outside the country. There are risks to this, but also rewards.

Global investing is sound investing

For several reasons, taking a global approach to one's investments makes considerable sense. One thing it does is add diversification, and diversification adds a measure of safety. Even though, in this age of globalization, they are becoming more dependent on each other, the financial markets of various nations seldom all move in the exact same direction at the same rate for a lengthy period of time. While on a particular day they may have influence over each other, in the long run they are more likely to be moved by basic economic fundamentals. One country's economy may be well into a recovery or even a boom at the very time another is in the midst of recession. In situations such as this, investing in a variety of nations may make a stock portfolio more stable.

HINT

Another factor is that some foreign markets are growing at a much more rapid rate than others. Countries such as the United States, Great Britain, and Japan have mature economies. In terms of dollars, their economies must show large increases just to produce a few percentage points of growth. Emerging markets such as Mexico, China, India, Thailand, Argentina, or the Czech Republic, with smaller but rapidly growing economies, are capable of growing at much greater percentage rates. As a result, the possibilities for financial gain may be much larger.

> *note* Those nations which are the targets of their investments receive the vital capital so necessary to build their economies, raise the standard of living, and bring about political stability.

There are other personally satisfying reasons for investing in foreign lands, especially those now trying to develop and modernize their economies. Such investments can be your own individual foreign aid project, and one not based on a hand out but a genuine helping hand which benefits everyone. The investors will reap personal profits. Global investing also links countries closer together and encourages them to live together in peace and work for their common benefit. It is unlikely we will see another Arab oil embargo such as occurred in the early 1970s. Arab nations have too much money invested in the United States and other Western countries to want to disrupt their economies.

For those who desire it, another advantage is the opportunity to learn about the various places where our money goes. Invest in Korea, France, South

Africa, or Canada and you may discover a new, much deeper appreciation for these nations and their people. Wise investors, large or small, study their investments. The global approach gives you knowledge and can help make the planet seem more friendly and less alien.

Disadvantages to global investing

The pitfalls to foreign investing are as real as the opportunities. Before you send your money on a journey, it would be a good idea to know what these pitfalls are, in order that your money might eventually return home! With junk bonds, the antics of the Savings and Loan institutions in the 1980s, and corporate merger mania American markets have at times been filled with speculative excess. Despite this situation, they are among the most carefully regulated in the world. That which is tolerated in some countries simply is not here. It can be enough to make even veteran investors run for cover.

What is admittedly an extreme case of this sort of thing is discussed by David Lamb in his fascinating book *The Arabs: Journeys Beyond the Mirage.* Just a little over a decade before Desert Storm, some of Kuwait's oil-rich citizens decided to start a stockmarket, largely because they did not know what else to do with their surplus petrodollars. A stock exchange was set up in the lobby of a downtown parking garage and listed about three dozen Arabian Gulf companies, many of which existed only on paper. Although the listed tire company never made a tire, its stock

> *note* Foreign securities can sometimes be an effective hedge against a falling dollar, although some mutual funds prefer to hedge against currency fluctuations.

and that of other companies began to be bid up to insane levels by Kuwaitis and others who arrived in town with suitcases full of money. Share prices sometimes tripled in as short a period as a day. Students left classes to trade stocks, and checks postdated as much as two years were accepted in payment. A passport clerk woke up one morning to discover that he had a paper worth of $38 billion!

Of course, the entire thing was as much a mirage as anything ever spotted on the desert. By mid-1982, the entire market had collapsed, and the same passport clerk who had once been worth $38 billion filed a bankruptcy petition listing $25 billion in debts!

Speculation is one thing, but even the most prudent of investors can lose money in foreign markets, and at the very time shares are rising in price. This occurs because of currency fluctuations. For example, if you buy Japanese stocks which show a modest increase at the same time that the dollar is making large gains at the expense of the yen, you will have a loss rather than a profit. Of course, if the reverse were to happen, it would be to the investor's advantage.

Still other problems await our would-be global investor. It may be difficult or virtually impossible to get all the information you would normally expect to study before making a careful investment. Even if you are successful in obtaining a copy of their annual report, the figures may be confusing or misleading when compared to the ones you may be used to studying. In some cases, the report may not be available in English, and some foreign companies simply will not make available the kind of information on their operations that American concerns will supply on a routine basis. Finally, various governments severely restrict or prohibit completely investments by anyone other than their own citizens. In his unique book, *Investment Biker*, Jim Rogers explains the lengthy and complex task he had to endure in order to buy the securities of companies based in Ecuador. Rogers is an experienced, highly sophisticated investor and money manager. Most people would have given up in confusion and frustration long before the process would have been completed. It is not always this difficult, and the problems we noted can be overcome in most cases without too much difficulty, but it is best to know they are there. If you do, then planning a strategy to circumvent them becomes a realistic goal, even for the person with relatively small amounts of money to invest.

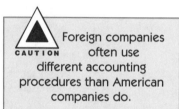

Foreign companies often use different accounting procedures than American companies do.

Becoming a global investor

The easiest way for everyone to make their first investment beyond America's borders is through mutual funds. In this way, the obstacles of obtaining adequate information about foreign companies and gaining access to foreign markets are no longer a problem. The mutual fund effectively handles these for the investor. Expect to pay for this convenience and assistance. All mutual funds charge a management fee. If the fund is doing its job well, the price will be worth it and probably less expensive than you would be able to do it for yourself. Mutual funds investing abroad come in essentially four varieties:

1) Global funds

Global funds honestly do give you the world. They will invest in the United States as well as anywhere else they find a good investment. Typically, about twenty to perhaps as much as fifty percent of their holdings may be American, although at times it could be even more or less, depending on how management sees the financial environment.

HOT spot Mutual funds that deal primarily or exclusively in foreign stocks will normally charge a higher fee, since their work and expenses are greater. Those focusing on emerging markets, the developing-world economies, will assess still higher fees.

Global funds offer solid diversity and thus a measure of safety. In addition to owning domestic securities, they usually will own stocks in several of the more developed foreign markets, and then have a certain amount of exposure to the emerging markets, where both risk and opportunity may be greater. There is possibly only one real drawback to the global fund. Since it normally charges a higher management fee than the pure domestic-stock mutual fund, you are paying somewhat more for the domestic portion of its portfolio than you would elsewhere. If you already are investing in one or more mutual funds which concentrate on American securities, you may want to consider an international fund as an alternative to a global one. However, if you come across a global fund you really like, then it may be a good choice for you, even if you do already own some domestic funds.

2) International funds

The international fund functions much like the global fund except that it does not buy American securities. As in the case of the global funds, most will concentrate on the more mature international markets, with their remaining assets invested in

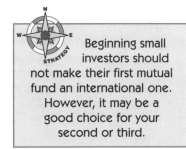 Beginning small investors should not make their first mutual fund an international one. However, it may be a good choice for your second or third.

developing economies. Once you have some exposure to American markets, an international fund gives you diversity and thus security.

3) Closed-end funds

Some mutual funds focus on a particular region such as the Pacific Rim or Latin America. Others may invest in only a single country, perhaps Japan or Russia. In many cases, these specialized funds are a particular type known as closed-end funds. These may be so important to the small investor seeking foreign opportunities otherwise not available, that they will be treated in detail later. For now we will limit our discussion to the typical or open-end fund that can be redeemed at nearly any time for its net asset value, the actual value of an individual share.

4) Regional funds

When you invest in a regional or single-country fund, you are giving up much of the diversity that global and international funds offer. As a result, you should expect more volatility in the price of fund shares. Funds concentrating on developed markets such as Europe will show less of this than those investing in emerging ones, such as Latin America. Funds investing in a single country of course offer the least diversity, although if the country is a developed one, such as Germany, volatility and risk may actually be less than for an emerging-market fund.

> Begin your trip outside America's borders with an international or global fund. Once you have that in place it may be time to carefully consider a fund with a more narrow focus.

Regional and single-country funds are not for everyone. Investors need to ask themselves if they are really comfortable with the roller-coaster ride some of these provide. However, they offer access to markets and companies that otherwise would probably be beyond the grasp of the small investor. For the courageous and the patient, they may also offer considerable reward, as you can focus some of your investment dollars on those specific parts of the world where you feel there is the greatest opportunity for dramatic and rapid growth. A regional or single-country fund should not be your first mutual fund. It probably should not be your first mutual fund for international investing either.

Other global funds

Still other kinds of mutual funds provide the small investor with a growing variety of ways to invest globally. Some may invest around the world, but limit their stocks to the developing markets or those in a single industry, such as telecommunications. Others buy foreign bonds, currencies, or other kinds of investments. These may offer still additional opportunities for diversification and hedging against a possible decline in the dollar. However, as with any kind of investment, make sure you fully understand it before you buy it. No

> **HOT spot** An ever-increasing number of foreign companies are listing their shares on our domestic stock exchanges and the Nasdaq system. Meanwhile, American companies are doing the same overseas.

one needs every type of mutual fund available, and few could afford them. Buy what suits your personal interests and needs.

When you're ready to invest

Earlier we examined some of the factors that should be considered before buying any mutual fund. It is not necessary to repeat these here, except to note that obviously all of these apply to funds involved with foreign markets, and these funds will, in almost all cases, have higher expenses which must be passed on to the investor. Nevertheless, mutual funds are still an excellent way for many small investors to get their initial foreign exposure. Nearly all the larger fund families now have funds which do invest abroad. With them you have the convenience (sometimes for a fee) of moving your money in and out of a particular fund should your investment objectives change. Other foreign-oriented funds are also available.

While mutual funds may be the ideal global investment, sooner or later you may be tempted to look at the stocks of individual foreign companies. Actually, buying many of these is quite easy, no more difficult than purchasing shares of a major American corporation. Look through the listings of the New York Stock Exchange and, among the companies, you will find there are Japanese giants Sony and Honda Motor Company, British Petroleum, the Dutch electronics manufacturer Philips, and Swedish car manufacturer Volvo.

While some European, Japanese, and Canadian companies have been around for quite awhile, recent years have seen companies in emerging markets also entering American markets. Popular with investors is Teléfonos de México, on the New York Exchange. Look for BHI Corporation, operating in the Central American country of Belize, on the Nasdaq. The American Stock Exchange also has its share of international listings, including a number of Canadian mining and petroleum companies.

ADRs

When buying a foreign company on a domestic exchange, you may sometimes discover that what you are actually purchasing are American Depository Receipts (also referred to as American Depository Shares), commonly known as *ADRs*. These represent the actual shares of stock which are held by banks (a very few companies trade in both ADR and stock forms). While the price for an ADR will not always be precisely the same as the shares of foreign stock it can claim, the small investor can treat ADRs just like regular stock. You can buy and sell them anytime the exchanges or Nasdaq are open for business, and you will be charged the commission you would be for a similar domestic trade.

DEFINITION

note Companies listing either their stock or ADRs in America will provide the kind of information about their operations that investors here would usually expect to receive from a domestic concern.

Owners of ADRs receive the same dividends they would if they owned the actual stock. ADR dividends and capital gains are subject to the normal tax laws. In the end, ADRs are primarily a device which makes life easier for companies beyond our borders who wish to make their stock readily available to investors here. The small investor need not worry about the technical factors that pertain to them.

note There is also the possibility that the security laws of the nation where the exchange is located severely restrict or prohibit entirely ownership by foreigners.

There is one matter the small investor should take into consideration before acquiring any ADR. Quite a few ADRs still do not have a dividend reinvestment and cash purchase plan. Increasingly, the banks that sponsor ADRs are making such plans available, but unfortunately they often come with a rather high fee structure which might make them unattractive, especially to the small investor. Therefore, unless you have enough money to buy a round lot (100 shares) of an ADR, or the ADR does have a cash purchase plan with modest fees, you may want to think twice before purchasing it. Round lots can be cheaper to buy or sell and usually give you enough of a stake in a company to feel it is worthwhile. It is relatively cheap and easy to build one gradually through a low-fee cash purchase plan. Without one, the commissions or high fees you pay each time you go to add shares to your holdings will make it a costly endeavor.

Small investors take note

Buying shares of a foreign company not found on a domestic exchange is far more complicated and, in many cases, simply not practical for the small investor. Some brokers, particularly the discount variety, will not fill such orders, except for Canadian companies. Others accept them, but charge higher than their regular commissions. There may also be additional fees for currency conversion and other matters. What is often the greatest single obstacle for the small investor is that, on foreign securities, the brokerage house will insist on a substantial minimum order if it is to be accepted. This is likely to be more than the small investor can or should invest at any one time in a single company of this kind.

There may be still further complications. If the stock you are seeking trades in a place such as London, Paris, Tokyo, or Toronto, you can find a broker who can obtain it, providing you are willing to pay the expenses involved. If it is found only on some exotic emerging market, chances are good your broker will be unable or unwilling to handle the transaction.

Regardless of the above, all is not lost. There is a convenient, practical way for even small investors to own securities in foreign markets that otherwise would be inaccessible to them. That way is through the purchase of shares in closed-end funds. These are important enough to deserve a rather thorough examination of what they have to offer, so let us begin!

Closed end funds—a passport to the world

Do you want to invest in the economies of Peru, Vietnam, Morocco, Pakistan, Ghana, the Czech Republic, Costa Rica, Portugal, Turkey, Thailand or almost countless other places? Closed-end funds make it possible to have your money working in these lands as well as at home and more common ports of call, such as Germany and France, if you wish. There are very few, if any, countries on the planet where Americans can legally own securities in some form that some closed-end fund has not already discovered. Ultimately, there definitely will be no such lands. In certain cases, even big investors may find the closed-end fund the easiest or only way to enter these markets.

DEFINITION

A *closed-end fund* is not a complicated device. It resembles a typical mutual fund except that its shares must be purchased and sold on a stock exchange rather than by dealing directly with a mutual fund company. The market value of these shares may be more or less than their net-asset value, the actual value of the portion of the fund's total assets which a single share can claim. A few funds may make provisions for directly redeeming shares on a limited basis, but they are the exception and, even then, redemption is likely to be available only with restrictions and during a brief period of time. Normally, if you wish to dispose of your shares you will have to have a broker sell them for you.

> HINT Many closed-end funds have dividend reinvestment and cash purchase plans which let you add to your holdings with minimum brokerage expenses.

Closed-end funds invest not only in emerging or developing markets, but virtually every foreign market and that of the United States as well. Many are regional. Others limit their portfolios to a single country. Still others may invest in only certain industries, such as utilities. Many closed-end funds are bond funds. These need not concern us here.

Advantages

The advantages of closed-end funds are numerous. In certain instances, governments have closed their securities markets to foreigners except for closed-end funds. In other cases, only closed-end funds can practically meet the restrictions on investing and the repatriation of funds which foreign governments may impose.

All closed-end funds, even those limiting most or all of their investments to the United States, can provide certain unique opportunities. As previously mentioned, funds frequently trade at a discount to their net-asset value. If you buy one trading at 10 percent below net-asset value (20 percent or more is possible) you need invest only 90 cents for every dollar you have working for you. Closed-end funds have another valuable advantage. The standard mutual fund share, except under very exceptional circumstances, will be redeemed by the company issuing it for its net-asset value at any time the shareholder requests it. This is usually a desirable attribute and one of the things that makes mutual funds attractive. However, there are times when it can create problems. Closed-end funds can avoid these.

As mentioned, shares in closed-end funds are not normally (there are occasional exceptions) directly redeemable. If you want to dispose of them, they must be sold through a broker like any other stock. As a result, in times of sharp sell-offs or outright panic, managers of closed-end funds cannot be forced to sell at distressed prices stocks they want to retain in order to raise the necessary cash to pay investors who wish to liquidate. This provides considerable stability. It is especially helpful when the funds have invested heavily in emerging markets. These often are not very liquid, and large blocks of securities being put up for sale could depress prices rapidly and dramatically, if they can be sold at all. The patient investor, like the patient fund manager, will have the ability to wait until the environment returns to a more normal condition.

Disadvantages

Closed-end funds do have some disadvantages. With very rare exceptions, a closed-end fund investing either here or in foreign lands should usually not be purchased until it has been on the market at least three and probably more like six months. The underwriters who sell the initial stock offering will have a large quantity of shares they need to get out of their inventories. They will enter the stock market to maintain the resale price during the initial offering period in order to keep their shares attractive. After they have disposed of their stock, the price in most instances will drop, although it may do so gradually over a period of time.

> **HINT** Should you own shares in a closed-end fund converted to open-end status against the will of its management, you may want to consider selling your shares as quickly as possible.

Another problem is that if you want to buy into a fund that has access to an otherwise closed market, which is sometimes the case with emerging markets, you might have to pay a price above net-asset value no matter when you make the purchase. For the small investor, there may be no other practical way to enter these markets.

One problem associated with closed-end funds is seldom discussed. Certain investment firms are concerned about short-term profits. They may have little or no interest in long-term investments at home or abroad. Should they find a closed-end fund selling at a substantial discount they will accumulate shares. Then they will attempt to force a vote by stockholders to convert to open-end status. If successful, they will quickly redeem their shares at net-asset value and depart with a nice profit. The fund at best will be left in a severely weakened state and sometimes simply does not survive. Two former funds, the Scandinavian Fund and France Fund, were destroyed in this manner. The Japan Fund, probably because of its large size and successful management, was able to continue as a regular, open-end mutual fund. Other funds, such as the Brazil Fund, appear to have been considered for takeover. While many funds have adopted practices to make these tactics more difficult in the future, that does not make them impossible.

> **note** If you do not want to obtain more stock, nontransferable rights may be allowed to expire, as they have no cash value.

It does not happen very often, but occasionally you might discover a closed-end fund selling at a price well above net-asset value, perhaps twice as much or even more. If this is the case it is possible that the stock is being manipulated to put pressure on those who sold it short and hope to buy it back at lower prices. Instead, they may have to pay a significant premium to purchase the shares they need to close out their shorts. This kind of situation developed with some funds investing in Germany in the late 1980s. It is one of those very rare instances when a small investor may want to be a short-term trader rather than hold for the long term. If you sell your shares and take a profit, most likely before too long you will be able to buy them back again at a much lower price. Just remember that, for various funds, a certain premium over net-asset value is a normal situation, not a trading opportunity.

Rights offerings

DEFINITION

Anyone seriously considering closed-end funds should be aware of possible *rights offerings*. Rights entitle the possessor to buy additional shares of stock. Unlike warrants, which may not expire for a number of years, they usually have only a brief life of several weeks during which time they may be exercised. While other companies may issue them, closed-end funds seem to be particularly inclined to use them in order to raise additional capital to invest.

Although rights offerings vary, a typical example would be to extend to the shareholder one right for each share of stock previously owned in the fund. Three rights may then be used to permit their owner to purchase one new share of stock. Funds will sometimes make this a tempting purchase by offering the new shares at a price below the current net-asset value of existing shares. In other instances, the price may be a percentage of the average price for shares on the secondary market over a period of several days, or simply the net-asset value (which could be less than the secondary market price) on the day the rights offering is closed. The transaction will be free of regular brokerage commissions, although a sales load may be included in the share price.

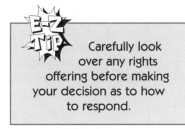

Carefully look over any rights offering before making your decision as to how to respond.

Rights may be transferable or nontransferable. If transferable, they will be listed on a stock exchange and, if requested, the fund will sell for you any you do not wish to use. If you receive transferable rights, do not let them expire without making a decision. Either exercise them to buy more shares, or sell them. Otherwise, they will become worthless.

One could debate at length whether rights are a blessing or a curse. You are never required to use all or any of them to increase the number of shares you own. If you decide to do so, they may provide you with what looks like a very attractive price at the time. Transferable rights can be sold for cash. However, what rights give with one hand they often take with the other. Their issuance will certainly lead to some dilution of the value of the shares you already own. Funds also tend to make rights offerings at the very times their share prices are at or near record highs. It is to their advantage to do so. Invariably, it appears that not too long after a rights offering is completed, the price on the secondary market declines, and shares could have been acquired there at a lower cost. Their chief value to the small investor may be that they provide a convenient way to buy a small amount of stock without paying commissions. Some brokers prefer not to handle orders for a few shares, and, if they do, must charge at least their minimum commission.

Help for closed-end funds

A list of the commonly traded closed-end funds along with their net asset values and market prices can be found in *Barron's* and weekly in the *Wall Street Journal.* Summaries of most of them can also be found in the *Standard and Poor's Stock Guide*, and many are also included in *Value Line. Morning Star* now has a special publication devoted to closed-end funds. Some or all of these resources should be available at your local library. They can be valuable in helping you select closed-end funds you may wish to consider for purchase. Closed-end funds are not without their problems. However, they can be a convenient and useful tool for the small investor wishing to diversify into foreign markets. They may also have some place in the domestic part of your portfolio as well.

Other opportunities

In recent years, several new products appeared on the market which are not closed-end funds but have certain things in common with them. They may be of interest to small investors looking for international possibilities. These include Country Baskets, traded on the New York Stock Exchange, and World Equity Benchmark Shares, commonly known as Webs, which are listed on the American Stock Exchange (Amex). In many ways they both resemble stocks, as they are bought and sold in a similar fashion and pay dividends. If you buy Webs or Country Baskets, you are buying something that looks much like a stock index fund for a particular country, as each share represents a collection of stocks in various companies located in the country you choose. There are also domestic varieties, including Standard and Poor's Depository Receipts (referred to

HOT spot Webs and Country Baskets are available for only a limited number of countries, and the included stocks are likely to remain the same even if conditions in the foreign market undergo change.

as *Spyders*), which mirror the Standard and Poor's 500 Index, and Diamonds (DIAs), which enable you to buy the stocks in the famous Dow-Jones Index. Both trade on the Amex.

Webs, Country Baskets, Spyders, and Diamonds have some solid advantages. They are both convenient and liquid, and you do not have to worry about them selling at a premium or a discount the way you do closed-end funds. However, like an index fund, you will not get the benefit of professional management. If you keep these limitations in mind, they are worthy of your consideration.

Around-the-world investing

Before leaving the subject of foreign investing, it could prove helpful to note some of the various markets around the globe which are available to even small investors through the various methods we have already explored. Let us begin close at home.

North America

- **Canada**: If looking for corporations involved in mining, petroleum, forest products, or other natural resources, Canada is an important market. These companies often do well in an inflationary period. A number of Canadian businesses are also available which are in telecommunications, manufacturing, and services.

- **Mexico**: In spite of the collapse of the peso in early 1995 and continuing insurgencies in the South, Mexico promises to be one of the most rewarding of all emerging markets in the years to come. The North American Free Trade Agreement (NAFTA) has boosted the opportunities for Mexican exports, and many Mexican companies have taken advantage of it. Various political and economic reforms, both enacted and proposed, should also help. There may be bumps along the road, but Mexico should do well.

- **Elsewhere in North America**: A post-Castro Cuba could offer some very exciting investment opportunities. The closed-end Herzfeld Caribbean Basin Fund already has plans to invest in Cuba when it becomes legal for Americans to do so. Elsewhere in Central America and the Caribbean, a few companies are now listing their shares on American exchanges or are turning up in the portfolios of several mutual funds. Expect more of both situations in the future.

South America

The major markets in South America have all attracted increasing interest in recent years. These are Argentina, Brazil, and Chile. Of the three countries, Chile generally has the most stable economy and political system. Brazil is both a big and rich country, with one of the world's largest economies. If it can continue to make progress in its battle against inflation and political uncertainty, it stands to be a world economic power. Each of these states should have excellent potential for future economic growth.

Venezuela has received some attention from foreign investors. Now even Colombia, Peru, and Ecuador, are looking interesting to the more daring. South America has good potential.

Europe

Virtually any European country at one time or another may be a good place to invest. Economies range from the large, developed, and relatively safe ones of Germany, France, and Britain to those like Greece and Portugal, which still have at least a few of the characteristics of a developing nation. The impact of the European Union and the introduction of a common currency, the euro, for its member states may make Western Europe one of the most attractive places in the world for economic progress.

Among the emerging markets of the former Soviet bloc, probably the Czech Republic, Poland and Hungary offer the best opportunities. Russia and any other state which was once part of the old Soviet Union have to be considered very speculative, but in time rewards should be there for those investors willing to venture into these "frontier" markets. The best way for small investors to be active in the area most likely is through closed-end funds.

Middle East

The region is still hurt by its extensive political instability. Also, the small investor will find fewer ways to invest here than most other places. Several Israeli firms are listed on major stock exchanges, and Israeli companies involved in sophisticated technology could be interesting investments. There are closed-end funds that invest in Israel and Turkey. The Foreign and Colonial Middle East Fund, a closed-end fund, invests in Israel, Turkey and various Arab nations such as Egypt, Morocco, Oman, Jordan, and others.

Africa

The Republic of South Africa has a diversified, well-developed economy and stock market. Unfortunately certain parts of the African continent are economic basket cases and so politically troubled it could be said they have no functioning governments. However, several countries are showing significant signs of progress. These include Zimbabwe, Botswana, and Ghana. In predominantly Arab North Africa, Morocco has several companies which are receiving attention. In coming years, other African states such as Kenya, Namibia, the Ivory Coast, and the island nation of Mauritius may begin to draw more of a following among investors.

Asia

The 1990s have not been kind to Asian economies. Japan has been in an economic malaise throughout the decade. In 1997, the currencies of several Asian states collapsed, producing economic turmoil throughout the region. However, 21st century Asia may offer more investment opportunities than any other portion of the globe. Several of the world's largest economies and also some of its potentially most rapidly growing ones are to be found here.

Japan

Many people are aware of Japan's post-World War II economic miracle. The bursting of its speculative real-estate bubble, banking problems, economic recession, and trade disputes with the United States have managed to put considerable tarnish on it. At times, the rather high prices of many Japanese stocks have also tended to chase many people away. However, Japan has such a large, sophisticated economy, with so many world-class companies, that sooner or later it may be tempting to invest here. Ample opportunities are available through Japanese companies listed on our domestic stock exchanges or through mutual funds.

China

While governed by a Communist party, China is a country filled with seemingly countless people who are not only hard working but also have a strong sense for business success. The 1997 return of Hong Kong to Chinese control has made the country's large economy even larger, although Hong Kong does retain considerable economic autonomy. Eventually China's economy may become the world's largest. Certainly parts of this nation of well over one-billion people have seen at times economic growth few other areas can match.

India

China has been attracting attention for several years. Now India is also. Too many people see only its poverty and not its huge, growing middle class and surprisingly large number of advanced industries. It has a giant, diversified economy, which some believe has the potential to become even greater than that of China. Government reforms are helping, although more are needed, and religious and linguistic rivalries have hurt. So has political tension with neighboring Pakistan.

HOT spot When it comes to investing, clearly much of your money should stay home. However, the remainder may enjoy a most profitable journey if you are careful in planning a constructive itinerary.

The "little tigers"

South Korea, Taiwan, Singapore, and Malaysia have impressed the rest of the world with their economic strength and growth. South Korea, for example, is a major player in the economic activity of northern China. However, all were caught in the Asian economic turmoil brought on by the 1997 currency collapse. In time, stability should return to the region. The four "little tigers" may also be joined by Thailand, the Philippines, Indonesia, and possibly Pakistan and Vietnam. Indonesia, in particular, was mauled by the Asian collapse, but if you have a great deal of patience, Asia may offer potential rewards.

The Pacific

Australia and New Zealand with their stable economies and democratic governments should not be overlooked. Australia offers investment opportunities in natural resources as well as industry and services. Some see New Zealand as one of the world's nations with the greatest potential.

Even our brief journey around the world demonstrates that, if the dangers are there, so are great opportunities. The small investor who is willing to spend time in research and assume reasonable risk should be able to claim some of these.

Foreign currencies and the small investor

There was a time when life was much simpler. That was certainly true for the small investor, as well as nearly everyone else. If you bought stocks or bonds they were almost always American, and nearly everyone used the expression, "sound as a dollar." Our world is decidedly different. Mutual funds have made international investing easily accessible to any investor who wants to go globe-trotting, and there have been those days, when after pondering the news, we may have felt it would have been better to have taken our paychecks in

> *note* One year, dollars may be the currency of choice. The next, it may be euros. Increasingly, we will live with a global rather than a national economy, and so will everyone else.

Deutschmarks, yen, or Swiss francs rather than in dollars. There have been other days when only the old, familiar Yankee greenback seemed really secure. Such times are most likely here to stay in one form or another. Nations that seek to avoid this will probably be very few, and they are destined to become economic backwaters whose citizens will most likely have a standard of living well below that of what could have been theirs. But, the price we pay for being able to sell and buy goods and services in over 200 different countries is that, at least to some extent, what happens to them affects us as well. It is much like being a member of a large family. Many of

> **HOT spot** Foreign stock markets offer not only economic diversification but currency diversification as well. This can contribute to financial stability.

your relatives you enjoy seeing, but there is old Uncle George. He is loud and cranky. You would like him to go away, but he will not. After all, he is family!

International events affect investors much as a family might. Sometimes they bring good news, in fact far more often than we may think. Often the good news does not get as much attention as the bad. However, there are those times when the news is definitely not to our liking, but we will still have to put up with it anyway. On occasions the news, good and bad, will have an impact on our currency and that of the other countries with which we must live. Naturally, what we do will affect the situation as well as what they do. If we live beyond our means and begin to inflate our currency to cover our debts, we should not be surprised if other nations do not want to give us as much of theirs as they once did in exchange for ours, when it is time for everyone to settle their accounts with each other.

Investors are affected by currency exchange rates. If you buy a foreign stock directly, or you own mutual funds that own them, the value of your investments will, to some extent, depend on what the foreign country's money is worth in relation to the American dollar. Should the dollar weaken against the other currency, you might find yourself in the position of actually having made money, even

> **HINT** At times, foreign bonds may offer a higher yield than their domestic counterparts, which could be a better reason for considering them than for currency hedging purposes.

though in its native country the price per share declined! It works the opposite way as well. You may hear that business has been good for your foreign company, and you would expect your shares to have increased in value. The opposite may be the case. The foreign currency has declined against the dollar and taken your profit south as a result. Some mutual funds will hedge currencies through the purchase of currency options and other methods. This may work, but it could make the situation even more difficult if they guess incorrectly which currencies will rise and which will fall. They occasionally do.

Some experts would suggest you simply ignore currency fluctuations. In the long run, they will probably have little effect on the value of your stocks or mutual funds, as the variations ultimately tend to pretty much cancel each other out. You can take that approach if you wish, and you will probably not lose much, if anything, as a result. Certainly it will make your investing life much less complicated. However, if you are concerned about possible future declines in the dollar's value, then diversifying into some foreign stocks makes sense. This is one of the few ways small investors can responsibly hedge currencies, as they will not find it feasible to buy currency options or large amounts of foreign exchange.

Beyond this, the opportunities in the currency markets for small investors are rather limited. In nearly all cases, if you want to venture further, the only practical way will be through mutual funds. In addition to foreign stocks, some mutual funds are designed to invest in foreign bonds and short-term foreign money-market instruments. These offer a chance to diversify into nondollar financial investments. However, do not assume this offers a foolproof strategy should the dollar decline. These funds may hedge some of their holdings back against the dollar. If their view that the dollar was about to strengthen proves to be incorrect, you will have a loss rather than a profit. Some funds never hedge, simply allowing their portfolios to rise and fall with the fluctuations of the dollar and other currencies.

note It is unlikely you would buy a foreign stock primarily to hedge currency fluctuations, but it can be an attractive bonus.

The direct purchase of foreign bonds, money market instruments, or currency is either not possible or practical for the small investor in nearly all instances. Yes, without too much difficulty you can find a bank in your area which will be happy to sell you foreign exchange, either in the form of paper money or travelers' checks, but the exchange rate will be so unattractive that you will almost certainly not show a profit. It will be even more unattractive if they buy it back from you. You could also be stuck with worthless bills if a country changes its currency designs and demonetizes the old ones. Reserve such transactions only for those occasions when you may be fortunate enough to travel to another country and for the sake of convenience want some of the local currency to use upon your arrival. Mercantile Bancorporation of St. Louis, Missouri (telephone: 800-926-4922) does offer both certificates of deposit and bonds in a variety of international currencies. However, the account minimums are likely to be too high for most persons interested in the investment strategy this book offers. Forget all that stuff you may have read about foreign bank accounts. They are not for the small investor, are not insured, and are unlikely to make you any more money than you could have made more safely and conveniently at home. If you do not know what you are doing, you might also find yourself with some legal complications as well.

Leave currency speculation to others. Do not let the "Chicken Little" school of investment advice panic you into doing something you will probably later regret. There is no investment without some risk, and do not permit anyone to convince you otherwise. Certainly, there are risks for those investing in the United States, but they are still far less than in the vast majority of places in the world. Some currency diversification through foreign stocks and the appropriate types of mutual funds is certainly an acceptable approach. You may also wish to consider a mutual fund investing in mining stocks and precious metals for a very small percentage of your investments. Beyond this there is little or nothing you can do, or should do.

Chapter 20

Thoughts for Canadian investors

Although this book is intended primarily for an American audience, much of what it has to say may also prove helpful to Canadians. While many things about investing are the same in both countries, other matters, such as tax laws, do differ. It is impossible here to touch upon everything a Canadian should know, but certain matters may at least provide a starting point. They may also be of some use to the American who wants to diversify and feels our neighbor to the North may be a good place to look.

Canada's stock exchanges

There have been five stock exchanges operating in Canada. The largest in terms of dollar-trading volume is the Toronto Stock Exchange. Others are Montreal, Vancouver, the Calgary-based Alberta Stock Exchange, and a smaller exchange in Winnipeg. There is also an over-the-counter market in unlisted securities. As with nearly all the world's stock markets, Canadian securities prices are quoted in decimal form. Prices are never given in fractions (American exchanges switch to decimals early in the new century).

Traditionally, Canada has no equivalent to the American Securities and Exchange Commission. Regulation of the exchanges and security trading has been done at the provincial level rather than at the national level, as in the United States. While the laws have been essentially adequate, the effectiveness of enforcement has varied from province to province and from one exchange to another.

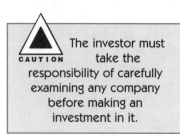

The investor must take the responsibility of carefully examining any company before making an investment in it.

Neither American nor Canadian exchanges can guarantee you that a company is sound or that you will make money. Nevertheless, exchanges in both countries can set certain standards for the companies they list. While the Toronto Exchange has not been exempt from problems, it has made efforts to establish reasonable standards as has the Montreal Exchange, which is the nation's oldest. Many excellent companies have been listed in both Vancouver and Alberta, but others must be considered speculative. Although price alone cannot tell you whether a company is financially solid or not, numerous companies on these two exchanges have sold for less than one or two Canadian dollars per share; they are so-called penny stocks. Many of these are speculative mining or oil drilling concerns. Others, particularly on the Vancouver Exchange, have been concept companies. They have a good idea, and often little else.

In an excellent article appearing in the 21 October, 1995, issue of the *Toronto Globe and Mail*, Gary Lamphier notes it is often the speculative listings in Alberta and Vancouver that have attracted the attention. They may be hyped by promoters claiming the sky is their limit. For a time, some do soar to great altitudes, only to eventually come crashing down again. Ironically, as Lamphier points out, both exchanges have listed some companies which are excellent values with a consistent record of actual and growing earnings. These are in less glamorous industries such as paving, food services, and real estate. Perhaps that is why they have been often overlooked.

Vancouver, for quite some time, had a rather unsavory reputation for listings that were peddled on both sides of the border to naive investors by unscrupulous boiler room operations. In recent years there appears to have been genuine attempts by both the exchange and the provincial government of British Columbia to clean up the situation. Vancouver stopped trading in one company which the Nasdaq permitted to resume business after only a brief suspension. However, even Toronto has had several embarrassing listings, including gold miner Bre-X Minerals, whose Indonesian gold find turned out to be fraudulent, and YBM Magnex International, a Pennsylvania-based magnet manufacturer who was accused of money laundering and connections to Russian organized crime.

The above situation does not mean that Canadian investments should be avoided. To the contrary, the country offers excellent opportunities. It simply serves as a reminder to always know what it is you are really buying before you purchase it.

In March 1999, plans were announced for the reorganization of the Canadian stock exchanges. While some details remain to be worked out, the proposal should financially strengthen Canadian markets, improve regulation, and benefit investors. Large companies would trade on the Toronto Exchange. Vancouver and Alberta would merge along with the Canadian Dealing Network, which trades unlisted securities. This new body would trade the stocks of smaller companies. Montreal would handle all the derivatives business, such as options and futures. Winnipeg is also expected to be included, and some sort of national regulation seems virtually inevitable. The result may be an excellent environment for all investors.

Should you wish to invest

When buying any stock listed on a Canadian exchange, it is always a good idea to check the spread before making your purchase. This is the difference between the bid price, what you will be paid for any shares you sell, and the asked price, what you pay for any shares you buy. In some instances it will not be significant. At other times, especially for stocks that trade less frequently, it may be large enough that you will at least want to consider it before making a final decision on what you want to do.

For the investor seeking solid investments rather than speculation, Canada offers a nice variety of opportunities. There are sophisticated

HOT spot You can even invest in the venerable Hudson's Bay Company, a corporation far older than Canada itself, and one which played a key role in its formation.

communications companies such as BCE and Nortel. The national economy is no longer oriented toward natural resources and mining to the extent it was in the past, but both are still significant components in it. Companies in these areas are often particularly attractive in inflationary times, since inflation usually brings an increase in commodity prices. One example is Alcan Aluminum, which is important in the metals business. Potash Corporation of Saskatchewan is another major natural resource producer. There are two large railroad companies. Canadian National Railways is the former government-owned railroad which has been privatized. The other is Canadian Pacific, which also has significant operations in hotel management and petroleum. Still other companies are found in everything from gold mining to automobile parts, banking, and insurance. Barrick Gold is a major and extremely efficient producer. The Toronto publisher Thomson Corporation is one of Canada's most successful. Montreal-based Bombardier is known around the world for its transportation equipment. Canada also offers a variety of opportunities in technology.

note Several funds make it possible to invest in a particular region of Canada, such as Atlantic Canada.

HINT In short, there is something for everyone. Americans will be pleased to learn that some large Canadian companies are listed on the American exchanges, making the purchase of their shares very convenient. Several hundred Canadian companies offer dividend investment plans which make it easy to gradually add to your holdings. Some of these are also open to share holders who live outside Canada. Nearly all brokers in the United States will handle orders for stocks listed on Canadian exchanges.

When buying a Canadian company listed on a Canadian stock exchange, as you would expect, you normally will find the price quoted in Canadian dollars. However, there are a few exceptions, and you might possibly be given a quote in U.S. dollars. Some companies may also pay a dividend denominated in U.S. dollars, Australian dollars, or British pounds or pence. Likewise, Canadian companies listed on American exchanges will trade their shares based on a price quoted in U.S. dollars, but probably pay a dividend based on the Canadian dollar. As always, know what it is you are buying.

Canadian mutual funds

Canadian investors will have access to a nice variety of mutual funds, including some that practice socially responsible investing, such as the Clean

Environment group. Eugene Ellman authored a book entitled *The Canadian Ethical Money Guide*. According to Ellman, Canada has fifteen socially responsible mutual funds which have attracted some 2.2 billion dollars from 90,000 investors. There is also a Toronto-based organization dedicated to the principles of socially responsible investing.

Make certain any mutual funds you are considering are based in Canada, as Canadian law prohibits the purchase of those which are not. For those who want to diversify and invest outside the country, mutual funds make this rather easy. Many Canadian-based fund families offer funds that invest in the United States. Still other funds provide opportunities to invest in Europe, Asia, and emerging markets. Many, but not all funds, are available for RRSP accounts. These are *Registered Retirement Savings Plans,* and offer tax benefits somewhat similar to American Individual Retirement Accounts (IRAs). Stocks and bonds are also eligible for these plans. Canadians can shelter as much as C$14,000 per year in RRSPs until age 69, when they must be cashed or converted. Some mutual funds are priced in U.S. rather than Canadian dollars so, again, make certain you know what you are buying.

Be sure to diversify. Not all the small investor's money should be in stocks and mutual funds, or even bonds.

There have been suggestions for closer regulation of the Canadian mutual fund industry in order to help investors know better what it is they are acquiring and what possible risks they are taking. In the past, the Ontario Securities Commissioner has been one that advocated such steps. Regardless of what has been done or may be accomplished in the future to improve and clarify disclosure, Canadian investors need to practice the same measures as American investors. Never buy any investment until you fully understand it and the risks involved.

Other Canadian investments

One instance where there is a need to fully understand before proceeding would be the case of *labor-sponsored venture capital funds.* These are a form of mutual fund developed by the Canadian government to assist both labor unions and small businesses. The idea for the funds originated with the Canadian Federation of Labour, and they are run by organized labor but open to anyone interested. Investors can receive substantial federal and provincial tax credits which help to recover a portion of their investment. However, the funds are not very liquid. You can lose the tax credits if you do not stay invested for five years and are under age sixty-five. Most of the funds' investments tend to be in companies that are not publicly traded, and this also adds to the potential lack of liquidity if a number of investors should opt out over a relatively short period of time. At least in some cases, there are probably better places for small investors to put their money.

Serious investors in Canadian stocks and mutual funds should find reading *The Financial Post* very enlightening. Published weekly, it covers Canadian markets in depth. Toronto daily *The Globe and Mail* is also an excellent source of financial information.

Through their banks and certain other financial institutions Canadians can buy *guaranteed investment certificates (GICs),* which are insured by the Canada Deposit Insurance Corporation, a federal Crown corporation, up to C$60,000 per account. These can be a good, safe place for some of your money, especially that which may be needed in the short term. The CDIC also insures savings and chequing accounts. To be eligible for coverage, term deposits, such as GICs, may not have a maturity date greater than five years. Additional information on CDIC policies can be obtained from member financial institutions or by calling 800-461-2342. A web site is also available (http://www.cdic.ca).

> **HOT spot** In certain instances, the differences between the tax law situation in Canada and that in the United States are considerable.

Canada Savings Bonds are another very safe option. They are 100-percent guaranteed by the Government of Canada and, unlike their American counterparts, they also guarantee a minimum interest rate. Rates are adjusted upward or downward every three months, but cannot fall below the minimum rate at the time of issue. The longer you hold the bonds the higher the minimum. Bonds can be cashed at anytime and cannot fall in value. Those issued since 1989 mature after twelve years. Further details can be obtained at 800-575-5151. A web site is maintained (http://www.cis-pec.gc.ca).

Taxes and Canadian investing

It is beyond the scope of this work to discuss Canadian tax law. Canadian investors need to be familiar with its basics, since to some extent taxation does affect even the small investor's strategies. As a rule, treatment of capital gains from the sale of stocks and other investments is not as favorable in Canada as in the United States. Also, Canadians who die owning stocks and other property pay tax on the capital appreciation (the increase in value over the time of ownership) when their final tax return is filed for them. In the United States this is not the case, and any federal taxes are levied on the total value of the estate. For the typical American small investor this means no federal (there could be state) estate taxes will be due since property inherited by a spouse is exempt as well as up to the first $1,200,000 of the estate, as higher exemptions are phased in over time.

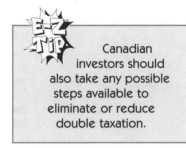

Canadian investors should also take any possible steps available to eliminate or reduce double taxation.

If you feel you need professional help in dealing with tax matters, be sure to get it. This can be an excellent investment for both Canadians and Americans. Additional information on Canadian tax matters can be obtained from Revenue Canada, 875 Heron Road, Ottawa, ON, K1A OL8 (telephone: 613-952-0384), and the Tax Court of Canada, 200 Kent Street, Ottawa, ON, K1A OM1 (telephone: 613-992-0901).

American investors investing in Canada and other countries, and Canadians investing outside Canada, need to remember that, in most instances, you will be subject to double taxation on dividend income. Currently, Americans have 15 percent of the dividends they receive from Canadian companies withheld. They are still subject to federal income tax on the entire dividend. However, this can be offset by claiming the foreign tax credit, which can be taken regardless of whether or not you itemize deductions. This credit can be taken for investment-related taxes paid to any foreign country by filing IRS Form 1116, Foreign Tax Credit, or on Schedule A if you itemize.

The future of Canadian investing

On 30 October, 1995, the province of Quebec by the narrowest of margins (50.6 to 49.4 percent) rejected a proposal to become a sovereign nation of its own. Should Canada be unable to resolve its constitutional crisis and create a formula which enables the French-speaking population of Quebec to feel comfortable being a permanent part of Canada, then most likely there would be another referendum. Possibly this time Quebec might vote to leave the Confederation. Certainly, for the majority of Canadians, this would be an event of grave consequences. No doubt it would also create considerable turmoil in Canada's currency and financial markets, at least in the short term. Investors need to pay serious attention to these risks. However, Canadians, and Americans for that matter, do not have to permit the problem to paralyze them. The political situation is cause for concern, but new efforts have been made since the referendum to try to resolve the crisis.

> **note** Even if Quebec ultimately did decide to leave, in all probability it would maintain strong economic links with Canada, perhaps a common currency and customs union.

HINT

Canada is a land rich in resources, and a country which continues to attract immigrants because it is considered one of the very best in the world in which to live. Successful steps have been taken by both the federal and provincial governments to put their financial houses in better order. This vast land has great potential. The smallest province, Prince Edward Island, for the first time in its history is linked to the mainland by a causeway and bridges. Mineral exploration continues in the Arctic regions, and Vancouver is taking its rightful place as a lively Pacific Rim port. Canada has challenges to meet. It also has the possibility of a brilliant future. Canadians who are willing to risk some of their resources by investing in their country's future, whether they do it out of a sense of patriotism or a desire for profit, or both, may reap considerable rewards.

Chapter 21

Considering collectibles

While some seem blessed by a natural immunity to the disease, others of us appear to be born collectors. We collect stamps, coins, baseball cards, and even such bizarre items as old glass insulators and barbed wire. For many this obsession started early in life, and previous efforts may now have been abandoned for new collecting pursuits. For others who thought they were safe, it may have come from almost out of nowhere. One morning you awakened and, for no good reason you could possibly discern at the time, you became obsessed with the idea of collecting antique books or trolley tokens! It happens all the time.

Perhaps every collector at one moment or another has wondered why bother, and where am I going to put all this stuff anyway? We really cannot answer that question except to say we enjoy it. It is fun, can be relaxing, and can lead to friendships with persons who share our interests.

The world of collectibles

If you are a collector, go right on collecting to your heart's content. The one thing that the collector needs to see clearly, however, is that collecting is definitely not investing. Certainly, wealthy investors may receive a profit from their collections of art, truly investment grade coins, or antique furniture. Even then, this is not guaranteed. What is clear is that investment-grade collectibles will be priced beyond the range of the small investor, and even many others for that matter. Yes, it is just possible you might find an original letter signed by George Washington tucked in a frame behind

> **HINT** Rarity alone will not assure you a profit when you want to sell a collectible, but do not expect one without it.

a cheap painting at the neighborhood garage sale. You might, but the odds of winning the lottery are probably better, and we know what that possibility is.

Unfortunately, numerous modern collectibles are advertised to collectors as having investment possibilities. They almost never do. One reason is that in many cases, the coins, collectors' plates, baseball cards, and various other items are often turned out in such large quantities that the resale market, if it exists at all, is saturated. What is advertised as a limited edition may be limited only by the number of people willing to respond to the offer.

As noted, even when some degree of rarity exists, the possibility of a profit may not. A collectible is only worth what someone else is willing to pay for it. The secondary or resale market in collectibles is subject to collectors'

> Collectibles are not necessities and, unlike stocks and bonds, they pay neither dividends nor interest.

interests, whims, and fads. It can change drastically and rapidly in some cases. What was in fashion one year may not be the next. Some items, although rare, may never attract a large following. For example, a number of foreign coins with mintages below that of American coinage command a much lower price, because collectors favor the domestic product over the imports. Interest in world currency could increase dramatically in the future, but there is no way to know that for certain.

Another problem with collectibles is that even when you buy an item that has not been mass produced, and for which there is some reasonably steady demand in the secondary market, it may still be difficult to make a profit, or at least it will take a very long time. The reason for this is that many collectibles are purchased from dealers, and dealers must make a living. Their markup may often be 50 percent or even more. Should you doubt this, buy a collectible from one dealer, and then offer it to another. One highly respected dealer in ancient coins even advises prospective customers not to purchase if their purpose is strictly to make a potential profit. Yes, you may do better if you can make your purchase directly from another collector. This is unfortunately not always possible or convenient. You can also hope for a better resale price if you in turn can sell to a collector rather than a dealer, but again such an approach has its challenges.

Few price guides can account for the variations that exist from one locality to another, and in various instances these may be considerable.

Still another factor that tilts the collectible market against the average person is that to make serious money in it you must compete against professionals, dealers, and others who have expert knowledge that takes both time and effort to acquire. Typical collectors may have difficulty even establishing what their collections are worth. Price guides, if available, may not be revised often enough. Prices may reflect the retail market rather than the wholesale, and wholesale is what collectors often receive when they become sellers. Guides may list unrealistically high prices, which can be obtained only under unusual circumstances or for pieces which are in superior condition.

Finally, we note that a serious problem with collectibles is that money spent on them is lost for real investments. The small investor does not have that many discretionary dollars to spend. Get caught up in collectibles, and you may find you have little or nothing left for savings or investing.

Collecting vs. investing

In summary, the small investor needs to know the difference between collecting and investing. If you enjoy collecting as a hobby and can afford to devote some funds to it, then do not hesitate to do so. There are also some things you can do to make your collecting more pleasant and possibly give you better resell value if, at a later date, you decide to dispose of your acquisitions.

Collect things you enjoy owning. Buy only from reputable sources. This helps reduce the chances of getting fakes or counterfeits. Avoid modern "limited editions," and stay away from current collecting fads, which usually tend to drive up prices. Buy the best condition you can afford, but not better than you can afford. Collectibles in near perfect condition hold or increase their value far better than those in lesser grades, but remember this is not an investment. Exploit inefficiencies in the markets if you are fortunate enough to find one. For example, modern commemorative coins offered by the United States Mint are often produced in smaller quantities in uncirculated condition than in the

> The idea is to have some fun. Study and read about your area of collecting interest. It will increase your pleasure and enable you to buy and sell more intelligently.

higher-price proof grade. As a result, the uncirculated coins, which cost less in the first place, occasionally can be resold at a better price than the proofs.

If your collection does begin to have some solid monetary value, it either needs to be insured or kept in a safe deposit box. Take steps to protect your collectibles from damage by careless handling, improper or inadequate storage, and breakage. To receive back as much of your original expenditures as possible, or to realize some profit, hold your collection for the long term.

If one good thing could be said about collectibles as an investment, it might be that, unlike most true investments, they tend to do best in an inflationary environment. However, should you be so fortunate as to make a profit by selling one, the tax man will want his share. Your losses in most instances are not deductible.

Chapter 22

If your rowboat comes in

What you'll find in this chapter:

- ⟶ Receiving an unexpected financial gift
- ⟶ How to realistically set your goals
- ⟶ The "financial hangover"
- ⟶ Work for money or have it work for you
- ⟶ Incremental saving plans

This chapter is not incorrectly titled. In the unlikely event your ship ever does come in, you probably will not be reading a book such as this. At that point, your goals and concerns are likely to lead you in a different direction from the one explored here. If it does happen, we will sincerely say "congratulations" and wish you the best of everything in the future. If the ship turns out to be more modest, in the rowboat or canoe category, perhaps what follows may prove helpful.

The unexpected windfall

Although it may never happen, there could be that moment in your life when you receive a sum of money which was at least partially unexpected. It might be on the order of a modest inheritance, some sort of prize, or a bonus from your employer. The sum might be as little as a $1,000 up to as much as $100,000 or more. The question is: what do you do now?

First, let us clarify things. We are talking about receiving money that is an extraordinary event, one not likely to be repeated. For an example of what we do *not* mean, if your employer is in the habit of paying you a bonus every Christmas, for all practical purposes, that is part of your regular salary. You probably treat it as such, anticipating its arrival in advance and planning on how it will be used. Were you to not receive it, you might experience serious financial pain, since it may be earmarked for certain needs or other expenses literally months in advance. Naturally, if an annual bonus would be unusually large one year, the amount above what you customarily receive would qualify. It also goes without saying that money received from an employer-sponsored or other retirement plan never counts. Any such funds should be transferred or rolled over as quickly as possible in order to insure they will be there when needed and to protect them from possible tax penalties.

note There is a difference between improving your financial condition and living more comfortably on the one hand and retiring to some sort of life of ease and luxury on the other.

Second, while $100,000 may look like the QE2 rather than a rowboat to numerous readers, and as pleasant as the receipt of that amount would be, in all reality (in many cases) it is not enough money to radically alter your lifestyle, at least in a permanent way. Were you to take the $100,000, refuse to spend any of it, but in turn prudently invest it, you could probably expect as an average reasonable return somewhere between 7 and 12 percent per year. You might do better occasionally, but other years may wind up with no earnings at all or even a loss. So, it is best to look at an average for a number of years. Were you to take the earnings your invested $100,000 produced each year, you can see that, at very best, you would probably have about $1,000 a month additional income to spend, and this is a before tax figure. While that would be welcomed and helpful, it is hardly enough to cause you to start looking at a new home in Palm Beach or Beverly Hills. That rowboat can be very useful in helping you accomplish the former; just do not try to travel all the way across the ocean in it.

Avoiding the "financial hangover"

All right, if choice ocean-front property on the Florida Gold Coast is out of the question, what can be accomplished? Perhaps the first thing is actually to do nothing! People who live primarily paycheck to paycheck almost inevitably have pent-up desires. Many may actually be things which, under more generous financial conditions, would be perfectly fine to pursue. Suddenly the money is there. There is a rush to spend it on a better home, new car, elaborate vacations, and other longed-for dreams. Soon the nest egg is seriously depleted or totally gone, and within a few years the same may be true of many of the things which it was used to purchase. We are right back where we started, maybe worse, as we suffer the pains of a "financial hangover."

 It takes discipline, commitment, and determination to change your spending habits. If you are truly determined to put your financial house in order then paying off some debt may be in order.

The urge is quite understandable. Resist it anyway, as there are very good reasons to do so. There are some ways to help. Actually, you do not want to be too rough on yourself. Depending on the size of the amount you receive, you might want to designate a certain amount of it, somewhere between 5 up to no more than 25 percent, as your "mad money." This you permit yourself to use in any harmless manner you choose. Perhaps you, at long last, take that trip to Switzerland, or buy a new living room sofa. At the same time, you promise yourself that you are doing this in order to protect the remainder, that it will be put to work to accelerate your investment program and help you achieve a better degree of financial security than you have now, and sooner than you otherwise would have anticipated.

Paying off debts

 Some might consider paying off or at least paying down the mortgage on the house. Others might think it is time to use part of the money to clean up those credit card debts. Both are commendable approaches to making the money work constructively, provided you keep one critical factor in mind. The money saved on monthly mortgage or credit card payments should go into a monthly investment plan, perhaps automatic payments to a mutual fund or at least a bank savings account. Unfortunately, all too often this never happens. It goes to cover regular expenses without us really realizing where it has gone and, before too long, those credit cards have balances similar to where they were before we paid them off. If you fear that in time you will once again yield to temptation, it may be better to leave the debt in place, handle it through the regular payments you have been making, and proceed with what follows below. Again, this is a case where investors need to know who they really are.

Your best bets

You can either work for money or it can work for you, making your life now or sometime in the future a little more pleasant. Probably, part of the unexpected windfall should go into low-risk investments such as bank certificates of deposit and United States EE Savings Bonds. It will slowly compound as it earns interest and can serve as a nest egg to provide security in the event of a genuine and unexpected emergency. It might also help to educate a child or be used to smooth the financial transition that can be quite challenging when retirement comes. Probably, the smaller the amount and the more risk adverse you are, the higher the percentage that should be invested in this way.

The remainder might go into stocks and mutual funds. At least some of this perhaps could be designated for nonspeculative but somewhat riskier investments than you otherwise might consider. For example, you might want to invest in a mutual fund that concentrates its investments in emerging foreign markets or buys stocks of small companies, either domestic or foreign. The pitfalls are greater than usual, but so are the potential rewards.

DEFINITION

Unless the amount is rather small, $1,000 or less, it would be a good idea to consider *dollar averaging*. Instead of investing the money all at one time, it is invested in installments over a period of months or even several years. In this way you avoid the danger of committing all your money just when prices may have peaked. You will not get the best price, but you will not get the worst either.

The trick is to keep your rowboat from springing a leak. If it remains dry on the inside, in time it can help take you on a pleasant voyage, perhaps one that otherwise would not have been possible. Happy sailing!

Chapter 23

When you do have to borrow

What you'll find in this chapter:

⟶ Sources to borrow from

⟶ Home equity loans and mortgages

⟶ Borrowing from your credit line

⟶ Questions to ask when borrowing

⟶ How to guard against negative amortization

Never borrow money to make an investment! The reason for this is quite basic. Even if your investment turns out to be a good one, it is highly unlikely it will earn you as much money as the loan will cost you. There are other reasons as well, and they are discussed elsewhere. Obviously, one should not borrow unnecessarily, but there are those times when borrowing money is necessary and makes sense. There are a few things to keep in mind that could save you money when a loan is a valid option.

If you must borrow

Always remember that when you borrow money what you are actually doing is buying money, or maybe, more correctly, renting money. You are paying an agreed price to use someone else's money for an agreed period of time. Understanding this can help eliminate unwarranted guilt and confusion about what you are actually doing, and thus make it easier to do the right thing. You would not feel guilty about buying an automobile if you needed transportation to get to work, but you might ultimately feel foolish if you bought a car which was bigger and more expensive than you were

---

comfortable driving or could afford. Borrowing money confronts us with similar decisions.

You would not rent a house unless you knew why you were doing it. Do not rent money frivolously or on a whim. That may seem difficult to do until you remember that credit cards make it quite easy, and expensive. However, perhaps you have a clear purpose in mind. You may wish to buy a home. You do want a car. There are

> **HOT** spot It should always be completely clear to you why you want to rent someone's money.

educational or medical expenses that must be paid, or some other situation which makes borrowing appear to be the only practical possibility. Few people who are potential small investors will ever be in a position to pay cash for a home, and most will probably find from time to time other situations which will strain the regular budget to the breaking point. If you have clearly and carefully identified a need (as opposed to a mere wish or want), then it is time to borrow.

Shop around

Most of us, when shopping for an item, especially an expensive one, would not automatically take the first one we see without comparing other similar ones. We want to look at quality and price, among other things. Renting money is the same kind of situation. Before you rent it, shop around, and leave the guilt at home. Banks and other lending institutions want your loan business. It is business. You are a customer. Make them work for your business by making the product as good a value as possible.

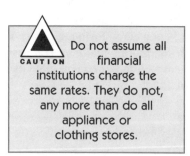

> ⚠ **CAUTION** Do not assume all financial institutions charge the same rates. They do not, any more than do all appliance or clothing stores.

If you are a member of a credit union, you may do well to make that the first stop on your comparison shopping list. Credit unions are nonprofit organizations and usually can offer very attractive loan terms to their members. Many even offer a special type of loan which is as economical as you are likely to find. If you have savings on deposit with the credit union, but are reluctant to withdraw them for fear you will not pay yourself back, the credit union will hold your money as collateral and loan you an equal amount at an attractive rate. Meanwhile, your savings will continue to earn interest, thus reducing the actual cost of the loan still more! Of course, if your account balance is minimal or nil, or you want to retain control of your savings for emergency use, or the amount you need is larger than you have on deposit, conventional loans are available, and often at interest rates lower than you will find elsewhere.

Many credit unions will even offer you a first or second mortgage.

HINT

Banks also are a good source for loans, but compare rates and terms. One bank may have a slightly lower rate than another, but will they loan you the money for as long a period as you think you will need to repay the loan? Avoid small loan companies and companies that offer to loan you money by mail. The reasons are basic. They usually accept borrowers who are much higher risks, and their interest rates are also much higher as a result. If you are employed (unfortunately, self-employed persons sometimes find it more difficult to borrow), and a bank or credit union will not make you a loan, there is a good chance you are financially overextended. Additional borrowing may only make the situation worse, or impossible.

The home-equity loan

DEFINITION

If you are already buying a home, the *home-equity loan* is another way to borrow money at reasonable rates. The lending institution loans you the equity you have accumulated in your home over the years you have been making mortgage payments. If you are in a position to itemize deductions on your income taxes (many taxpayers are not), home-equity loans are especially attractive, since your interest payments are deductible. However, there is one critical factor often overlooked with this type of borrowing—a home-equity loan is in fact a mortgage on the home, a second mortgage unless before the loan there was no other existing mortage. Lenders make home-equity loans at attractive rates because the loan is a secured one. It is secured by your house. If you default on this type of loan, the lender has the option to foreclose, and you could lose the home. This does not mean never take out a home-equity loan. It simply means know what you are doing before you do it. The loans can be a tempting source of relatively "easy money" which can encourage someone to borrow more than is wise or necessary, and thus become overextended. This is even more the case with the increasingly popular home

> **note** People enter into mortgage contracts every day. Few of us would ever own a home if we refused. Home-equity loans can make much sense.

loans that permit you to borrow more than your equity if the market value of your dwelling has increased. Avoid the temptation.

It will also pay to shop carefully and patiently for a home-equity loan if you do decide this is the best source of funds for you. Lenders normally charge various fees and closing costs to establish your account, much as they do on a regular mortgage. They will then extend you a line of credit, based on a percentage of your home equity, and you may borrow all or part of it. Additional loans up to the amount of the credit line may be made later without paying further closing costs. However, if you are not in a hurry, you will frequently find that home-equity loans often go on sale. The closing costs will be waived on new accounts opened during a limited period of time.

When you need a mortgage

If you are planning to buy a home, what you need is not a home equity loan, but a mortgage. The usual rules apply. Shop around to get the best price. There are some additional questions to ask:

- What closing costs will you be expected to pay?

DEFINITION

- Will *points* be charged? A point is 1 percent of the price of the home. You may get a lower interest rate if you are willing to pay points, but loss of the use of your "point money" may, in the long run, make this type of loan more expensive.

- Is there a penalty for paying the mortgage early?

- Is the mortgage assumable by someone who may later buy your house? Assumability is especially valuable should interest rates rise extensively in the future.

- What time periods are available? Most first mortgages will be for periods of from fifteen up to a maximum of thirty years. Naturally, the interest rate will be less on loans of a shorter duration and higher for those lasting thirty years.

• Finally, ask if you will be required to escrow insurance and tax payments, or be permitted to make them yourself. If you must set up an escrow account and have your lender make the payments, it may make budgeting for them easier on you. However, the lender rather than you gets free use of the money until the payments are made.

It will normally pay HINT you to do so if you can obtain a new loan for at least two percentage points less than the old one. Sometimes, even a smaller decline may make refinancing feasible.

A critical factor to consider is whether you want a mortgage with a fixed interest rate or one with an adjustable rate. The initial rate will always be higher if you select the fixed-rate loan, but you will be spared any nasty future surprises. Should interest rates drop in the future, you could always consider refinancing.

When interest rates are at unusually high levels, adjustable-rate mortgages become very attractive. First of all, the initial cost will be less than the fixed-rate type. Secondly, probably interest rates will ultimately decline, and this will reduce your future payments. When interest rates are low, avoid adjustable rate mortgages. They are, at best, a temporary bargain. Most likely in the future you will have larger payments to make. These loans have rate caps which limit the amount you must pay each month. However, in many instances, the interest rate cap is not the interest rate limit. Your monthly payment may be capped, but the amount you owe is not. If your payment is inadequate to cover the additional interest owed above the payment cap, the amount is added

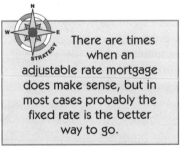

There are times when an adjustable rate mortgage does make sense, but in most cases probably the fixed rate is the better way to go.

DEFINITION into the mortgage balance. This can produce *negative amortization*, a situation where your mortgage balance becomes larger than the sum you originally borrowed.

Car loans

Automobile loans can produce a situation with characteristics similar to negative amortization. It is popularly called being upside down. If you buy a new car and have an accident which results in so much damage that it would cost more to repair the car than it is worth, the insurance company considers it "totalled." The company writes you a check for the value of the car, less any applicable deductible, and hopes for a better day tomorrow. However, the amount of the check is for the actual cash value of the automobile, not what you paid for it. Once you left the dealership with your new purchase, it was no longer a new car, but technically a used one, and its actual cash value declined accordingly. It is possible to finance a new automobile for up to 100 percent of the cost. If you did just that, and have had the vehicle for only a brief period of time, most likely you are *upside down.* The balance you owe on your car loan is greater than the check you received from the insurance company. You have no automobile, but you still have payments due on an automobile loan. Always make a down payment on an automobile at least large enough to prevent this situation. Ten percent may be adequate. Fifteen or twenty would be safer. The same logic also indicates that, in most instances, car loans of more than five years duration are not a good idea.

DEFINITION

Credit cards

One could preach about the evils of credit cards, but why bother. Let us face reality. Almost all of us are hooked. They are convenient, and probably a lot safer than carrying lots of cash. Still, it will again pay to do comparative shopping. Interest rates vary considerably. Be certain the rate quoted is the true one, and not just an introductory one, available for a limited period of time. Increasingly, card issuers are going to variable interest rates which, in some instances, seem to have the annoying habit of going up faster than they come down. However, you may still find some cards available with a fixed interest rate. If you tend to pay your balance every month (good for you!), then a card with no annual fee is a logical choice. If you make monthly payments on the balance, the lowest possible interest rate is usually more important. Premium or gold cards will offer a higher credit line and a larger annual fee. This credit could offer an unhealthy temptation. If the card offers additional services that you find useful or reassuring, then the greater fee may be worth the cost. Most people probably do not use or need these services, and do not need gold cards. Some may lack the credit rating to obtain one anyway.

note

Various types of cards have different advantages. **Visa** and **Mastercard** are by far the most widely accepted both at home and around the world. **Discover** has the nice feature of giving you a cash rebate based on a percentage of what you charged during the previous year. However, it is not accepted outside the United States. **American Express** costs more and has higher standards to qualify. If you do qualify, and are willing to pay the price, it does provide a variety of services and benefits that are especially useful to people who travel. Except for certain travel and other large expenses, the regular American Express card is a charge account rather than credit card. Your total bill is due and must be paid every month. The American Express **Optima** card functions like a typical credit card. If you qualify for the regular one, you will have no difficulty obtaining the Optima if you wish. You can then use both. Of course, you may also apply for just an Optima card. In addition to these cards, you will find some places also accept the **Diners Club** card.

> **HOT spot** Credit cards are about the most profitable form of banking business around, but not the healthiest for you, me, or the country.

Many retail stores and gasoline companies have their own cards. They come without annual fees and, obviously, these outlets would prefer that you use them, since they retain the percentage they would have to pay another credit card issuer. If you obtain these types of cards and use them simply as a charge card, paying the balance each month, there is no problem. If you use them for credit purchases, you may discover the interest charged is often even higher than that charged on your regular credit cards.

Increasingly, cards are being offered that provide certain enticements, such as reduced telephone charges, frequent flyer miles, rebates on automobiles, or other perks. Again, do comparative shopping. Are the extra "goodies" something you would actually use? Are they really a bonus, or do you have to pay for them with higher interest rates and annual fees? If they appear to offer genuine value, and you are going to get some sort of card anyway, then one of these may be the right card for you.

Keep your eyes open

Periodically, about every six months or so, carefully review the interest rates on all your credit cards. Many people are aware that card issuers will offer a "teaser" introductory rate for several months up to possibly a year in some instances. They realize that at the end of this period they will be charged the normal rate. What the lenders do not disclose is that sometimes this "normal" rate, which may have looked very competitive, is very quietly raised to a much higher one after a period of time. This may be done although you have never been delinquent on the account, and national interest rates have not risen. In fact, they may have actually declined. You will receive the required notification, but it is often easy to overlook.

Should this happen to you check first to make sure it is not the result of national interest rate increases which would ultimately affect all borrowers. If

> *note* As we begin to have investment success, it can give us the confidence and encouragement to improve our entire financial situation, including paying any outstanding loans as soon as possible.

it is not, but the result of the particular lender hoping you will either not notice or will endure it anyway, there is only one course of action. Close the account as quickly as possible, and tell the card company why you are doing so. If you had an account balance, find another card issuer that will arrange to pay off or transfer your balance (most are quite happy to do so) and, as soon as this has been accomplished, cancel the original account. Then keep just as careful a watch on the new company while making every reasonable effort to pay down that balance!

Remember that any kind of credit card is about the most expensive way to borrow money, unless you visit your friendly, neighborhood loan shark. That is why banks and other institutions are so eager to issue them to you and raise your credit limit if you request. As they used to say on the old television program *Hill Street Blues,* "Let's be careful out there!"

Other loans to avoid

Little needs to be said about borrowing money from friends and family members or making loans to them. There is only one short rule you need to remember, and exceptions to it should be about as rare as unicorns. "Thou shall not ever!" All parties involved may have the best of intentions at the start, but the situation invariably becomes an unpleasant one. Prevent that from happening by not giving it the chance to happen.

If you have outstanding loans, other than a mortgage and possibly an automobile loan, should you be investing at all before they are paid? Some might say "absolutely not." After all, it is a rare investment that will make as much for you in a year as a similar amount would cost you in interest if owed on a credit card. While this is surely correct, there is something else to consider. Many of us, if we wait until all our debts are paid, will never begin to invest. Therefore, we need to start now, even while we make every effort we can to reduce our debt.

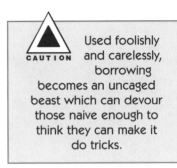

CAUTION

Used foolishly and carelessly, borrowing becomes an uncaged beast which can devour those naive enough to think they can make it do tricks.

HINT

For similar reasons, I would, if possible, avoid depleting savings to make loan payments. The savings give us a sense of security and are available if a genuine emergency should arise. Also, there are far too many cases of people paying off credit cards only to run up their balances once again. If you do that with your savings, then they are gone, but the loan balances are not. Likewise, consolidation loans are often not a desirable option for many people. There is a good deal of temptation to borrow again what we just paid, but now we have the additional consolidation loan payment to make. It is quite easy to know we should not do these things. It is much more difficult to resist doing them. The best plan of attack is not to give ourselves the chance in the first place. Obviously we can also help the situation by closing out unnecessary charge accounts once they are paid. A couple of credit cards may offer convenience and cash in an emergency, but do you really need six or seven?

If you have so much debt that you feel you need credit-life insurance to cover your loan balances in the event of your death, in most instances you could save a great deal of money by buying regular term insurance to cover the amount rather than the very expensive coverage offered by lenders and credit card companies. This also holds true if you want to make sure the mortgage is paid should you die. The younger and healthier you are, the more likely this is the case.

Borrowing money is part of your total financial situation, along with investing and obtaining necessary insurance. Used carefully and when necessary, borrowing can be a helpful tool, one which hopefully eventually we will need less and less, if at all.

Chapter 24

Insurance

What you'll find in this chapter:

- ➠ Types of insurance
- ➠ Why it isn't necessary to insure children
- ➠ How much insurance do you need?
- ➠ When to buy double indemnity
- ➠ Rating companies and systems

Insurance is in some ways much like death. Nobody likes to talk about it, but eventually everybody needs to do so. Certainly, the small investor is no exception. The subject could be a book in itself. Here, we simply attempt to cover the basics. Your local library may have some helpful resources should you find that you need additional information. However, regardless of whether your insurance requirements are the usual ones or somewhat more complex, they should be part of your overall financial planning. Determine what you need, and make your insurance premiums part of your overall household budget. Periodically review these needs, and if you find ways to cut insurance costs without sacrificing necessary coverage, the savings could then be designated for investments.

Insurance planning in most instances will work best if it is done along with your investment planning, not before or after.

Universal life insurance

The most critical thing to remember about insurance is that it is not an investment. This may be obvious in many instances. It is less so when dealing with the matter of life insurance, since life insurance is often packaged and sold as an investment. Good investments take what you already have and make it grow. There are some life insurance policies, known as universal life, which do a reasonably decent job of combining these two tasks. If you are the sort of person who will save and invest only when forced to do so, then perhaps you may wish to consider a *universal life policy.* Since you must make premiums regularly to keep your

note

Insurance is protection, nothing more. Insurance should be designed to help you keep what you already have.

policy from lapsing, the portion of that premium which goes into the policy's investment vehicle will also be invested regularly. Within certain limits, you can even decide how large a premium you will make each year.

Universal life policies usually have a larger savings component than do traditional whole life policies. Stay away from policies that offer unreasonably high yields, as this may mean the company is investing in junk bonds, high-risk derivatives, or other potentially dangerous instruments. Remember that any earnings estimate is simply a projection. If you expect a decent rate of return on a universal life policy, and many can provide this, you will need to hold it for the long term, probably at a minimum ten years.

Variable life insurance

Depending on the policy, variable life policies are really a form of either whole or universal life insurance that looks much like an annuity. The policy's cash value, and sometimes the death benefit, can vary as a result of how well the insurance company has done investing in stocks and other financial instruments.

Both universal and variable life policies (also single-premium life) can have tax benefits, especially for wealthy investors who wish to reduce tax liabilities on estates they wish to leave to their heirs. They may meet the needs of some small investors, particularly those who do need help in saving on a regular basis. As is the case with whole life policies, any earnings also have the advantage of being tax deferred until actually withdrawn, and death benefits should be entirely free of federal taxation (be sure to check current tax treatment before purchasing a policy). However, they are probably better as savings devices than for insurance.

Life insurance basics

While life insurance comes in many fancy wrappers these days, when you examine the real insurance part of nearly every policy it will be either *term* insurance or *whole life* insurance. Before looking at the differences, we need to understand what life insurance should do and who needs it. Not everybody does.

The task of life insurance is to provide adequate financial resources for those who are dependent on the income or services of the person insured, in the event that this person should die. If you are a single person supporting only yourself, in most instances you do not need life insurance. A possible exception may be if you believe future health or occupational changes could make you a high risk or uninsurable at some later date when you may need coverage. If you are married and you are the chief source of the family's income, you probably do need life insurance. A mother, not employed outside the home, may need it also. If she were to die, would someone have to be employed to care for young children while the father continues his regular occupation? If you are financially responsible for an aged parent, a relative, or someone else, again, life insurance may be necessary.

> **HINT** Many of us will find we can take better control of our financial decisions if we keep insurance separate from our investments. Usually this should enable us to make clearer decisions about both areas.

 Except in the most unusual of circumstances, do not insure a child's life. Children do not have dependents. They are dependents. About the only exception would be if the child already has some sort of health condition (not just your concern that this could develop in the future) which could make obtaining coverage later difficult or impossible. Some policies for adults may permit you to add small amounts of coverage for your children. The premiums for this are usually rather small. Such money is almost always better spent to provide additional coverage on the parents, but if it makes you feel more comfortable, purchasing this option is probably alright, especially if you would have difficulty handling the funeral bill or any possible remaining medical expenses. Retired persons who have pensions which are adequate and permanent may want to take any remaining policies and turn them in for any possible cash value, if it appears they will no longer be needed to meet future emergency expenses.

How much to get

How much life insurance do you need? That is seldom an easy question to answer. However, unless a double-indemnity provision is included at no additional charge, do not waste precious premium dollars on one. If you have this, it normally will pay twice the policy face amount if you die in an accident. Your dependents' financial needs will be the same regardless of how you die. Put the money saved into additional coverage. If double indemnity is offered to you at such a low additional premium that you find it difficult to refuse, there is no real harm in accepting it. This is especially the case if you are in your early thirties or younger, since you are probably

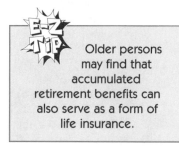

Older persons may find that accumulated retirement benefits can also serve as a form of life insurance.

more likely to die by accident than in any other manner. Just do not make the mistake of assuming that you now will have twice as much insurance.

For the same reason, policies that insure your life only in the case of accident make no real sense. Sometimes an organization which you join may make a small amount of this kind of insurance available at no additional cost. If it requires paying your dues on time or filling out a simple form to qualify, certainly you should do it and accept the coverage. If you are offered additional coverage for a fee, decline and buy insurance that protects regardless of how you die. The same approach should be taken toward insurance which covers hospital or medical expenses resulting strictly from accidents.

In considering how much coverage to purchase, take into account for what it will be needed and for how long. Are you trying to insure a child's education? What employment skills does your spouse have? What is the age and health condition of your spouse and children? In the end, you probably need to purchase as much coverage as you can reasonably afford. The old rule of six to ten times the family's current annual income can be used as a rough guide. Before making any final decisions, take into account other assets you may have. Is there any employer-provided group life insurance to help carry part of the load? If you have dependent children, Social Security benefits should be available.

The right type for you

DEFINITION

Buying the right kind of insurance will help you purchase an adequate amount. For most persons this means *term insurance*. Term insurance normally does nothing fancy. It just insures your life for a stated amount of dollars for a specific period of time. Because it does not try to do anything else than this, if you are in reasonably good health and do not smoke you may be pleasantly surprised at how attractive the premium rates may be. Maybe this is why you do not hear as much about term insurance as you should. It is usually more profitable to sell other kinds, but they may not do as good a job of providing the protection needed.

DEFINITION

Term insurance comes in two basic forms, *renewable* and *decreasing*. Renewable provides a steady level of coverage, for example $100,000. After the policy has been in force a certain number of years, typically five, it will automatically be renewed for the same amount of coverage and without medical examination but at a higher premium. The policy will continue to be renewed unless you choose to cancel it, or until you reach the age of 65 or 70.

Decreasing term insurance is more or less the mirror image of renewable term. The premium will remain constant over the life of the

HINT Decreasing term may be a good choice for persons who expect to have declining financial responsibilities as children leave home and permanent pension benefits gradually accumulate.

policy, which will normally expire after a period of 20 or 30 years. Each year the policy is in force, the amount of insurance in force will be reduced. Renewable term can be excellent for young people with considerable responsibilities and minimum incomes. In future years, earnings should rise to meet premium increases. Many or most term policies do permit conversion without medical examination to an ordinary or whole life policy.

Whole life insurance is sometimes called **permanent insurance**. Unless you choose a policy with a higher premium, which will be paid up at 65 or some other selected age, premiums on a whole life policy remain in effect until you die or reach the ripe old age of 100, at which time the policy matures, and the insurance company will send you a check for the face amount. Whole life policies contain a savings account feature which keeps your premiums at the same rate over the life of the policy, even though you are growing older. Basically, what this means is that in your early policy years you are paying an amount in excess of what is needed to provide the insurance coverage. These additional funds are put into your policy savings account and are invested by the insurance company, which will pay you interest on them. The money you save and earn will help pay the premiums as you age. If you are fortunate, there may be, in later years, an excess which will be returned to you in the form of either a premium reduction or a dividend.

Tax laws affecting insurance proceeds change from time to time, so check carefully with the insurance company or a tax advisor to clarify the situation.

Whole life policies offer several attractive options. The savings feature gives these policies a cash value. If, eventually, you no longer need the policy, it can be cancelled, and you will receive the money. Some of this may not be subject to federal income taxes, as it is actually a return of the excess premiums you paid. The interest you have earned on the excess premiums most likely will be taxable. If you prefer, instead of taking the cash, you may keep the policy in force at a lesser face amount as permanently paid-up insurance. No additional premiums will be required.

Borrowing to buy

Since the cash value is, in reality ,your own money, insurance companies are quite happy to loan it to you at very attractive interest rates, far less than you would pay for a regular loan. Furthermore, you have the option of paying the loan back over whatever time period you wish or never paying it back at all. Just remember, there is no Santa Claus. The amount of insurance you originally purchased is reduced by the amount of any outstanding loan plus any unpaid interest. Cash value can also be used to make premium payments through the option of an automatic premium loan, should you forget or be unable to make them. These also are subject to interest, just like any other policy loan.

Whole life insurance

The big problem with whole life is that the savings feature makes it very expensive to buy. You get far less protection for your dollar, and protection is what life insurance should provide. You may also find that what the insurance company pays you on your savings is less than what you could earn elsewhere. There are probably only two instances when you might want to seriously consider whole life:

1) If you are going to need coverage beyond the age of 65 (although the conversion of a term policy if and when the whole life policy is needed may provide a better option).

2) If you must be "forced" to save, whole life could make sense.

> **HOT spot** As already mentioned, unless it is an irresistible "bargain," do not pay additional premiums for double indemnity.

Purchasing a small whole-life policy to cover funeral and other expenses that could occur at the time of your death may also be something you might want to do, but if you wait too long to do this the premiums will probably be so high as to make this unattractive. Otherwise, most or all of your life insurance budget will stretch further if you purchase term insurance.

Special provisions and offers

Some policies may be available with extra "goodies," which are worth considering. A *disability provision* may be worth the extra money. This pays the premiums if you are disabled and cannot. A "cost of living" feature is especially nice. Under this you have the option each year to buy additional one-year term insurance to keep the purchasing power of the policy value roughly equal to what it was when you originally bought it and before inflation began to eat away at it. While you are never required to exercise this option, if you decline to do so, it will

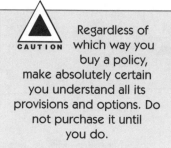

Regardless of which way you buy a policy, make absolutely certain you understand all its provisions and options. Do not purchase it until you do.

expire and may not be used in future years. A provision permitting terminally ill persons to completely or partly cash in policies before their actual death is an attractive feature and may be included without additional charge.

DEFINITION

Particularly if you read financial publications, you may from time to time come across an advertisement for something called *single-premium life insurance*. Its name reflects the fact that you only make one premium payment, and the policy remains permanently in force unless you decide to cancel it. It is usually purchased by people for purposes of earning interest which can be shielded from income taxes as long as it is not withdrawn. This income can eventually be left for beneficiaries, who will receive it completely tax free. Single-premium life functions in some ways like an annuity with a certain amount of life insurance added for good measure. The initial premium

will be considerable and, if you decide to terminate the policy, there could be substantial charges. As a result, and when other factors are considered, most small investors will probably want to look elsewhere for both their insurance and investment needs.

note Ratings information should be available from either an agent or the company itself.

Some life insurance companies normally sell their product through agents. Others market directly to the purchaser and may be able to offer somewhat lower premiums as a result.

Rates will vary considerably, so do some comparative shopping. When comparing policies, if possible try to obtain Cost Comparison Indexes. The calculation of these is somewhat complex, but all you really need to remember is the lower the figure the better the value.

Expect to be rewarded with lower premiums by virtually all companies if you do not smoke. Obviously, the younger you are the lower your rate will be. So if you really need life insurance, it will pay to not delay. If you do need the coverage, then this becomes an extremely important purchase. Do not allow yourself into being pressured to make it through a family member or friend unless they can offer what you truly need and at a competitive price.

Choosing the right company

Before buying any policy, you will do yourself a big favor if you check on the insurance company's financial stability. Remember, the federal government does not insure policy holders in the event your company goes bankrupt. There may be some state protection, but there will probably be considerable complications if the insurance company owed you or your beneficiaries money and, even if this is not the case, health or occupational changes may have left you uninsurable in the future. Several companies evaluate the financial health of insurance companies. Probably best known is *A. M. Best Company. Standard & Poor's, Moody's Investors Service*, and *Duff & Phelps Credit Rating Company* also provide information. If you prefer a more independent source, your local library may have publications produced by the ratings services or be able to help you get directly in contact with them. Each service's rating system is slightly different. Best's highest rating is A++, Standard & Poor's is AAA, Moody's is Aaa, while Duff & Phelps is AAA.

> **HOT spot** Every few years it would be a good idea to review your life insurance situation to determine if more coverage is needed or if old policies could be dropped.

Weiss Research, Inc., is known for its extremely tough ratings criteria, some might say overly tough. However, a good rating from Weiss has been earned by a number of companies. Weiss Research is located in the West Palm Beach, Florida, area and is completely independent of either the insurance or banking industries. You can reach them at 800-289-9222 and receive a written report for a reasonable fee. Weiss can also furnish you with a report on your bank, if you wish.

Be in it for the long haul

You may keep a life insurance policy for literally decades. Make certain that the company issuing the policy is healthy enough to be there when it is needed. Periodically check to make sure it is retaining its ratings.

HINT

Think at least twice before replacing an old policy with a new one, especially if you are considering buying a new whole life policy to take the place of the one you now have. You may have paid too much for the old one, but most of the overhead costs are paid the first two or three years the policy is in force. After this, cash values do begin to build up. If you drop the policy to buy a new one, you will pay these costs a second time.

note If the company has a solid financial rating and offers you an attractive price for the policy you want, it should meet your needs regardless of which type it is—stock or mutual.

It may sometimes pay to cash in an existing whole life policy and replace it with a greater amount of term insurance. However, never cancel any kind of life insurance until the new policy is definitely in force. If you do, there could be the possibility of finding you have no coverage.

Types of insurance companies

Insurance companies come in two forms: Many are **stock companies**, organized like any other business corporation. If they make a profit, they may pay their shareholders a dividend. **Mutual companies** are the other type. Technically, they are owned by their policy holders. If they pay dividends, they are paid to the policy holders either in the form of lower premiums or cash. Mutual companies may appear to offer the insurance purchaser a better deal and often do, but this is not always the case. With a stock company you always know what your premium will be.

Mutual companies will project dividend payouts, but these are never guaranteed. They could be more or less than the company's estimate. Your premiums will reflect this and may fluctuate from year to year. Some stock companies are strong and efficient enough to offer rates quite competitive with those of mutual companies. Generally, stock companies also find it easier to raise additional capital if they need it. They can always consider a stock offering. Mutual companies cannot. The typical insurance purchaser need not worry too much about any of this. There are both stock and mutual companies that are competitive and financially sound.

Unless you are rather elderly or normally not insurable, there is one kind of life insurance you definitely do not need. This is the **credit life insurance** offered by lenders and credit card issuers. Credit life insurance is not necessarily such a bad idea, but the premiums charged for it are. If you have loan balances that you want to be certain will be paid in the event of your death, buy a regular term life insurance policy for the necessary amount instead. Take the considerable savings and invest them to help pay off those loans early.

Other insurance

Health insurance

Health insurance has become so complex and rapidly changing that not much can be said on the subject here. By all means check with your employer to see what options are available to you. If you are self employed, be sure to take any federal or state tax deductions that may apply to the premiums you pay. On your federal return, the deduction can be taken on form 1040 regardless of whether or not you itemize on Schedule A. Tax laws on this matter sometimes change, so be careful to check what the current situation is.

These days, health insurance comes in a variety of forms including traditional coverage plans, preferred providers, and health maintenance organizations, or HMOs. You may have access to only one or all of these. Obtain as much information as you

A visit to the doctor's office for a cold will not financially destroy you; a needed kidney transplant could if you do not have adequate coverage.

can on any plans available, and study it carefully. An Internet site (http://www.ncqa.org) may also be helpful. Once you make a decision, you will probably have to live with it for at least a year.

Regardless of which plan you choose, there are two things to keep in mind:

1) Unless you have a generous employer who still pays all the premiums for you and your dependents, you may be able to save some money by agreeing to take a higher deductible, the amount you pay before your plan pays. What you need is coverage for the major expenses you could not pay or could pay only with difficulty.

2) The second matter is somewhat related to the first. Bells and whistles are fine if they are free or you can afford them, but what is essential is coverage for major and catastrophic illnesses. Check any plan offered to you carefully for how thoroughly it will provide this. If you do not understand it, get someone who does to explain it to you. It is vital.

Of limited value are privately offered insurance plans that pay you so much per day for every day you are in the hospital. Few hospitalizations last long enough that such insurance will pay more than a very small portion of your expenses. Policies that insure you for only a particular kind of illness, such as cancer (some may also include other diseases), are also of questionable value although, if there is a strong family history of the particular illness, you may want to reconsider. If this kind of policy is all that is available, rather than a supplementary major medical policy, which would pick up where your regular insurance stops, it again may be worth a second look. Some coverage may be better than none at all. However, if you feel your regular coverage is inadequate, try to obtain a major medical policy which will provide benefits regardless of what kind of medical needs you have and how long you are in the hospital. You really cannot predict what sort of medical treatment you will require in the future.

HOT spot If your company does not periodically automatically adjust your coverage to cover inflation, you will need to ask it to increase your insurance by the additional amount needed.

Long-term care and disability insurance

Coverage for long-term nursing home care, which Medicare does not pay, can be obtained with various options available. However, it is very expensive.

> **E-Z TIP**
>
> If your employer will pay for disability coverage, you may want to take the premiums you would not have to pay and invest these on a regular basis.

If you anticipate someone in your family may need this kind of care, it may be helpful to consult with an attorney to see what if any possibilities are available to limit the drain on financial assets. The sooner this is done the better, ideally several years before you expect the care will be needed, although obviously this is not always possible.

Some people may need disability insurance as badly as they need life and medical insurance. This covers you if you become disabled and are unable to work. Unfortunately, if you have to go buy your own individual policy it is quite expensive, and coverage may be limited. Again, you can save money by taking a higher deductible. If your employer provides disability coverage at no cost, consider yourself fortunate. If it is offered at some charge think seriously about taking it.

If you pay the premiums for disability insurance yourself, the benefits are currently free of federal income tax. If your employer provides coverage and pays the premiums, benefits are subject to taxation. Some companies will permit you to make the choice. Usually it will be better to permit the employer to pay, but which

> **note**
>
> Social Security can provide limited disability benefits, and many people are covered by their employer's Workers' Compensation insurance if they are injured at work.

is best for you will depend on your particular situation, taking into consideration your health, probability of being injured, and other financial obligations.

Home and auto insurance

What was said about life insurance applies to automobile and homeowner's insurance. Check the financial soundness of the company you

HINT

are considering and compare the rates. If you possibly can, try to obtain information on how satisfied the company's policyholders are with claims and other services. When considering automobile coverage, always take uninsured motorists coverage if it is available. Few people will ever need it, but disasters have happened because it had not been obtained. This covers you if you are in an accident caused by someone who has no insurance or is underinsured.

Conventional wisdom says take the highest deductible you can afford on both your automobile and homeowner's coverage. Conventional wisdom is usually correct on this one, but in some cases you may find only a limited number of deductibles offered and the savings minimal. In such instances, a lower deductible may make sense, unless you want to look at what another company has to offer. Your automobile collision coverage will pay no more than the actual cash value of your car, what you could reasonably expect to receive if you sold it. As a result, in many instances, once an automobile reaches an age of seven to ten years, it may no longer be practical to retain the collision coverage, when you consider your deductible amount plus the premium charged. Some companies may advise you to drop it. Others may refuse to write it.

Should you have occasion to rent a car, you may not need those expensive daily collision damage waivers the rental companies encourage you to buy. Often regular automobile insurance policies provide rental-car coverage, as well as for the cars you own. However, your regular deductibles will remain in effect. Many premium or gold credit cards also cover this. Do carefully check to be certain that you are covered in some way, before you rent the vehicle.

Try to obtain homeowner's or renter's insurance which covers you for all perils other than those specifically excluded. Some policies provide protection only for the limited number of perils indicated. They are usually cheaper, but could leave you vulnerable to a serious loss. Insurance against flood or earthquake is not included in either type of policy. If you feel the need, it will be extra, somewhat expensive, and possibly not available. You should still explore the possibility of obtaining it. Buy replacement coverage when you purchase your homeowner's (or renter's) policy. The additional cost is worth it. Otherwise, the company is only obligated to pay you the fair-market value of your possessions should they be destroyed or stolen. The new furniture you bought last month is now used furniture. Used furniture has a fair-market value well below what you paid for it. Likewise, make certain your home is insured for an adequate amount that, if totally destroyed, it would be replaced. Keep in mind that most policies pay only very limited amounts for such items as jewelry, furs, silverware, coin and stamp collections, firearms, and computers. If you want to cover these things for an additional amount, you will have to buy a *personal property floater*, and professional appraisals of the things to be covered may be required at your expense. Unless you can conveniently secure these items in a safe deposit box or safe, the additional cost may be worth it. There is little reason to have things you do not feel comfortable or safe using.

Liability insurance

 One place you definitely do not want to be penny wise and pound foolish is on your automobile and homeowners liability insurance. *Liability insurance* is what pays the damages you would be obligated to pay if you are at fault in an accident. Never drive with just the minimum coverage required by your state to meet its financial responsibility laws. Buy as much as the company will sell you and you can reasonably afford. Additional amounts cost surprisingly less than you may think after you have paid for the initial minimum required coverage. Adequate liability coverage makes sure you will not lose everything you have should you have the misfortune to be involved in a major accident. It also encourages the insurance company to stay and legally defend you rather than pay a claimant the limit on a small policy and then run, leaving you to defend yourself against any suits for a larger settlement. Carry as much homeowner's liability insurance as you do automobile, if you can possibly afford it. Most companies

Buy the insurance coverage you really need. Consider its cost a normal, continuing expense.

will offer to their better risks policy limits of up to $300,000. Some offer more. Unfortunately, your homeowner's insurance does not normally cover you for liability which may result from your job or business. Unless you are self employed, most likely your employer's policy covers you. Check to make sure. Should you start a business of your own, even part time, you will probably need to obtain coverage.

Title insurance

When you sell your home, do not destroy the title insurance policy you probably received when you purchased it. While it is extremely rare, it is possible to be sued over an alleged faulty title, even though you no longer own the property. You are still covered under the policy you had when you bought the home, and there are never any additional premiums to pay to keep that coverage in force.

> **note** Probably the mortgage lender required title insurance in order to approve your loan. If you deal with one that does not, insist on it anyway.

Umbrella policies

DEFINITION

As certain court settlements have ballooned into astronomical amounts, some people felt the need to obtain *umbrella liability policies*. These provide coverage, usually up to one million dollars, after your regular automobile or homeowner's coverage is exhausted. Insurance companies are naturally very particular about who are their customers for these. A single speeding ticket within the last three years may be enough to disqualify you. You may also feel you really have no need for such extensive insurance. However, if you do want it, and the company will sell it to you, it is not particularly expensive.

Many companies will offer you a discount if they insure both your home and your automobiles. Do not be too quick to change companies just to save a few dollars, if you are satisfied with the service you have been receiving. While it does not happen very often, you could have difficulty obtaining the coverage you want elsewhere. For example, since Hurricane Andrew hit Florida in 1992, some insurance companies have been reluctant to write new homeowner's or renter's coverage in that state, or at least parts of it. However, many of them have permitted present policy holders to renew. If you have had the same automobile insurance company for a while, it may be more willing to cover a new teenage driver than another would be. And yes, though it may be quite boring, read your policies. Many are standard, but not all of them are. For example, you could discover that your automobile insurance does not cover you if alcohol or racing are involved. Most policies do, although do not expect the company to be in a very good mood at renewal time.

If you are fortunate enough to have a boat, a piece of rental property, or even a very modest vacation home, you will need additional insurance, including liability coverage, as do people in certain occupations and professions. Discuss any special needs you may have with an insurance agent whom you feel you can trust. It is obvious, but sometimes forgotten. Do not take foolish risks. Do not buy coverage you do not need or for risks so small you can safely insure yourself.

Should you ever have difficulty in making an insurance claim or settling any other dispute with your insurance company, try to resolve it first by discussing the situation with the company's representatives. However, if all else fails you can ask the office of the Insurance Commissioner of your state to intervene on your behalf. You should be able to find the telephone number in your phone book. There is no charge for their services, but they will need copies of all your bills, correspondence, and any other documentation pertaining to your claim, so be sure to make copies of everything before sending originals to insurance companies for reimbursement.

With realistic effort and study, the mystery can be taken out of insurance matters. Nearly all of us need some insurance. Once we understand what we need and how best to obtain it we can go on to more interesting financial matters.

Chapter 25

Taxing matters: planning for retirement and taxes

What you'll find in this chapter:

- How much Social Security pays
- Pensions and salary reduction plans
- Employee stock ownership plans
- Individual retirement accounts
- Some IRA and annuities considerations

So much could be and has been written about both retirement planning and dealing with taxation, that all we can really do here is cover a few key points. Depending on your situation, you may want to do some further research on either or both of these subjects. We treat them together here, because they sometimes are closely linked.

Social Security

Let us begin by dealing first with the basic area of Social Security. Unfortunately, there are numerous rumors circulating about the program that have many people needlessly worried. Social Security began in the 1930s, and has been in force for over 60 years. At times, reserves to pay for future benefits have been strained, and claims the program will eventually "go broke" can be heard almost daily. When Social Security encountered troubles in the past, Congress and the President have always stepped in to deal with them. There is little reason to believe they would refuse in the future, or that the difficulties would be so great they cannot be resolved. This does not mean changes will not be made to Social Security. Some of these may be dramatic, but the essentials of the program are almost certain to continue. You can count on your Social Security benefits to be there when you are ready to retire. What you should not count on is Social Security adequately covering all your retirement expenses. In fact, it was never intended to do that. Unfortunately, millions of Americans have little else.

Currently, you qualify for Social Security retirement benefits by earning 40 credits of work. The formula for determining credits changes slightly each year, but essentially full-time workers can expect to earn four credits per calendar year. For disability benefits you need 30 credits, 20 of which must have been earned within the last 10 years. Social Security will also pay certain family and survivor benefits to the spouse and young children of workers who have 30 credits. At 65, those eligible for retirement benefits are also eligible for Medicare hospital and medical insurance even if they continue working. There is also a very small one-time death benefit payable

> **HOT** spot Both of America's major political parties are firmly committed to protecting Social Security. It is too popular and too vital to be permitted to die.

to a worker's spouse or young children. As you can see, Social Security can do quite a lot of different things. It is a good idea to familiarize yourself with its benefits.

Reduced retirement benefits are available as early as age 62. For full benefits, you must wait until age 65 and, in the year 2003, the age for full benefits will gradually increase until it reaches 67 in 2027. How much you receive each month depends on what age you start receiving benefits and how much you earned. Social Security uses your 35 best years of earnings to determine the benefit amount. A married person may receive either his or her own work benefit or 50 percent of the spouse's benefit, whichever is higher. Upon the death of a spouse, the survivor receives the higher of the two benefits. Widows' benefits can be received as early as age 60, and divorced persons are also eligible to receive payments based on the record of the former spouse. Until you reach age 70, benefits are reduced if you continue to work. How much of your Social Security income will be taxable in your retirement years depends on the amount of other income you have at that time. At present, single persons with incomes of $25,000 or less (including Social Security) and married couples with incomes up to $32,000 pay no taxes on Social Security benefits. Those with greater incomes are taxed, but not on the entire amount.

HINT

There is one critical step everyone needs to take in regard to Social Security. That is to periodically check the record of your earnings for possible errors. Given that Social Security must keep track of millions of people, it is not surprising that these are by no means rare. Making the check and correcting an error, in theory, appears rather easy. In reality, it may take some persistence. You start the process by requesting Social Security to send you the necessary form to request a "Personal Earnings and Benefit Estimate Statement." This can be done by either calling or visiting your local Social Security office, or by telephoning 800-772-1213 between the hours of 7 a.m. and 7 p.m. EST on weekdays. The first challenge you may

Because of frequent changes in Social Security regulations, it is best to check with your local office for details on your personal eligibility and benefits or that of your family.

encounter is simply getting through to someone, even an automated service. Lines are especially busy early in the week and early in the month. It may also be best to avoid Fridays.

Once you are successful in requesting the form and receive it, carefully provide the basic information requested and return it. It may take a while, so again patience is necessary. Eventually, however, you should receive the statement. This will furnish you with some theoretical estimates of what benefits you could receive, and most important will include a detailed report of your earnings reported to Social Security for every year you have worked.

It is important to check each year's entry. The best way to do this is to compare the figures with your past W-2 forms and federal income tax returns. You should never dispose of these no matter how old. Be especially careful to check any self-employment earnings. Errors are far more likely to occur with these than with wages and salaries reported on a W-2.

Copies of past
HINT returns may possibly be obtained from the Internal Revenue Service, but this will require further time and inconvenience.

Should you find errors, it will be necessary to contact your local office or the telephone number indicated in the statement. You will be advised as to what information you will need to furnish in order to get your account corrected. Be prepared to supply exactly what is requested, and be ready for the possibility of having to discuss your situation with more than one person before problems are completely resolved. Patience and determination will enable you to eventually prevail. Social Security benefits are simply too important not to do so. And, remind your spouse to also check his or her account. It would be a good idea to repeat this process about every five years. Social Security maintains a web site (http://www.ssa.gov) which may provide some helpful information.

Pensions and salary reduction plans

DEFINITION

In addition to Social Security, many workers will be eligible for some sort of pension benefits. Recent years have seen a drastic change in these. Most companies that maintained pension plans did so on what is known as a *defined benefit basis*. Based on your salary and years of service, the company promised to pay a certain amount each year once you retired. In many cases, all payments made into the pension fund were made by the employer.

Today, defined benefit plans are rapidly going the way of the dinosaur. Eventually, virtually all pensions will be *defined contribution plans*. Employees are not guaranteed any specific amount when they retire. Instead, the employer agrees to contribute a certain amount of money to the employee's account each year. Some of these plans are known as *cash-balance pensions*. If your company has one of these, make sure you understand both its benefits and limitations. How much you receive on retirement will depend on how successfully the plan trustees have invested the contributions.

HOT spot How much all of these contributions by either employer or employee will yield depends on how well they are invested, and increasingly today that may depend on the employee.

Not all, but many defined contribution pension plans are linked to 401k plans, or in the case of not-for-profit organizations, 403b plans. In addition to any amounts contributed by the employer, frequently the employer will also match up to a certain point additional contributions made by the employee. Some plans may require employees to contribute a particular amount each year if they wish to participate.

Many plans require that employees determine how retirement money will be invested. A typical plan may have a menu of five or six choices, each one resembling a mutual fund. One may be a money-market fund, another bonds, still another for stocks, along with several other choices which may include various kinds of stocks, bonds, real estate, or

> *note* Stocks should provide greater returns if left alone to allow their profits to compound.

international markets. The participants determine what percentage of their money will be invested in each fund. Details vary from plan to plan, but periodically the percentages may be changed, and it may be possible to shift funds from one account to another.

Previous chapters in this book can serve as an introduction to the various kinds of investment choices and also the need for asset allocation many 401k participants will confront. Again every family's situation is different, and so are the plans. It is impossible to devise a formula for investing retirement funds that will be suitable for everybody. Still, a few general rules may prove helpful. Normally, the younger you are the greater the percentage of your retirement money should be in stocks. Workers in their twenties or thirties have quite a few years to recover from any possible market downturns, and also many years to benefit from the higher average returns stocks pay over other kinds of investments. As you get older, you can begin to shift a greater percentage of your money into bonds or even a money-market fund. However, older workers normally should have some money in stocks. Many of us can look forward to a rather lengthy retirement, and we also need to provide for the surviving spouse.

Even older workers should not make the mistake of putting too much money into a pension money-market fund. Yes, the principal is safe, but the returns are meager. If you are faced with the reality that all you will have at your retirement is your pension and Social Security, then you do need to be more conservative as you get closer to retirement age. However, if you have other savings and investments, you can accept somewhat more prudent risk.

Other funds and retirement plans

Some plans offer a particular type of fund known as a **stable-value fund** (or **guaranteed-investment contract**). Several IRA programs also offer it as an option. It looks something like a bond or money-market fund, but really is not either. Unlike the other investment choices you may be given, this one guarantees to pay a particular rate of interest for a specific period of time, perhaps as much as a year. After that, the rate may be raised or lowered. There may also be a guarantee that at no time will the interest rate be permitted to drop below a certain specified point. In addition, as in the case of a money-market fund, the value of your principal is guaranteed not to decline. Other than for shifts in the interest rate, there is no market risk. This type of fund almost always pays a higher rate of interest than a money-market fund, and at times may provide a better total rate of return than a bond fund, which of course is subject to market risk.

HOT spot When it is finally time to retire, you will have to make critical decisions about how you will receive your 401k money. Once made these cannot be changed. It is important to begin to prepare for that day now.

If a fund with some of the above guarantees is available, it is a good choice for a certain core portion of your retirement account. In a bull market, it is true, stocks will outperform it, but in stagnant and bear markets, it will help you sleep better. Again, what percentage of the contributions to your retirement account should be invested in this manner differs from individual to individual. Probably, the less risk you can afford to take the greater the amount you might want to protect here.

Guarantees do come with a price. Retirement plans that make them available are able to do so because they are putting your money in stable, long-term investments. For example, they may be buying thirty-year Treasury bonds which they plan to hold all the way to maturity. These yield a predictable stream of interest, are very safe, and will be worth their face value when they finally mature. Mortgages are another place some of the money might be invested.

note

For this approach to work, the plan's investments have to be undisturbed for long periods of time. As a result, if you do commit money to such a fund, unlike your other options in many cases, it may have to stay there permanently or, at best, can be shifted to other investment choices only gradually over a number of years. Therefore, a stable-value fund is a good place for some of your retirement contributions, but definitely not all of them. To put all of your money here is to lose too much choice and potential opportunity.

For many employees, their 401k plan will ultimately be the most valuable asset they own. It is wise to know as much about it as possible. Read and carefully study any literature that is provided about it. When you receive account statements be sure to review them. If your company has a resource person to assist you with understanding the plan or makes seminars available to help explain it, take advantage of these opportunities to learn as much as you possibly can.

Something should be said about taxes and 401k plans. Any money contributed by your employer or you in the form of a salary reduction is not taxable in the year the contribution is made. There are legal limits on the amount that can be contributed in a single year but, as usual, these will affect very few small investors. Your employer should be able to provide you with details on limitations. What your account earns in the years before retirement is also free from taxation until it is withdrawn. It is the ability to defer taxes that makes these plans so desirable, and why many, if not most, people should contribute as much to them as they possibly can. The younger you are and the more years you can contribute, the greater the advantage. If a 401k or or 403b plan is available to you, take advantage of it. Especially if your employer matches contributions, try to make yours as large as you can. The employer's part may be the equivalent of a first-year return of as much as 50 percent! There are few opportunities elsewhere to earn that kind of money.

> **note** Because taxes are being deferred both on the original contributions and what they are able to earn, you have considerably more money working for you than you would otherwise.

Obviously, there are some drawbacks as well. Money you put into 401k or 403b plans is money that should not be touched. It is now possible to borrow from your account, but such a loan should be made only as a last resort, when there is no reasonable alternative other than the loan shark or his sometimes legal near-equivalent. If your loan is not paid back within five years, or ten to thirty when it is used to help purchase your principal residence, the IRS considers it a permanent withdrawal. You will then be assessed both regular taxes on the amount plus penalties.

Except under certain very limited circumstances, if you receive money from your plan (and it is not a loan) before you are 59 and one-half, or before you permanently retire at age 55, you will be subject not only to the ordinary rate of taxation that applies, but a penalty of 10 percent of the amount received. Avoid such situations at all costs. If you receive a lump-sum distribution from your plan, it could occur because you left your job, the employer terminated the plan, or some other reason usually beyond your control. The IRS will give you 60 days to roll over the money into some other tax-deferred plan such as an IRA or another 401k. If you do so, you avoid both the penalty plus any regular taxation. If you are not sure what to do, get help from an employer, tax professional, or financial consultant. Delay can be extremely costly.

> **HOT spot** Should an employer terminate any kind of pension plan, profit sharing plan, or employee stock ownership plan (ESOP), you also need to make a rollover on any lump sum cash received in order to escape taxes and possible penalties.

Employee stock ownership plans

Some companies make available employee stock ownership plans as part of a 401k or as a separate benefit. Participation in them is optional, but they are often good deals for both employer and worker. Employers offer them because they have concluded that employees who own some of the company are more likely to be better and more motivated workers. The plans can also save the company money when they can be used for part of the employer's contribution to a 401k.

Employees benefit because they will usually obtain shares at prices below the market cost, may receive additional ones free, and can pay for the shares they do purchase with modest sums over a period of time. In some cases, employees may be able to purchase stock in excellent companies that are otherwise privately held and whose shares are not available to the public. Florida-based Publix Supermarkets is such an example. Its stock has not been traded either on an exchange or in the over-the-counter market. However, employees who wish to do so can obtain limited amounts. Should they leave the company, they can either sell it back to the company, almost certainly at a profit, or retain it until they do wish to sell. Few who have participated in the Publix plan ever regretted doing so, and many are quick to sign up to buy more shares whenever they become eligible.

There can be much satisfaction in working for a not-for-profit organization, and many 403b plans, which they offer instead of a 401k, are excellent. Unfortunately, not-for-profits do not have ESOPs. They have no stock to sell. This is one place where their employees are at a definite disadvantage. Perhaps someday a creative and caring not-for-profit corporation may attempt to devise a reasonable substitute which would benefit its employees. While there would undoubtedly be various legal obstacles and ethical questions to face, it might not be impossible. Maybe one in the health care business could devise a plan which gives employees the option to purchase shares in several pharmaceutical companies, who would elect to participate and make shares available at a favorable price. Educational institutions might devise one made up of publishing companies. Quite possibly some sort of plan might even be developed for government workers. Employees working in not-for-profits are usually already making a sacrifice by receiving lower salaries and wages. It would seem these organizations have some sort of moral obligation to do what they can to assist those making the financial sacrifices, when it may cost them little or nothing to do so.

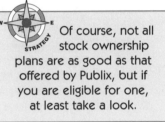

Of course, not all stock ownership plans are as good as that offered by Publix, but if you are eligible for one, at least take a look.

Individual retirement accounts

Individual retirement accounts, or IRAs as they are more commonly called, are a convenient way for small investors to defer taxes on money they put aside for investments. Starting with the 1998 tax year, two types are available, the Traditional IRA and the new Roth IRA. Let us first turn to the Traditional IRA.

Before opening an IRA account with a financial institution, it would be best to check with it on the current rules, as changes in legislation may modify past regulations.

If you, or, in the case of a married couple, your spouse is employed, you may put money into a Traditional IRA account. Currently the limit is $2,000 for a single person and $4,000 for a married couple ($2,000 for each), provided you have at least that much income from employment. Individuals covered by an employer-sponsored pension plan and with adjusted gross incomes of $30,000 or less have a fully deductible contribution, while those with incomes no more than $40,000 will find them partially deductible. Married couples will be able to deduct their contributions if the couple's adjusted income is no more than $50,000. Contributions are partially deductible with an adjusted income up to $60,000. An individual not in an employer-sponsored pension plan may deduct his or her contribution even if the spouse is, provided their combined adjusted gross income is no more than $150,000. Partial deductions are permitted up to $160,000. If a single person is not covered by a pension plan, or neither spouse is, then contributions are always

> **HINT** Even nondeductible contributions should be worthwhile, as earnings in a Traditional IRA account are not taxed until the money is withdrawn.

deductible. With the new, more generous income limits, many small investors should be able to make deductible contributions.

Once you reach age 59 and one-half, money may be withdrawn from the account without penalty and is taxed as ordinary income. You must start to make withdrawals by age 70 and one-half. Certain amounts may be withdrawn at any age without penalty for a first-time home purchase or for higher education expenses.

If you are self-employed you may put self-employment income either into an IRA or a *Keogh plan*. Keoghs are quite similar to an IRA, but permit considerably larger contributions per year. How much in part depends on the kind of plan you have. Many institutions that sponsor IRAs also sponsor Keoghs and, if you think you are eligible and interested, they will be happy to provide you with the details.

> **HOT spot** It is possible to have both a Keogh plan and an IRA, provided you have some self-employment income.

There are income limits for the Roth IRA, but they are high enough that they should affect few small investors. As in the case of Traditional IRAs, single taxpayers may contribute up to $2,000, and married couples $2,000 each. Contributions are not tax deductible, but earnings in the account are tax free. They may be withdrawn free of penalty once the account is five years old and you are at least 59 and one-half. Limited earlier withdrawals are permitted for home purchase, and withdrawals may be made for some educational expenses. There is no mandatory age at which withdrawals must start. Subject to various limitations, Traditional IRAs may be converted to Roth IRAs.

Some IRA considerations

Deciding on an IRA requires the small investor to make some critical decisions. Obviously, the first is whether you want a Roth or a Traditional account. If you already have a Traditional IRA do you want to convert it to a Roth IRA? The financial institution which will manage the account should be able to help with these decisions. However, a few general guidelines can be given. If you have fewer than ten years to retirement you probably will do better with the Traditional IRA and should not convert an existing one. Taxpayers with more than ten years to retirement in most cases will benefit more from the Roth IRA. You might also want to convert a Traditional IRA, but be aware that you will have to pay the taxes (not penalties) that will be due on the conversion amount. Since you never have to make contributions to an IRA, you may want to leave your Traditional IRA alone and open a second Roth IRA. This can legally be done.

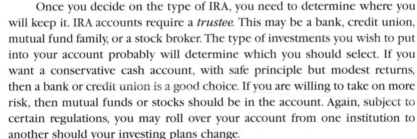

Once you decide on the type of IRA, you need to determine where you will keep it. IRA accounts require a *trustee*. This may be a bank, credit union, mutual fund family, or a stock broker. The type of investments you wish to put into your account probably will determine which you should select. If you want a conservative cash account, with safe principle but modest returns, then a bank or credit union is a good choice. If you are willing to take on more risk, then mutual funds or stocks should be in the account. Again, subject to certain regulations, you may roll over your account from one institution to another should your investing plans change.

Some types of investments, such as general partnerships and collectibles, may not be placed in IRA accounts. Some other types which may be, such as limited partnerships, United States gold coins, and platinum, should not be. IRAs are not the place to speculate. Small investors should not be doing that anyway, but if you lose money on an investment in an IRA you have no tax-deductible capital loss, which you would have on the same investment outside the IRA. They are a nice place for bonds and stocks with high dividends, since the interest and dividends are shielded from immediate taxation. For the same reason, they are also a good place for mutual funds that tend to make extensive capital gains distributions each year. Likewise, capital gains from stocks you sell at a profit are tax-deferred.

One factor often overlooked with the Traditional IRA (and also 401k and 403b plans), is that the money coming out of the account is taxed as ordinary income. As a result, it may be taxed at a higher rate than if the account were not an IRA and any profits were eligible for capital gains tax rates. Currently capital gains are taxed at no higher than 20 percent, while many taxpayers with even modest incomes may be in the 28 percent bracket. There is also the possibility that at some future date Congress may lower the capital gains rate even lower. This does not mean do not contribute money to a Traditional IRA. It does mean that, to benefit from the account, you need to leave the money untouched for as long as you reasonably can in order that tax deferral has time to do its magic.

Annuities

Annuities are another matter which really can only be touched upon briefly here. Pension and insurance benefits are often paid fully or partially as a kind of annuity (an income for life or a stated number of years), but that is not what we are discussing at this point.

HOT spot If you are interested in annuities, you would be advised to seek professional financial advice to help you make the right decision about which one to purchase.

DEFINITION

What we are dealing with now are annuities that are available for purchase by individuals as an additional vehicle for saving and tax deferral. *Annuities* are sponsored by banks and insurance companies, possibly in conjunction with mutual fund companies. Some have various death benefits, but their real advantage is that while the money you contribute to them is not free from taxes, once it is in your account what it earns is tax deferred until you withdraw it, and it is taxed as ordinary income. Unlike an IRA or a 401k plan, you may make unlimited contributions. There are essentially two types: One pays you a fixed rate of interest for a particular period of time, after which the rate can be adjusted. The other, known as the *variable annuity*, will normally invest in stocks or mutual funds. Its returns will fluctuate.

There are limitations on withdrawals, and some have severe surrender charges if you close the account within the first couple of years. However, for people who need to defer money from taxation or provide additional retirement income, they may be useful. After you are 59 and one-half there is no tax penalty for early withdrawal, so they may be

Annuities can offer some nice payout options, including a monthly income for the rest of your life.

particularly useful for elderly persons who wish to use an annuity as a sort of tax-deferred bank account. Make sure you understand all options, charges, fees, and restrictions before you buy. Be certain the sponsoring institution is financially sound.

Some conclusions

Your retirement planning is often the most important financial planning you will be called upon to do. If done wisely, retirement years can be fulfilling and provide considerable opportunity. It is never too early to start. In fact, the earlier you start the more you can take advantage of the small investor's most powerful weapon, compounding.

Wise retirement planning can also save taxes. Take advantage of this as much as possible. However, no investment should ever be made solely on the basis of tax considerations. Many persons, who lost all sense of reason in a desperate attempt to avoid taxes, have discovered that questionable tax shelters are the only places an otherwise rational individual will throw away a dollar in order to save fifty cents. You want sound investments inside your retirement vehicles. Choose carefully, and they will serve you well.

Chapter 26

Final matters: wills and living wills

Why you need a will

Not much needs to be said on this subject. What is said is terribly important. It is essentially this: Unless you are an absolute pauper with no assets at all, you need a will. You need that will not when you are older, or next year, or next month. You need that will *now*. If you die without a will, at the

CAUTION

very least, you will cause your family or other heirs much inconvenience, delay, and unnecessary expense. You may also cause them to lose all or part of what you wanted them to have. You will lose forever the opportunity to make a final declaration about who and what are important to you. If you refuse to make a will, you will still die someday (there are people who refuse to believe this), but instead of you, the

note It would be a great tragedy to apply successfully what this book has attempted to teach, and then abandon the estate you worked so hard to establish by refusing to make a will.

state will determine who receives what was yours. If you do not like what the state would decide, there will be absolutely nothing you can do about it.

Contrary to what you may have been told, having a will made is not expensive. If you doubt this go now to the telephone directory and find the telephone numbers of several attorneys in your area. Call their offices and ask what they charge for a basic will. You will probably be surprised. The laws of each state vary; sometimes they are complex, and from time to time they change. The modest amount you save by having an attorney write your will is definitely worth the cost to make certain it is done properly. Have your will written by an attorney in the state which is your legal residence. If you move to another, have a new will drawn up. Normally, you should leave the original with your attorney, and keep a copy in your safe deposit box.

> **E-Z TIP** Periodically review your will to see if any changes are necessary or desirable. These also should be made by an attorney. In many cases it is not necessary to rewrite the entire document

The real expense involved in estates is not in having the will written, but in having it probated once you have died. Regardless of who wrote it, the will must be probated before its provisions can be carried out. In almost all cases this will require an attorney. This is why it is often best to leave the original document with an attorney in the first place. There will be no problems in finding it when it is needed, but the attorney that wrote the will does not have to be the one who probates it. For probating a will and the additional legal work required to settle the deceased's estate, attorneys receive either a percentage of the estate or will negotiate some other fee arrangement, usually an hourly rate. Depending on where you live, there may also be possible estate and inheritance taxes which must be paid. At least to some extent these expenses are usually unavoidable. Property jointly owned as joint tenants with rights of survivorship should normally be exempt from probate (this may not be true of all other legal forms of joint ownership). Life insurance proceeds should also escape probate.

Subject to any legal limitations in your state, you may do whatever you wish with your assets in your will. Consider leaving something to the charitable organizations you have supported during your life. You are making a final declaration of what you believe is important. While you will probably want to leave assets to family and relatives, you are not obligated to leave them to persons you believe would use them harmfully or irresponsibly. If you feel it is necessary to put restrictions on their use, such as to pay educational expenses, an attorney can help. You have worked hard for what you are now giving away. Give it away carefully and lovingly. If you do, a portion of you does, in its own special way, continue to live.

Under no circumstances ever attempt to draw up any kind of trust without an attorney.

Living trusts

These days, there is much talk about living trusts as a way to avoid probate. Living trusts and other kinds often do make much sense for people with considerable assets. However, even they will still need a will. For the average person, a living trust could wind up costing more than it would save, and may create certain inconveniences. If you still think you might benefit from one, certainly discuss it with an attorney.

Living wills

Finally, a few words might be said about living wills. A living will is a simple document which advises family and medical personnel what medical

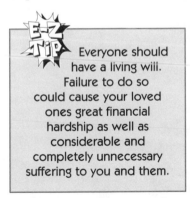

Everyone should have a living will. Failure to do so could cause your loved ones great financial hardship as well as considerable and completely unnecessary suffering to you and them.

and surgical treatment you want and do not want, in the event you are in such physical condition that you can no longer communicate that information. It can be revoked or changed at any time you wish. For a small fee an attorney can help you make one. A hospital or physician may also be able to provide you with helpful information on this matter. *Choice In Dying, Inc.*, 200 Varick Street, 10th Floor, New York, NY 10014-4810 (telephone 212-366-5540) may be able to bring you up to date on the current legal regulations pertaining to living wills in your state. In some instances, certain legal situations may make it necessary for medical personnel to act as if no living will existed. However, if you have one which makes your wishes clearly known, you will have done everything possible to assist physicians and family in carrying out your requests whenever they possibly can.

DEFINITION

Legally, living wills are a type of document known as an *advance directive*. You may want to consider expanding your living will to include other advance directive provisions. Among these are your instructions to cover conditions where you may not be conscious or able to respond, but the condition is not life threatening, and also those involving artificial nutrition and hydration. You may want to designate a "health care surrogate" who would be able to make health-care decisions for you when you cannot. You can also provide instructions on possible organ donation. Living wills and other advance directives may not be perfect documents but, in certain situations they could be of considerable value to both you and your family. Give copies to your spouse, attorney, physician, health care surrogate, and anyone else you feel might have to make decisions about your medical treatment in the event you could not make these for yourself.

Chapter 27

When nothing seems to go right

You may want to wait until a later time to read this chapter. It is really intended for one of those periods when nothing seems to be going your way. If you are not having that kind of day, be thankful and consider going on to something else. However, if you are, then maybe this can help. I must admit I am writing these words after having had about a week full of days I would have been quite happy to cancel. So hopefully there is something here for both of us.

Sometimes, when things go wrong, we know we could have gone about them in a better way. Sometimes, despite our very best effort, nothing seems to turn out right. Perhaps you have been struggling to put aside $50 each month to start an investing nest egg. After all, does not this book urge you to begin now and to begin with modest amounts if that is all there is with which to begin? You have been proud because through real sacrifice you have been doing this for a full year, and you have invested the grand sum of $600 in your first mutual fund. Then the next month comes the unexpected and absolutely unavoidable car repair. You guessed it. The bill is $600 plus, of course, sales tax. You are right back at the starting gate, or even a step or two behind it.

Sometimes it gets worse. The month after the car repair, the $300 medical bill, which you thought was covered by insurance but is not, arrives in your mail box. Everything seems to be going in reverse. At times such as this, there can be an understandable urge to either give up and just curl up into a ball or to take what few remaining resources we have and exhaust them on one final binge before we lose them anyway. Those sound like reasonable alternatives to me.

 Resist the urge. An old Japanese proverb declares: "Fall down seven times; stand up eight." We have got to get up and go forward even though we do not want to do it and feel it is impossible anyway. You and I both are going to ask, "Why?" That is both a fair and honest question. Believe it or not (and let us admit there are those moments when we do not), it is a question that can be answered.

If you read to this point, you ARE probably aware by now that all financial markets and thus, all investments, involve risks. Markets never go forever in just one direction. If they did, there would be no risk, and it is reasonable risk, not foolish speculation, that financial markets reward you for taking. No risk means no rewards. We love the rewards, but we tend to forget that if markets never went south there would be none. Some days they do indeed go down.

> **note** It is tough to be an investor. It takes courage, good judgement, and especially patience.

Even more painful is that sometimes they stay that way for lengthy periods of time. Those that do not understand risk, or have taken on too much risk, will give up, and usually just about when things have reached the bottom.

Yes, investing is often difficult. So is life. And your life comes with no owner's manual. You have to learn how to live it by doing just that—living it. Maybe investing can give us some insights that can help us accomplish this successfully. Financial markets do not always go up because they involve risk. Human beings must face numerous risks every day. Inevitably, some days are going to be downers. No matter how hard we try to prevent that, it is essentially inevitable. The trouble is, if you give up and quit, chances just may be you are bailing out when things are about at their bottom. You could miss out on your own personal bull market that lies shortly ahead.

If you are not easily convinced (and maybe I am not either), then let us take our worse-case scenario. No honest person can ever guarantee you success in investing or anything else. That is where the risk factor again comes to play. Yes, there is always that possibility that you and I, despite real sweat and pain, will not be successful. In fact rather than gain we may wind up with less than when we started. We might even wind up with nothing. That is not pleasant, but it needs to be admitted. So does the alternative. Should we get in there and make it a good fight we might be dealt a knock-out blow. It will hurt badly. But at least, if nothing else, we will have earned the right to get back up and walk out of the ring with our heads held high and no sense of shame in our hearts. We fought the good fight, and nobody, including ourselves, ever has the right to demand more from us than that. We fell down seven times, but we got up eight.

> **HOT spot** Life is full of risks. It is more likely to reward in a variety of ways those who take them rather than those who refuse.

Now look at the alternative. Leave that ring without a fight, without so much as a scratch, and in the long run it is going to hurt a great deal more. For the rest of our lives, we will be haunted by the "Ghost of What Might Have Been" and his faithful traveling companion "If Only." They are a mean-spirited couple. They will give us no quarter. The only possible defense is to give them none. So do not.

If life, including our investing life, is going to bring those inevitable dark nights no matter what we do, we are faced with another decision. We can lie there flat on our backs and curse the darkness, hoping somehow we can find the strength to get up, or we can use that same darkness as a time for reflection, rebuilding, and finding new strength. Maybe there was nothing more we could have done, but maybe a second look reveals there was something we honestly missed the first time around. Perhaps a little more preventive maintenance could have made that car repair unnecessary. Maybe the vacation, while well deserved, was just a bit longer and more expensive than we should have attempted this year. Maybe that "it can't miss" investment which bombed was not researched as thoroughly as it could have been. This is a time for learning, not for wallowing in guilt. Consider

note Remember, even the most successful players never get a hit every time they come to the plate.

the money and time you may have lost as tuition. If you learned something from the experience, such as perhaps you need to start an emergency fund, then it truly was. Sir John Templeton has remarked that fully one-third of his investments turned out to be disappointments. But, do not dwell on his failures. Look at what he accomplished with his two-thirds that were successes. The Templeton Mutual Funds achieved a kind of legendary greatness for their success long before their founder decided to sell them.

Then, when things are at their darkest, it may be time to take inventory of what you accomplished. This does not mean some sort of nauseating, shallow call to "count your blessings." Rather, it is a reminder that though lately we may have been in something of a slump, in the past we may have pitched some pretty good games that we may have forgotten. Sit down to write a book about investing on one of those "bad" days and you may ask yourself why bother. Bills seem to increase at a far more rapid rate than family income. The big folks may not understand that plight. Many would-be small investors have been there. Do I honestly have anything to say? If I say it, is anybody going to care? If anybody would care, is anybody else going to be willing to risk enough to publish it? Who am I to give suggestions to others on how to handle their financial concerns? After tossing such depressing thoughts around for a while, I started to look over a portfolio of stocks and closed-end funds I had put together over a period of some years. Despite my pessimism, it looked better than I had dared hope. The vast majority had done reasonably well, and only a few were disappointing. I was quite satisfied with the total profit which would have been available had I chosen to liquidate everything.

> **HOT spot** We have all had our victories. Sometimes we forget to claim them, but they are ours, and we should not be embarrassed to savor them. They are the food that gives us the strength to go forward.

Certainly, many others have done better, but I had done this on my own, through trial and error and with limited funds, able to take only limited risk. Furthermore, I knew by doing it there was no magic involved. Others could do it also, and it might help if someone gave them some insight as to how. So, I kept on writing, and if you are now reading these words you will know that this book, once a dream, became a reality.

Maybe your past accomplishments have not been of a financial nature. Maybe you have taken on the far more challenging job of raising children, and when you look at them you are rather pleased at what you see. Perhaps in a time of crisis you were the only person in whom a friend could confide. Maybe you are a local hero in your neighborhood because you can fix broken things most other folks cannot. Possibly, despite that discouraging car repair, you found the vision to see that your determined efforts to invest may not yet have produced a profit, but they did substantially cut your losses. You are in a position to do battle again, if you have the will.

In his uplifting book *Discovering the Laws of Life,* John Templeton quotes the old Buddhist saying, "If you are facing in the right direction, all you need to do is keep on walking." There is much wisdom in these words. We may have temporary setbacks, but that is what they are, just temporary. If we have a sound plan for financial life and for the rest of our life, in time our journey should be a profitable one. "Fall down seven times. Stand up eight."

Feeling good about it all

Some readers may wonder why this chapter is included. Others, after they have been investing a while, may come to see it as absolutely essential. Saving and investing simply for the sake of saving and investing are of little or no value. As individuals, we cannot change the entire world even if we had the wisdom to know what sort of seemingly perfect place we would create. But there is none of us so powerless that what we do has absolutely no effect on others or our own future. If we are aware of that simple fact we can use it to make life a bit better and happier for ourselves and more people than we may think possible.

When fear and greed are kept in check, the investor is in an advantageous position to make sound decisions which over the long run prove profitable.

One of the initial places to start is by giving some of our money away. Yes, strange as it may first seem, one of the secrets to being a successful investor is to give some of our resources to others. John-Roger and Peter McWilliams, in their delightful and encouraging book *Do It! Let's Get Off Our But's,* provide us with a solution to understanding this seeming paradox. When you give some of your money away you are in effect saying to yourself, "I have more than I need." That can be beneficial in several ways. However, for the investor, it probably is most helpful in caging those two most dangerous monsters of all—fear and greed.

How much should we give? One possibility is the traditional tithe or 10 percent of your material increase. That is a fine goal if you can meet it, and indeed some people may even be able to exceed it. However, for a number of small investors the percentage will probably have to be adjusted downward with the hope and expectation that it can gradually be raised. You do not act prudently giving money away when the tires on your car are so badly worn they are dangerous. You do not act prudently giving money away while failing to provide adequate medical insurance for your family. You do not act prudently if you give so much money away that you have nothing left for occasional pleasures and thus make life dreary, monotonous, and discouraging. Again, common sense is the order of the day. Determine what you can comfortably give. Then try to give a little more. Leave it at that. Periodically review the situation to see if the figure needs adjusting up or down.

To whom should you give? Choose the recipients of your giving as carefully as you do your investments. If your money goes to causes in which you really believe, that will provide a sense of satisfaction. Your giving becomes still another investment. Should you have an interest or membership in a particular religious organization it can, of course, be one cause you support. However, it does not have to be the only one. Perhaps you may find organizations working to save the environment worthy of your support. Groups that feed the hungry both at home and abroad may also get your attention, or possibly it may be one that works at healing the physical and mental wounds of those who in one way or another have been abused. You can help with disaster relief, caring for abandoned animals, medical research, or educating disadvantaged minorities. The needs are numerous. Select ones that are personally meaningful to you.

> **note** Giving should be a part of your overall saving and investment program, but not all of it or none of it.

Should you give all your support to a single organization, or should it be spread around? There is no easy way to answer that question. Some feel that giving most or all of what we have to give to a single cause is more practical and efficient. Organizations will cut administrative overhead if they are acknowledging larger gifts. On the other hand, seeing your money working in a variety of places can generate your personal enthusiasm to do still more. Some charities will assist you in having a small amount automatically withdrawn by your bank from your checking account each month. That makes it economical for them to handle small gifts and, by the end of the year, your series of monthly modest contributions looks considerably larger.

Read the material that charitable organizations send you in response to your giving. If they provide you with an annual report, go over it as carefully as one from a business corporation.

While there may be an occasional exception, in most instances it is probably far better to give your money to a recognized organization than Cousin Harold, who is down on his luck and needs a lift. Responsible charities, including religious bodies, are organized as not-for-profit corporations. As such, they must submit to audits, file reports, and make themselves otherwise accountable. They may not be perfect, but misuse of funds is held to a minimum. Furthermore, gifts to such organizations are tax deductible if you are able to itemize your deductions on your federal income tax return. Cousin Harold may be well meaning, but you really cannot hold him accountable if he is not, and gifts to him are never deductible for tax purposes.

In addition to charities, you may find certain civic organizations are worthy of your support. Some help to preserve and restore historic buildings or in other ways improve the city. They may not always qualify as a tax-deductible charity, but if you find their

> HINT Make sure the charity is using your money effectively and efficiently. Determine if you want to continue supporting it or consider increasing your support.

work satisfying consider helping them. Naturally, review what they do and how well they do it as carefully as anything else you may support.

There is one group of organizations that you may wish to strike from consideration. These are the ones that engage in the obnoxious practice of making unsolicited telephone calls. You may want to make an occasional exception if it is an organization that you already know and feel genuinely deserves support. But groups that use these sort of fund-raising tactics can be considered first-class pests and, in addition, they often have high expenses because of the way they raise their money. They should not be encouraged to continue doing this.

Giving done reluctantly or out of a sense of duty may still manage to do the recipients some good. However, it does not do anything for the giver. Try to use your giving as a tool that adds meaning to your investing and as a source of personal growth and satisfaction. Take pride in the fact that you are financially secure enough to help others. Such an approach can contribute to results which, in turn, will produce still more satisfaction.

You may find several publications helpful in determining which charitable organizations you wish to support. These may be available at your local library or can be obtained directly from the publishing organizations. One is Gale Research's *Charitable Organizations of the U.S.: A Descriptive and Financial Information Guide*. Another excellent source is the *Wise Giving Guide* published by the National Charities Information Bureau. They can be reached at 19 Union Square West, New York, NY 10003. Publication 78, *Cumulative List of Organizations*, can be requested from the Internal Revenue Service. It includes thousands of charities which qualify for tax-deductible contributions. Your library may have still additional resources or be able to advise you where you can find them.

Helping-hand investments

For the reasons previously discussed, charitable giving belongs in every investment program. Why not go a step further and consider investments which have a positive, direct impact on the lives of other people? The opportunities for these may not be as numerous as in the case of traditional charities, but they exist. One of the best examples anywhere is Chicago's South Shore Bank, a truly amazing institution.

HOT spot Know that as your investing enables you to prosper, it will also enable you to do more to assist those you would like to help.

South Shore has been so successful it has attracted depositors from all fifty states and now serves as a consultant to other financial institutions in both rural and urban areas which seek to help those who need it the most. It is a successful bank with over twenty years of experience and one which, like conventional banking institutions, fully qualifies for the federal government's FDIC insurance on depositors' accounts.

note What makes South Shore distinctive is that it targets its loans for the rehabilitation of housing and for the establishment of small businesses. Most of the loan recipients probably would not qualify for assistance from other banks either because of their low income levels or declining neighborhoods or both. South Shore has found that such persons, if given an opportunity, are usually good financial risks. Indeed the bank has a lower loan default rate than most conventional banks. South Shore's programs in Chicago have been so successful that its parent organization, Shorebank Corporation, has also established a presence in both Cleveland and Detroit.

One of the most pleasant things about helping South Shore Bank help others is that it really does not cost you anything. Not only are the bank's deposits insured, it pays competitive interest rates. Every small investor needs some liquid, safe, stable investments such as bank accounts and certificates of deposit. A bank such as South Shore is worthy of consideration for some of this money. It can be contacted at 7054 South Jeffery Boulevard,Chicago, IL 60649-2096 (telephone: 800-669-7725).

Throughout the country are a number of credit unions which offer good terms to their depositors and provide excellent loan and other banking facilities, including financial counseling, to their members. Some of these are especially commendable because they serve groups who otherwise would have no or limited access to such help. Among them are American Indian tribes, residents of isolated rural areas, and others often overlooked by the typical financial institution. Should

> **note**
> About the only thing wrong with South Shore Bank is that it cannot be everywhere.

you be interested in helping these credit unions help others by depositing some of your money with them, you will find that if legally feasible they usually will welcome you as a member. A Supreme Court decision, based on a 1934 law, threatened to make it more difficult for them to do so than in the past, but Congress was supportive of efforts to make qualifying for membership as easy as possible. Legislation passed in 1998 by both houses of Congress and signed by the President should enable many people to join any credit union in which they wish to participate. As in the case of South Shore Bank, credit unions will normally provide deposit insurance and pay competitive rates of interest. Banking by mail makes them readily accessible

You may be able to obtain information on this kind of credit union from the New York office of the *National Federation of Community Development Credit Unions.* Over 150 credit unions who focus on serving low-income populations belong. Nearly all welcome persons of any income level as members. You can contact the Federation at 212-809-1850. It also maintains a web site on the Internet (http://www.natfed.org/) where you can find further details. In addition, you may read or hear about one of these credit unions or a similar institution in the financial media. You may also come across the office of some on your vacation travels, or there may be one not far from where you live. If one of these attracts your interest, why not make contact with it and consider becoming a member? This is a relatively painless, actually financially rewarding way to help those who really will benefit from it.

Accent the positive

Although it may still be something of a quiet calling rather than a thundering voice, the socially responsible investing movement is gaining strength, adherents, and respect these days. Its followers see investing as far more than a way to make money. Rather it is a tool to help heal the world and move it forward in a positive direction.

According to one of its chief advocates, financial counselor and author Gary Moore, the movement rests on three major principles:

1) Socially responsible investors engage in charitable giving.

2) Socially responsible investors also postpone some material rewards in order to stay out of or reduce debt, which Moore sees as a form of bondage.

3) Finally, socially responsible investors invest for the good of their neighbors as well as themselves.

The third principle essentially leads socially responsible investors to examine what products and services are provided by the companies whose stocks they are considering. If these do not benefit people or might actually harm them, the investment should be avoided. Traditionally such investors have avoided the so-called "sin" stocks, namely companies who derive all or much of their revenue from alcohol, tobacco, and gambling (now commonly referred to as gaming).

> **HOT spot** Investing in the economies of developing countries appeals to those investors who want to have a positive impact beyond the borders of their own country.

Various other "social screens" are also employed by different socially conscious investors these days. Some shun companies whose environmental records they consider poor. Others avoid stocks in the defense industry and nuclear power. Publishers of sexually exploitive or excessively violent material are rejected by some investors. Still others favor with their investments companies who make strong efforts to treat their employees fairly and avoid discrimination against women and minorities. On socially responsible grounds, concerned investors will invest in health care and mortgage-based securities (which help to finance housing) while avoiding junk bonds and other high-risk speculative investments which can fuel excess in the financial market place.

Deciding your social stance

What social and ethical standards investors should uphold is not a matter on which there is common agreement. One may see absolutely no wrong in owning shares in defense companies. Another might even argue that, when properly employed, junk bonds can have a positive impact. In the end, all investors are called upon to examine their own principles and wrestle with their conscience.

 Perhaps one concept that may be helpful is to ask yourself if you would avoid using a product or service because you thought it would be personally harmful. If the answer is yes, then should you, through your investing, encourage others to use it? The reverse of this is, of course, to seriously consider investing in companies who produce things you have found to be useful, helpful, and of high quality.

If you decide to establish some social criteria for your personal investing, it is not too difficult to apply it when investing in individual companies. The situation becomes somewhat more complex when considering mutual funds, as the individual investor has no control over the content of the fund's portfolio.

Gary Moore notes that there are a number of quality mutual funds which do screen their investments. These include such well-established ones as many of the Templeton funds, the Calvert Group, the Pioneer Funds, and the Washington Mutual Investors Fund of the American Funds group. There are others as well. However, not all have the same social standards, and investors will have to match theirs to that of the fund. As with all mutual funds, their investment records are varied. Some have have been outstanding.

CAUTION Many mutual funds, which maintain high standards in their dealings with their investors and have excellent portfolios, may hold a few securities which particular investors would not feel comfortable purchasing if shopping for themselves.

note

Many socially responsible funds are load funds with a sales charge or other fee, but some are no-load. An example is the Pax World Fund, which even avoids U.S. Treasury securities because these can be used to finance defense spending. Another one is the Social Choice Fund, a balanced fund consisting primarily of a mix of stocks and bonds, which is sponsored by the College Retirement Equities Fund, commonly known as CREF. However this particular CREF fund is normally available only to those employed in higher education, although CREF does have other funds (without screens) open to anybody. Still another group, Domini Social Investments, includes both load and no-load versions, while Citizens Funds are no load.

In the end, investors are called upon to develop their own goals and standards. Are they willing to impose any social screens at all? At certain times those who have avoided tobacco and nuclear power have probably been thankful that they did so. A few years ago many wished too late that they had never heard of junk bonds, but it has to be admitted that certain investors who would categorically refuse all social and ethical screens have done quite well. In fact sometimes the "wages of sin" have been rather good. Tobacco and gambling stocks have been known to provide some investors with rather nice returns. Investors must ask themselves what they wish to accomplish. Are they at peace with their hearts? Do their investments give them a good feeling? Are they willing to pay a load or other charges to purchase mutual fund shares in socially responsible funds? Are they willing to accept some "contamination" in order to invest in a fund which targets its investments to a developing country? For example, the fund may help provide much needed capital while at the same time holding stock in the nation's tobacco company. Some investors may feel that, while they can avoid distasteful companies when purchasing individual stocks, for a variety of reasons it is not really practical when buying mutual funds. Others will just as strongly disagree.

note

There is no absolute standard. All investors may find it enlightening to pause from time to time and ask what their money is doing besides trying to earn more money. The answers may be disturbing. They may also be a source of much satisfaction.

Those with Internet access may find helpful information on funds with a conscience at SocialFunds.com (http://www.socialfunds.com). Some companies that market socially responsible funds, such as Citizens Funds and Domini, also have web sites focused on ethical investing.

Chapter 28

Putting it all together

As we noted, Adam Smith in *The Money Game* gave the classic comment, "If you do not know who you are, the stock market is an expensive place to find out." When we hurt physically, mentally, or spiritually, we really are not our true selves. We may not, at least for the moment, know who we are. Not only is that a painful state of affairs, but one in which our decision-making process is very likely to be flawed. At such moments, we may have far more critical things on our mind than our investments, but quite clearly people who are hurting in any major way should probably avoid financial decisions as much as possible until the pain subsides. Even people who are not severely hurting, but feel more than ordinary stress or other problems, may find making investment decisions difficult.

> **E-Z TIP** Obviously, there are countless other factors besides stress which may be affecting us, but if you wish to be an intelligent investor, you would be wise to first take care of yourself.

Good health leads to good wealth

Like investing, taking care of yourself is something that works best if it becomes habit forming. Adequate exercise, regular medical and dental care, and some time for fun and relaxation all help to keep the mind fit as well as the body, and that is what we need if decisions are to be based on sound thinking, not faulty emotions. Stephen Covey refers to the need to "sharpen the saw." If we do not provide the maintenance our minds and bodies need, we grow dull and unable to complete our tasks. Two of Covey's books, *The Seven Habits of Highly Successful People* and *First Things First*, may prove helpful in sharpening your saw and effectively managing your priorities and time. They are available in bookstores or through Franklin Covey Company, 2200 West Parkway Boulevard, Salt Lake City, UT 84119-2099 (telephone: 800-863-1492).

Maintaining a positive attitude is also important. It is difficult to be a successful long-term investor if you dread the thought of tomorrow and what it might bring. Helpful for giving you the right outlook on life may be some of the books authored by one of the greatest investors of all time, John Marks Templeton. A good place to start is with his work *The Templeton Plan*. Then go on to absorb *Treasures for the Mind and Spirit*, *Discovering the Laws of Life*, and *Worldwide Laws of Life*. The books may not make you financially rich, but they definitely do provide riches for the mind. These titles and others authored or edited by John Templeton can be obtained by contacting Templeton Foundation Press, Two Radnor Corporate Center, Suite 330, 100 Matsonford Road, Radnor, PA 19087-9166 (telephone: 800-621-8476).

Mental health is important, too

It should be obvious that when we need professional help, we should get it. That includes assistance from physicians, dentists, accountants, and attorneys. Competent help does not come cheaply but, as noted, we usually get what we pay for.

Some people take care of their physical bodies and will seek the assistance of an attorney when closing on a house or drawing up a will. However, they may be very reluctant to call upon professional help when they are mentally hurting. Often help is sought only after a crisis occurs, and the task of healing becomes more difficult. If you feel you need assistance, do not wait, and avoid unwarranted excuses such as you cannot afford it.

You may feel you have no major concerns but might want to explore some of your psychological needs and feelings through some reading. One suggestion is Thomas Moore's *Care of the Soul: A Guide for Cultivating Depth and Sacredness in Everyday Life*. The title could be intimidating to some. In reality, the work is really a journey into personal growth and understanding of oneself. Another source might be the works of Joan Borysenko, such as her *Guilt is the Teacher, Love is the Lesson*. It is a book to heal "heart and soul," as are all her books. Further information about Dr. Borysenko's work can be obtained from Mind/Body Health Sciences, Inc., 393 Dixon Road, Boulder, CO 80302 (telephone: 303-440-8460).

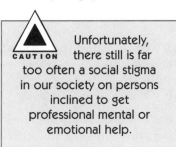

CAUTION Unfortunately, there still is far too often a social stigma in our society on persons inclined to get professional mental or emotional help.

Wayne Dyer is another writer whose insights may prove helpful. Browsing occasionally through a local bookstore should turn up various titles that can point you toward both mental wellness and a positive outlook. But, be discriminating. There are the literary equivalents of junk bonds out there, which can do more harm than good.

Those with a religious tradition may find it helpful to either return to it or explore it at a new depth. Again, it could be a source of growth and healing. For persons who may have had painful or even harmful religious experiences in the past, have no religious tradition, or feel they have outgrown the one that was given to them earlier in life, an exploration of a work such as John Spong's *Rescuing the Bible from Fundamentalism* or Sam Keen's *Hymns to an Unknown God* may be fruitful. Keen has the uncanny ability to meet you where you are and teach you to "trust the luminous darkness." He encourages one to go forward on a spiritual rather than a religious quest.

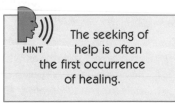

HINT The seeking of help is often the first occurrence of healing.

In the end, what matters is that you take care of yourself. Do not deprive your mind and body of what they need. Properly nurtured, in most cases they will serve you well. The result will be a happier and more fulfilled you, no matter what it is you are doing. That includes your investing decisions as well as nearly everything else

Putting it all together

If you started at the first page of this book and read all the way to this point, it may about now seem a little overwhelming. In reality it does not have to be. No person needs to do everything we have outlined here. Knowledge is indeed power. The more you know the more options you have to select the strategies that are best for you. In the end, however, there are only a few basic approaches that are absolutely essential. We will look at these now.

 Every small investor needs the safety of **diversification**. This can be done very simply by putting some of your investments into things like savings accounts and money market funds while the remainder might go into a single quality mutual fund. Obviously, more intricate approaches are possible if you decide to try them, and this book should have introduced you to many of them. Take a careful look again at the chapter on asset allocation. Then review the various kinds of investments that are readily available to the small investor. Decide where you want to put your money and what percentage will be in each type of investment. Periodically review your plan and fine tune it if necessary. Should your needs and goals change over the years you can of course modify it accordingly. Occasionally, you may have to shift funds from one investment to another in order to restore your original percentages. This is not psychologically easy, but it will take you out of those areas where probably there is now the least value. You will

> Do not try to time markets, but when better value comes along do not hesitate to sell and buy it.

be rewarded by the safety and superior financial returns that diversification in time should bring.

Next, develop a **dollar averaging** approach to investing. This means each week, month, or whatever time period you select, commit yourself to invest a particular sum of money in the various ways your asset allocation plan calls for you to invest it. Maybe 50 percent will go into your savings account, with the remaining half going into stocks or mutual funds. Only in the event of a genuine emergency (not inconvenience) would you not make your commitment. What dollar averaging does, especially with stocks and mutual funds, is enable you to purchase more when prices are depressed but will have you obtaining less when prices per share are higher. If, after a ten year period, the price of a stock was exactly where it was when you started to acquire shares a decade ago, assuming the price had fluctuated over the years, you would still have a profit, thanks to dollar averaging. Even when the money goes into something as basic as a savings account, it helps you acquire the habit of regular saving and investment and will probably make you a more effective money manager in all your financial dealings.

Finally, **buy value**. If purchasing stocks, buy sound companies out of favor and those with low price to earnings ratios. Buy mutual funds that use a value approach and which are slow to turn over their portfolios. If you have hung on to good stocks and funds which have been beaten up for one reason or another, do not sell at distressed prices. Be patient, and in time, if they truly are good, they should recover.

Final thoughts

It is worth repeating myself in order to make the critical point that market timing and value investing are definitely not the same thing. Most people simply cannot determine the direction of stock markets, interest rates, or prices of raw materials. However, with effort and research it is possible to determine if something offers reasonably good value or better yet is undervalued. Those are the things you want to buy. If gross exaggeration can be forgiven in order to clarify this, if you lived in a beautiful dream house that you loved, but somebody came along and offered you three times what it was worth, sell it to them as quickly as possible! Then go buy another dream house at a realistic price. Just remember that any kind of financial market can remain over or undervalued for a rather lengthy period of time. So, it is often necessary to wait, but the wait should be rewarding.

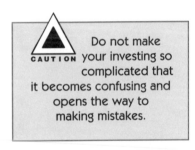

Do not make your investing so complicated that it becomes confusing and opens the way to making mistakes.

For those who are comfortable going a step further, you can add to your diversification and possible returns by also taking a look at global and international mutual funds, real estate in the form of real estate investment trusts (REITS) and real-estate mutual funds, and also mortgage-based securities such as Ginnie Maes. All of these, as well as other things we examined, provide additional opportunity, but none of them is necessary. Be patient and confident, in a realistic manner. Give yourself time, do some research, select the things you like and understand, and ultimately you will grow in financial knowledge and assets.

 After you have planned to do all of these things, then do one more—take some time to dream a little bit. Dare to think of a time when you are fully in command of your life's decisions, and your financial house is in good order. Certainly you might not be rich, but you would not be living paycheck to paycheck either. There would be time and resources to do some of the things that are meaningful for you, and they would also be there to enable you to be a positive force in the lives of others. This is the possible dream, one that can become a reality, and without winning the lottery.

Who knows, if enough of us made that dream come true we could literally change our nation and even the world. We could make a place where people are a little kinder to each other, where they are quicker to lend a helping hand, and where it is just more exciting to get up each morning and begin a new day.

Dare to start living that dream now. Perhaps some morning you will wake up to the exhilarating discovery that you are no longer dreaming. For you at least, it is now a reality. Let us wish each other well as we journey toward that tomorrow.

Resources

••• Online Resources •••

◆ **American Association of Individual Investors (AAII)**

http://www.aaii.org

◆ **American Stock Exchange (AMEX)**

http://www.amex.com

◆ **Barrons**

Dow Jones & Company, Inc.

http://www.barrons.com

◆ **Bloomberg.com**

http://www.bloomberg.com

◆ **Bureau of the Public Debt Online—U.S. Savings Bonds**

http://www.publicdebt.treas.gov/sav/sav.htm

◆ **CNN America**

   http://www.cnnfn.com

◆ **Dividend Reinvestment Plans (DRP) Authority**

   http://www.moneypaper.com/publications/drpauthority/index.html

◆ **Dow Jones & Company, Inc.**

   http://www.dowjones.com/corp/index.html

◆ **FannieMae**

   http://www.fanniemae.com

◆ **Federal Home Loan Mortgage Corporation—Freddie Mac Home Page**

   http://www.freddiemac.com

◆ **FinanceWise**

   http://www.financewise.com

◆ **Frank Russell Company / Russell 3000 Stock Index Forecast**

   http://www.russell.com/toc/toc.htm

◆ **Government National Mortgage Association. (Ginnie Mae)**

   http://www.ginniemae.gov

◆ **Investor's Business Daily**

   http://www.investors.com

◆ **John Templeton Foundation**

   800-621-8476

   http://www.templeton.org

◆ **Morningstar.com**

   http://www.morningstar.net

◆ **National Association of Investors Corporation (NAIC)**

http://www.better-investing.org

◆ **Nasdaq (National Association of Security Dealers Automatic Quotation System)**

http://www.nasdaq.com

◆ **National Association of Real Estate Investment Trusts (NAREIT)**

http://www.nareit.com

◆ **Nightly Businesss Report**

http://www.nightlybusiness.org

◆ **Pacific Exchange**

http://www.pacificex.com

◆ **Social Security Administration**

http://www.ssa.gov

◆ **Standard & Poor's**

http://www.stockinfo.standardpoor.com

◆ **Templeton Investment Management Limited**

http://www.templeton.co.uk

◆ **U.S. Department of Labor—Consumer Price Index, frequently asked questions**

http://www.bls.gov/ppifaq.htm

◆ **U.S. Treasury Department**

http://www.ustreas.gov

◆ **Wall Street Directory**

http://wallstreetdirectory.com

◆ **Wall $treet Week With Louis Rukeyser**

http://www.pbs.org/mpt/rukeyser

◆ **The Weiss Group**

800-289-9222

http://www.weissinc.com

◆ **Yahoo Business and Economy**

http://dir.yahoo.com/Business_and_Economy/Finance_and_Inve stment

••• Investing Publications •••

◆ **Amazon.com**

http://www.amazon.com/exec/obidos/subst/home/home.html/0 02-6753087-2327451

◆ **Better Investing—National Association of Investors Corporation**

http://www.better-investing.org/bi/bi.html

◆ **National Association of Investors Corporation (NAIC)**

http://www.better-investing.org

◆ **Bloomberg Personal Finance**

http://www.bloomberg.com/personal/index.html?sidenav=front

◆ **Business Week**

http://www.businessweek.com

◆ **Chase Global Data & Research—part of Thomson Financial's Wiesenberger division**

http://www.chaseglobaldata.com

http://www.wiesenberger.com

◆ **The Economist**

http://www.economist.com

◆ **Far Eastern Economic Review, The**

http://www.feer.com

◆ **Financial Times, The**

http://www.ft.com

◆ **Franklin Covey Company**

2200 West Parkway Blvd., Salt Lake City, UT 84119-2099

800-863-1492

http://www.franklincovey.com

◆ **Fraser Publishing Company**

Box 494, Burlington, VT 05402, 800-253-0900

http://www.fraserbooks.com

◆ **Forbes**

http://www.forbes.com

◆ **Fortune**

http://www.pathfinder.com/fortune

◆ **Grant's Interest Rate Observer**

http://www.grantspub.com

◆ **Kiplinger's Personal Finance Magazine**

http://www.kiplinger.com/magazine/maghome.html

◆ **Louis Rukeyser's Wall Street**

http://www.pbs.org/mpt/rukeyser

◆ **Money**

http://www.pathfinder.com/money

◆ **The Moneypaper, Inc.**

http://www.moneypaper.com

◆ **Morningstar**

http://www.morningstar.com

◆ **National Post Online**

http://www.nationalpost.com/financialpost.asp

◆ **Smart Money**

http://www.smartmoney.com

◆ **Value Line**

http://www.valueline.com

◆ **The Wall Street Journal Interactive Edition**

http://interactive.wsj.com

◆ **Worth**

http://www.worth.com/frame.html

••• Related Sites •••

◆ **Choice In Dying, Inc.**

200 Varick St., 10th Floor, NY, NY 10014-4810, 212-366-5540

http://www.choices.org

◆ **Citizens Funds**

http://www.citizensfunds.com/live/default.asp

◆ **Domini Corporation**

http://www.domini-inc.com

◆ **Duff & Phelps Credit Rating Company**

http://www.dcrco.com

◆ **Fiscal Agents Financial Services Group**

http://www.fiscalagents.com

◆ **Gale Research**

http://lindex.gale.com/trials/termsofuse.html

◆ **Internal Revenue Service**

http://www.irs.gov

◆ **Mercantile Bancorporation of St. Louis, MO**

800-926-4922

http://www.mercantile.com

◆ **Mind/body Health Sciences, Inc.**
Institute of Technical Energy Medicine

393 Dixon Road, Boulder, CO 80302

303-440-8460

http://www.item-bioenergy.com

◆ **Moody's Investors Service**

http://www.moodys.com

◆ **National Charities Information Bureau**

19 Union Square West, NY, NY 1003

http://www.give.org

◆ **National Federation of Community Development Credit Unions**

212-809-1850

http://www.natfed.org

◆ **Pax World Fund**

http://www.paxfund.com

◆ **Social Choice Fund-College Retirement Equities Fund (CREF)**

   http://www.tiaa-cref.org

   Social Funds.com

   http://www.socialfunds.com

◆ **South Shore Bank**

   7054 S. Jeffery Blvd., Chicago, IL 60649-2096

   800-669-7725

   http://www.sbk.com

••• Canadian Sites •••

◆ **Alberta Stock Exchange (ASE)**

   http://www.ase.ca

◆ **Canada Deposit Insurance Corporation (CDIC)**

   800-461-2342

   http://www.cdic.ca

◆ **Canada Investment and Savings**

   800-575-5151

   http://www.cis-pec.gc.ca

◆ **Financial Post, The**

   http://www.nationalpost.com/financialpost.asp

◆ **Globe and Mail, The**

   http://www.globeandmail.ca

◆ **Registered Retirement Savings Plan**

   http://www.fiscalagents.com/rates/rrsp.htm

◆ **Revenue Canada**

875 Heron Road, Ottawa, ON, K1A OL8

613-952-0384

◆ **Tax Court of Canada**

200 Kent St., Ottawa, ON K1A OM1

613-992-0901

◆ **Toronto Stock Exchange (TSE)**

http://www.tse.com

Appendix:
Recommended reading

What follows is not intended to be a complete or definitive bibliography of financial books. Even a quick glance will reveal it has numerous omissions, such as in the area of retirement planning. Rather, it is simply a compilation of titles that over the years I have found useful for one reason or another. Perhaps there will be some here that you also might find helpful and, in certain cases, even entertaining. Many of these are unfortunately out-of-print. However, they can often be obtained from bookstores and Internet providers who will do out of print book searches without charge or obligation. Your local library may have several, and occasionally you may come across a title or two at a bargain price in a thrift shop. For some, other editions rather than the one indicated here may exist. If you come across these, they should serve you just as well or nearly so as those listed.

While I found all these works beneficial in some way, that certainly does not mean that I advocate everything that they advise. Indeed that would be impossible, since various authors take approaches which contradict those of others. On occasion they may also offer counsel which is sound for the wealthy or even institutional investor, but would be detrimental for the typical small investor. Still, the more you read the more you should be able to separate the wheat from the chaff. For the sake of brevity, some titles discussed elsewhere and not directly related to financial matters are omitted here.

Abromovitz, Les. *Family Insurance Handbook: The Complete Guide for the 1990s.* Blue Ridge Summit, PA: Liberty Hall Press, 1990. Somewhat dated, but a very thorough and easily understood treatment of a sometimes rather complicated subject.

Basso, Thomas F. *Panic-Proof Investing: Lessons in Profitable Investing from a Market Wizard.* New York: John Wiley & Sons, 1994. Not a magic cure-all, but sound, practical advice for virtually anyone.

Bernstein, Jake. *The Investor's Quotient: The Psychology of Successful Investing in Commodities and Stocks.* 2nd ed. New York: John Wiley & Sons, 1993. Small investors should not trade commodities, but they can benefit from Bernstein's insights into the psychology of investors' behavior.

Berryessa, Norman and Eric Kirzner. *Global Investing: The Templeton Way.* Homewood, IL: Dow Jones-Irwin, 1988. No one has been more successful at global investing than John Templeton. Here is an excellent introduction to the methods he used.

Blanchard, James U., III. *Silver Bonanza: How to Profit from the Coming Bull Market in Silver.* New York: Simon & Schuster, 1993. Blanchard may be too optimistic about silver's prospects, but this thorough treatment is probably the best you will find on that particular precious metal.

Bogle, John C. *Bogle on Mutual Funds: New Perspectives for the Intelligent Investor.* Burr Ridge, IL: Irwin Professional Publishing, 1993. The founder of the highly-respected Vanguard family of mutual funds has written a superb work on the subject.

Engel, Louis and Henry R. Hecht. *How to Buy Stocks.* 8th ed. Boston: Little, Brown, & Co., 1994. Any book in its eighth edition is obviously a classic, and many consider this the best possible source of information for the beginning investor. Just remember, small investors should stay away from options.

Fridson, Martin. *Investment Illusions: A Savvy Wall Street Pro Explodes Popular Misconceptions About the Markets.* New York: John Wiley & Sons, 1993. The title pretty much says it all.

Galbraith, John Kenneth. *A Short History of Financial Euphoria.* New York: Whittle/Penguin, 1990. A brief but powerful look at how leverage creates excess in financial markets.

Gates, Bill, with Nathan Myhrvold and Peter M. Rinearson. *The Road Ahead.* revised ed. New York: Penguin USA, 1996. Microsoft's founder gives the reader an intriguing introduction to the world of the future.

Gibson, Roger C. *Asset Allocation: Balancing Financial Risk.* 2nd ed. Burr Ridge, IL: Irwin Professional Publishing, 1996. Although written for the professional, this work is understandable by almost any serious investor. It is one of the most valuable books you could read. Wise use of effective asset allocation can do as much as anything to help you have investment success and keep losses to a minimum. Highly recommended.

Goldfluss, Howard E. *Living Wills and Wills.* New York: Wings Books, 1994. Good basic treatment of two important subjects.

Graham, Benjamin. *The Intelligent Investor: A Book of Practical Counsel.* 4th revised ed. With a New Preface and Appendix by Warren Buffett. New York: Harpercollins, 1997. First published in 1949, this vintage classic should be read by all investors before ever purchasing a single share of stock in anything. Graham's work is the last word on value investing and is still quite timely. Highly recommended.

Grant, James. *The Trouble with Prosperity: The Loss of Fear, the Rise of Speculation, and the Risk to American Savings.* New York: Times Books/Random House, 1996. Grant reveals how economic boom inevitably leads to bust, which paves the way for the next boom.

Haugen, Robert A. and Joseph Lakonishok. *The Incredible January Effect: The Stock Market's Unsolved Mystery.* Homewood, IL: Business One Irwin, 1988. Fascinating study of the characteristics of small-capitalization stocks.

Henriques, Diana B. *Fidelity's World: The Secret Life and Public Power of the Mutual Fund Giant.* New York: Scribner's, 1995. A penetrating look at the dark side of the mutual fund industry, but do not let it scare you away from mutual funds, including Fidelity's.

Herzfeld, Thomas J., and Cecilia L. Gondor, ed. Thomas J. Herzfeld 1997/1998 *Encyclopedia of Closed-End Funds.* Miami: Thomas J. Herzfeld, 1997. An expensive but superb work by the leading expert on closed-end funds.

Hill, Frederick Trevor. *The Story of a Street.* Burlington, VT: Fraser Publishing Co., 1969. First published in 1908, this is an intriguing history of the birth of Wall Street and the early days of its securities trading activities.

Huff, Darrell. *How to Lie with Statistics.* New York: W. W. Norton & Co., 1954. Reissued in 1993, this little book is recommended reading before you study any company's annual report to stockholders.

Kilpatrick, Andrew. *Of Permanent Value: The Story of Warren Buffett* 1998 Edition. Birmingham, AL: Andrew Kilpatrick Publishing Empire, 1998. It has become trendy to write books about the legendary Buffett these days. This self-published effort is one of the more interesting.

Krieger, Andrew J., with Edward Clafin. *The Money Bazaar: Inside the Trillion-Dollar World of Currency Trading.* New York: Times Books, 1992. A good introduction to the huge, round-the-clock currency trading market.

Le Bon, Gustave. *The Crowd: A Study of the Popular Mind.* Atlanta: Cherokee Publishing Company, 1982. Originally published in 1895, this is a brilliant work which will help the reader understand market manias and excesses and also avoid being caught up into them.

Lefèvre, Edwin. *Reminiscences of a Stock Operator.* New York: John Wiley & Sons, 1994. This 1923 classic, based on the life of speculator Jesse Livermore, provides excellent insight into the psychology of markets and their tragically sometimes less than ethical practices.

Lehman, Michael B. *The Irwin Guide to Using the Wall Street Journal.* 5th ed. New York: McGraw-Hill, 1997. A very helpful guide to the effective use of a valuable investment tool and also for understanding economic cycles.

Lewis, Michael. *Pacific Rift: Why Americans and Japanese Don't Understand Each Other.* New York: W. W. Norton & Co., 1991. Helpful insights for the international investor. Those who wish to study the dark side of the financial markets can take a look at two other titles by Lewis, *Liar's Poker* and *The Money Culture.*

Loeb, Gerald D. *The Battle for Stock Market Profits.* New York: Simon & Schuster, 1971. This is essentially a companion work to Loeb's earlier work, *The Battle for Investment Survival,* which first appeared in 1935 and was reissued in 1996 by John Wiley & Sons. Some of Loeb's methods are not practical for the small investor, but there is also some tested wisdom here from a man who lived and survived through difficult financial times.

Lynch, Peter, with John Rothchild. *Beating the Street: The Best Selling Author of One Up on Wall Street Shows You How to Pick Winning Stocks and Develop a Strategy for Mutual Funds.* New York: Simon & Schuster, 1993. The legendary former manager of Fidelity's Magellan Fund advocates you buy what you know and gives you help on how to learn more.

Lynch, Peter, with John Rothchild. *One Up on Wall Street: How to Use What You Already Know to Make Money in the Market.* New York: Simon & Schuster, 1989. Lynch's original book does exactly what its title claims it will.

Mackay, Charles. *Extraordinary Popular Delusions and the Madness of Crowds.* Introduction by Andrew P. Tobias. New York: Crown Publishing, 1995. First published in England in 1841, it has become one of the great classics of all time. The legendary investor and speculator Bernard Baruch wrote a foreword for a 1932 edition, in which he claimed the book had saved him millions of dollars. Highly recommended.

Malkiel, Burton Gordon. *A Random Walk Down Main Street: Including a Life-Cycle Guide to Personal Investing.* 6th ed. New York: W. W. Norton & Co., 1995. Another classic. If Malkiel cannot convince you it is almost impossible to regularly time financial markets, then no one can. Essential reading for both the begining and experienced investor. Highly recommended.

Mamis, Justin. *The Nature of Risk: Stock Market Survival and the Meaning of Life.* Reading, MA: Addison-Wesley, 1991. Not all that Mamis, a market technician, relates is appropriate for the small investor, but there is much food for thought for anyone in this book.

Mayer, Martin. *Markets: Who Plays, Who Risks, Who Gains, Who Loses.* New York: W. W. Norton & Co., 1988. Mayer concludes that ultimately all markets are, at least to some extent, controlled by insiders.

McClain, David. *Apocalypse on Wall Street.* Homewood, IL: Dow Jones-Irwin, 1988. A sobering study of the 1987 stock-market crash.

Mobius, Mark. *The Investor's Guide to Emerging Markets.* Burr Ridge, IL: Irwin Professional Publishing, 1995. No one knows emerging markets better than Mobius.

Moore, Gary D. *The Christian's Guide to Wise Investing.* Grand Rapids, MI: Zondervan Publishing House, 1994. Those who share the author's sincere theological approach will especially enjoy this book with its clear, thorough, and careful guidance and its socially-responsible position. However, anyone could greatly benefit from it.

Moore, Gary D. *End-Times Money Management: Protecting Your Resources Without Losing Your Soul.* Grand Rapids, MI: Zondervan Publishing House, 1999. An excellent guide for managing your financial resources at the start of the next millenium.

Moore, Gary D. *Spiritual Investments: Wall Street Wisdom from the Career of Sir John Templeton.* Philadelphia: Templeton Foundation Press, 1998. Based on the philosophy of his well-known and highly respected friend, Sir John Templeton, the author offers a delightful book full of help for successful investing and living.

Moore, Gary D. *Ten Golden Rules for Financial Success. Foreword by John M. Templeton.* Grand Rapids, MI: Zondervan Publishing House, 1996. In a more detailed examination of the investment strategy of John Templeton, Moore once again provides another work full of vital, sound, and ethical investment insight. Highly recommended.

Morris, Kenneth M. and Alan M. Siegel. *The Wall Street Journal Guide to Personal Finance.* revised ed. New York: Lightbulb Press, 1997. A good, basic place to start on an investment education. But stay away from options.

Needleman, Jacob. *Money and the Meaning of Life.* New York: Currency/Doubleday, 1994. Helpful understanding of the constructive role financial success can play in society.

Nichols, Donald R. *Starting Small, Investing Smart: What to Do with $5 to $5,000.* 2nd ed. Homewood, IL: Dow Jones Irwin, 1988. Useful advice for the beginner.

Nichols, Jeffrey A. *The Complete Book of Gold Investing.* Homewood, IL: Dow Jones-Irwin, 1987. A readable and sensible look at investing in this precious metal.

Rogers, Jim. *Investment Biker: On the Road with Jim Rogers.* New York: Random House, 1994. I do not share Rogers' political views, but this is one of my favorite books. The author takes you on a worldwide tour by motorcycle, pointing out along the way places you might want to invest and others that are financial nightmares. Highly recommended.

Rothchild, John. *The Bear Book: Survive and Profit in Ferocious Markets.* New York: John Wiley & Sons, 1998. Possibly destined to become a classic, this book should be read by every investor. Highly recommended.

Rowley, Anthony. *Asian Markets: The Inside Story.* Hong Kong: Far Eastern Economic Review, 1987. Needs updating, but an early and still enlightening examination of Asian financial markets. The Far Eastern Economic Review, which published the book, is an excellent source of current information on these same markets. You may find it in the periodical collection of a university or college library.

Rugg, Donald D. *The Dow Jones-Irwin Guide to Mutual Funds: How to Diversify Your Investments for Maximum Return and Safety in Any Kind of Market.* 3rd ed. Homewood, IL: Dow Jones-Irwin, 1986. Needs updating, but an excellent treatment of the subject of mutual funds.

Schwab, Charles. *How to Be Your Own Stockbroker.* reissued. New York: Dell, 1994. Basic, helpful advice, especially for the beginner and anyone who wants to use a discount broker.

Schwed, Fred. Jr. *Where Are the Customers' Yachts? Or A Good Hard Look at Wall Street.* New York: John Wiley & Sons, 1995. This classic was first published in 1940 and is a revealing, eye-opening look at some of the more disturbing aspects of the financial markets.

Smith, Adam. *The Money Game.* New York: Vintage/Random House, 1976. Adam Smith is the pen name of George J. W. Goodman. Many consider this book to already be a classic. Every small investor needs to read the chapter on Odd Lot Robert. Any book by Smith is interesting reading. Highly recommended.

Sobel, Robert. *The New Game on Wall Street.* New York: John Wiley & Sons, 1987. This book appeared as many new investment and derivative products were begining to come on the market. Sobel helps you understand them, and that should help convince the small investor to avoid most of them.

Stigum, Marcia and Frank J. Fabozzi. *The Dow Jones-Irwin Guide to Bond and Money Market Investments.* Homewood, IL: Dow Jones-Irwin, 1987. A very helpful look at these types of investments.

Templeton, John Marks, ed. *Looking Forward: The Next Forty Years.* New York: Giniger, 1993. An intriguing and optimistic look at the future.

Thurow, Lester. *The Future of Capitalism: How Today's Economic Forces Shape Tomorrow's World.* New York: William Morrow & Co., 1996. Thurow examines those factors that are remaking our planet and how they will affect us economically well into the next century.

Thurow, Lester. *Head to Head: The Coming Economic Battle Among Japan, Europe, and America.* New York: William Morrow & Co., 1992. There do not have to be any total losers in Thurow's world of the mid-21st century, but he explains why Europe may be the big winner.

Tobias, Andrew P. *The Invisible Bankers: Everything the Insurance Industry Never Wanted You to Know.* New York: Simon & Schuster, 1982. Dated, but still interesting reading.

Tobias, Andrew P. *Money Angles.* New York: Simon & Shuster, 1984. Entertaining along with helpful advice for all investors. Any book by Tobias is worth reading.

Tobias, Andrew P. *The Only Investment Guide You'll Ever Need.* 2nd ed New York: Harvest Books/Harcourt Brace & Co., 1999. The expanded and updated edition of Tobias' classic. Excellent for the beginner or almost anyone. Highly recommended.

Tobias, Andrew P.. *The Only Other Investment Guide You'll Ever Need.* New York: Simon & Schuster, 1987. More helpful insights from one of the best financial writers around.

Vicker, Ray. *The Dow Jones-Irwin Guide to Retirement Planning.* 2nd ed. Homewood, IL: Dow Jones-Irwin, 1987. Needs some major updating, but contains some timeless investment advice for those planning for retirement.

Waggoner, John M. *Money Madness: Strange Manias and Extraordianry Schemes On and Off Wall Street.* Homewood, IL: Business One-Irwin, 1991. An entertaining book that can help readers strengthen their survival instincts.

Zweig, E. Martin, with Morrie Goldfisher. *Martin Zweig's Winning on Wall Street.* revised and updated ed. New York: Warner Books, 1997. Interesting insights from one of the smartest men on Wall Street.

Save On Legal Fees

with software and books from Made E-Z Products available at your
nearest bookstore, or call 1-800-822-4566

Fast answers to 90%
of your legal questions

Clear, reliable & up-to-date

Save costly legal fees
& protect your rights

More than a reference...
a complete do-it-yourself tool!

Stock No.: BK311
$29.95 8.5" x 11"
500 pages Soft cover
ISBN 1-56382-311-X

Everyday Law Made E-Z

The book that saves legal fees every time it's opened.

Here, in *Everyday Law Made E-Z*, are fast answers to 90% of the legal
questions anyone is ever likely to ask, such as:

- How can I control my neighbor's pet?
- Can I change my name?
- What is a common law marriage?
- When should I incorporate my business?
- Is a child responsible for his bills?
- Who owns a husband's gifts to his wife?
- How do I become a naturalized citizen?
- Should I get my divorce in Nevada?
- Can I write my own will?
- Who is responsible when my son drives my car?
- How can my uncle get a Green Card?
- What are the rights of a non-smoker?
- Do I have to let the police search my car?
- What is sexual harassment?
- When is euthanasia legal?
- What repairs must my landlord make?
- What's the difference between fair criticism and slander?
- When can I get my deposit back?
- Can I sue the federal government?
- Am I responsible for a drunken guest's auto accident?
- Is a hotel liable if it does not honor a reservation?
- Does my car fit the lemon law?

Whether for personal or business use, this 500-page information-packed book
helps the layman safeguard his property, avoid disputes, comply with legal
obligations, and enforce his rights. Hundreds of cases illustrate thousands of
points of law, each clearly and completely explained.

MADE E-Z
PRODUCTS

ss 1999.r2

Whatever you need to know, we've made it E-Z!

Informative text and forms you can fill out on-screen.* From personal to business, legal to leisure—we've made it E-Z!

PERSONAL & FAMILY

For all your family's needs, we have titles that will help keep you organized and guide you through most every aspect of your personal life.

BUSINESS

Whether you're starting from scratch with a home business or you just want to keep your corporate records in shape, we've got the programs for you.

* Not all topics include forms   ss 1999.r2

E-Z to load, E-Z to run, E-Z to use!

For our complete list of titles, call 1-800-822-4566
or visit our web site: www.MadeE-Z.com

LEGAL

Easy to understand text explains how to fill out and file forms to perform all the legal tasks you need to—without all those legal fees!

TRAVEL & LEISURE

Learn health tips or travel all around the world, and then relax with a good crossword puzzle. When your work is done, we've got what you need!

MADE E-Z™
PRODUCTS

Made E-Z Products, 384 S. Military Trail, Deerfield Beach, FL 33442
(800) 822-4566 • fax: (954) 480-8906
web site: http://www.MadeE-Z.com

ss 1999.r2

By the book...

MADE E-Z PRODUCTS

MADE E-Z BOOKS provide all the forms you need to take care of business and save on legal fees – *only $29.95 each!*

Everyday Legal Forms & Agreements Made E-Z ISBN 1-56382-301-2
A do-it-yourself legal library of 301 ready-to-use perforated legal documents for virtually every personal or business need!

Corporate Record Keeping Made E-Z ISBN 1-56382-304-7
Keep your own corporate records current and in compliance... without a lawyer!

Managing Employees Made E-Z ISBN 1-56382-302-0
Over 240 documents to manage your employees more efficiently and legally!

Vital Record Keeping Made E-Z ISBN 1-56382-300-4
201 simple and ready-to-use forms to help you keep organized records for your family, your business and yourself!

Collecting Unpaid Bills Made E-Z ISBN 1-56382-309-8
Essential for anyone who extends credit and needs an efficient way to collect.

Available at:
Super Stores, Office Supply Stores, Drug Stores, Hardware Stores, Bookstores, and other fine retailers.

ss 1999.r2

	Item#	Qty.	Price Ea.†
★ **E•Z Legal Kits**			
Bankruptcy	K100		$23.95
Incorporation	K101		$23.95
Divorce	K102		$29.95
Credit Repair	K103		$21.95
Living Trust	K105		$21.95
Living Will	K106		$23.95
Last Will & Testament	K107		$18.95
Buying/Selling Your Home	K111		$21.95
Employment Law	K112		$21.95
Collecting Child Support	K115		$21.95
Limited Liability Company	K116		$21.95
★ **Made E•Z Software**			
Accounting Made E-Z	SW1207		$29.95
Asset Protection Made E-Z	SW1157		$29.95
Bankruptcy Made E-Z	SW1154		$29.95
Best Career Oppportunities Made E-Z	SW1216		$29.95
Brain-Buster Crossword Puzzles	SW1223		$29.95
Brain-Buster Jigsaw Puzzles	SW1222		$29.95
Business Startups Made E-Z	SW1192		$29.95
Buying/Selling Your Home Made E-Z	SW1213		$29.95
Car Buying Made E-Z	SW1146		$29.95
Corporate Record Keeping Made E-Z	SW1159		$29.95
Credit Repair Made E-Z	SW1153		$29.95
Divorce Law Made E-Z	SW1182		$29.95
Everyday Law Made E-Z	SW1185		$29.95
Everyday Legal Forms & Agreements	SW1186		$29.95
Incorporation Made E-Z	SW1176		$29.95
Last Wills Made E-Z	SW1177		$29.95
Living Trusts Made E-Z	SW1178		$29.95
Offshore Investing Made E-Z	SW1218		$29.95
Owning a Franchise Made E-Z	SW1202		$29.95
Touring Florence, Italy Made E-Z	SW1220		$29.95
Touring London, England Made E-Z	SW1221		$29.95
Vital Record Keeping Made E-Z	SW1160		$29.95
Website Marketing Made E-Z	SW1203		$29.95
Your Profitable Home Business	SW1204		$29.95
★ **Made E•Z Guides**			
Bankruptcy Made E-Z	G200		$17.95
Incorporation Made E-Z	G201		$17.95
Divorce Law Made E-Z	G202		$17.95
Credit Repair Made E-Z	G203		$17.95
Living Trusts Made E-Z	G205		$17.95
Living Wills Made E-Z	G206		$17.95
Last Wills Made E-Z	G207		$17.95
Small Claims Court Made E-Z	G209		$17.95
Traffic Court Made E-Z	G210		$17.95
Buying/Selling Your Home Made E-Z	G211		$17.95
Employment Law Made E-Z	G212		$17.95
Collecting Child Support Made E-Z	G215		$17.95
Limited Liability Companies Made E-Z	G216		$17.95
Partnerships Made E-Z	G218		$17.95
Solving IRS Problems Made E-Z	G219		$17.95
Asset Protection Secrets Made E-Z	G220		$17.95
Immigration Made E-Z	G223		$17.95
Buying/Selling a Business Made E-Z	G223		$17.95
★ **Made E•Z Books**			
Managing Employees Made E-Z	BK308		$29.95
Corporate Record Keeping Made E-Z	BK310		$29.95
Vital Record Keeping Made E-Z	BK312		$29.95
Business Forms Made E-Z	BK313		$29.95
Collecting Unpaid Bills Made E-Z	BK309		$29.95
Everyday Law Made E-Z	BK311		$29.95
Everyday Legal Forms & Agreements	BK307		$29.95
★ **Labor Posters**			
Federal Labor Law Poster	LP001		$11.99
State Labor Law Poster (specify state)			$29.95
★ Shipping & Handling*			$
★ **TOTAL OF ORDER**:**			$

See an item in this book you would like to order?

To order :
1. Photocopy this order form.
2. Use the photocopy to complete your order and mail to:

MADE E-Z PRODUCTS

384 S Military Trail, Deerfield Beach, FL 33442
phone: (954) 480-8933 • fax: (954) 480-8906
web site: http://www.e-zlegal.com/

†Prices current as of 10/99

Shipping and Handling: Add $3.50 for the first item, $1.50 for each additional item.

**Florida residents add 6% sales tax.

Total payment must accompany all orders.
Make checks payable to: Made E-Z Products, Inc.

NAME

COMPANY

ORGANIZATION

ADDRESS

CITY   STATE   ZIP

PHONE (   )

PAYMENT:

❏ CHECK ENCLOSED, PAYABLE TO MADE E-Z PRODUCTS, INC.

❏ PLEASE CHARGE MY ACCOUNT: ❏ MasterCard ❏ VISA

EXP DATE

ACCOUNT NO.

Signature:
(required for credit card purchases)

-OR-

For faster service, order by phone:
(954) 480-8933

Or you can fax your order to us:
(954) 480-8906

SS 1999 r2

CHECK OUT THE

MADE E·Z® LIBRARY

MADE E-Z GUIDES

Each comprehensive guide contains all the information you need to learn about one of dozens of topics, plus sample forms (if applicable).

Most guides also include an appendix of valuable resources, a handy glossary, and the valuable 14-page supplement "How to Save on Attorney Fees."

TITLES

Asset Protection Made E-Z
Shelter your property from financial disaster.

Bankruptcy Made E-Z
Take the confusion out of filing bankruptcy.

Buying/Selling a Business Made E-Z
Position your business and structure the deal for quick results.

Buying/Selling Your Home Made E-Z
Buy or sell your home for the right price right now!

Collecting Child Support Made E-Z
Ensure your kids the support they deserve.

Collecting Unpaid Bills Made E-Z
Get paid–and faster–every time.

Corporate Record Keeping Made E-Z
Minutes, resolutions, notices, and waivers for any corporation.

Credit Repair Made E-Z
All the tools to put you back on track.

Divorce Law Made E-Z
Learn to proceed on your own, without a lawyer.

Employment Law Made E-Z
A handy reference for employers and employees.

Everyday Law Made E-Z
Fast answers to 90% of your legal questions.

Everyday Legal Forms & Agreements Made E-Z
Personal and business protection for virtually any situation.

Incorporation Made E-Z
Information you need to get your company INC'ed.

Last Wills Made E-Z
Write a will the right way, the E-Z way.

Limited Liability Companies Made E-Z
Learn all about the hottest new business entity.

Living Trusts Made E-Z
Trust us to help you provide for your loved ones.

Living Wills Made E-Z
Take steps now to ensure Death with Dignity.

Managing Employees Made E-Z
Your own personnel director in a book.

Partnerships Made E-Z
Get your company started the right way.

Small Claims Court Made E-Z
Prepare for court...or explore other avenues.

Traffic Court Made E-Z
Learn your rights on the road and in court.

Solving IRS Problems Made E-Z
Settle with the IRS for pennies on the dollar.

Trademarks & Copyrights Made E-Z
How to obtain your own copyright or trademark.

Vital Record Keeping Made E-Z
Preserve vital records and important information.

KITS

Each kit includes a clear, concise instruction manual to help you understand your rights and obligations, plus all the information and sample forms you need.

For the busy do-it-yourselfer, it's quick, affordable, and it's E-Z.

ss 1999.r1

Index

WARNER MEMORIAL LIBRARY
EASTERN COLLEGE
ST. DAVIDS, PA. 19087